D1374921

4

b **ONE WEEK LOAN**

EDITION
4

basic personal

a training manual for counsellors

counselling

David Geldard Kathryn Geldard

Prentice
Hall

Pearson Education Australia
Unit 4, Level 2
14 Aquatic Drive
Frenchs Forest NSW 2086

www.pearsoned.com.au

Acquisitions Editor: Diane Gee-Clough
Senior Project Editor: Carolyn Robson
Cover and text design by Carol Hudson Graphic Design
Index by Russell Brooks
Typeset by Midland Typesetters, Maryborough, Vic.

Printed in Malaysia, LSP

10 11 07 06 05 04

National Library of Australia
Cataloguing-in-Publication Data

Geldard, David.
Basic personal counselling: a training manual for counsellors.

4th ed.
Includes index.
ISBN 1 74009 574 X.

1. Counseling. I. Geldard, Kathryn. II. Title.

158.3

An imprint of Pearson Education Australia

contents

Introduction to the fourth edition

Readers familiar with earlier editions of this book will remember that it was written by only one of us, that is, David. However, some readers of the third edition may have noted David's acknowledgment of the help Kathryn (his wife) gave him in preparing that edition.

When the time came for this edition to be prepared we, David and Kathryn, decided that it would be most useful if we worked together as co-authors. We very much enjoy writing together, having co-authored the books *Counselling Children, Counselling Adolescents*, and *Working With Children In Groups*. We believe that working jointly enhances the quality of our writing as we have differences in our knowledge bases and counselling practice.

We decided to revise *Basic Personal Counselling* with the goals of expanding it, ensuring that it was up-to-date, and including some important material that we recognised was not included in earlier editions. Most importantly, we recognised the need to include a discussion of cultural issues and post-modern approaches to counselling. An understanding of cultural issues is essential for counsellors if they are to join with and help their clients. This is particularly so as we live in a multicultural society. We also recognised the need to discuss the processes of change in counselling in greater depth.

From time to time, new theoretical models of counselling are suggested. Even though counsellors generally may not adopt these new models as their preferred models, many counsellors may find it useful to incorporate ideas from them into their counselling practice. In recent years, counselling models that are known as the 'post-modern approaches' have been developed. We have therefore decided to include chapters on two of these, that is, solution-focused counselling and narrative therapy. Many clients and counsellors find these two post-modern approaches very helpful.

We hope that readers will find this book useful, and, most importantly, will also enjoy reading it. We have tried as far as possible to avoid the use of jargon, to retain the conversational style of previous editions, and to make this book as user-friendly as we can. This is because we do not believe that counselling needs to be based on complex theories; rather, we believe that effective counselling is dependent on the quality of the client–counsellor relationship.

David Geldard and Kathryn Geldard

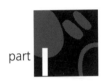

part I

Counselling—
an overview

chapter 1

What is counselling?

As we started to write this chapter, we asked ourselves the question, 'What is counselling?'. In seeking to answer this question we realised that to understand the nature of counselling we needed to think about the reasons why people might come to see counsellors. Generally, people who live satisfying and fulfilling lives, and who are not confronted by any particular crisis, do not seek counselling. However, even people who live satisfying and fulfilling lives will at particular times in their lives be troubled emotionally and may seek help. Many people, if not all people, will at some time encounter physical and/or emotional crises. It is at times like these that people may seek counselling.

It needs to be recognised that people deal with problem times in their lives in their own unique ways. Some people are very adaptive, and are able to resolve their emotional problems by thinking things through on their own. Other people may talk with a partner, family member, or friend. However, there are many people who either have no one to talk to about personal issues, or who prefer to deal with their issues by talking to a counsellor rather than someone who knows them well. Sometimes, it may be easier for a person to talk to a counsellor about extremely personal matters than to risk straining a relationship by disclosing intimate personal information to someone who knows them well.

Our personal experience suggests that the most common reasons why people come to see counsellors relate either to relationships or to developmental life changes. Many people experience emotional crisis when they are in a relationship which is troubled, when they have lost a relationship, or when they seek a relationship but are unable to find a satisfactory one.

Similarly, developmental life changes frequently cause high levels of stress and/or emotional distress. Examples of such developmental changes include getting married, having a first child, being promoted at work, and reaching mid-life. Of course, there are many other reasons why people might seek counselling. These include having experienced physical or emotional trauma, illness, and many types of loss.

Clearly, people usually come to see counsellors when they are emotionally troubled, and believe that they are unable to solve their problems and resolve their distress without outside help. In coming to counselling, they expect that they will be able to talk to someone else in confidence about their problems with the hope of finding solutions and feeling better. It follows that central to the counselling process is the client–counsellor relationship.

Counselling involves a relationship

Counselling involves a special type of relationship between the counsellor and the person seeking help. The characteristics of this relationship will be discussed in detail in Chapter 2. Sometimes the client–counsellor relationship is a face-to-face relationship and sometimes it is conducted by phone. Occasionally, a counselling relationship will be a relationship which is limited to writing letters between the client and counsellor. In our modern Internet world, this may occur electronically. Whatever the way in which the relationship is conducted, it is a relationship with a purpose.

In this book, we will try to parallel some of the qualities of the counselling relationship by remembering that you, the reader, and we, the authors, are engaging together in a relationship with a purpose. We also need to remember that we each have our own unique personalities, so inevitably we will sometimes think similarly and sometimes differently, and that is OK.

People receiving help from counsellors like to know something about the person who is helping them so that they can have confidence in the help being offered. Sometimes it is sufficient for them to know that the counsellor concerned works for a reputable agency. When this is not the case, they may want to know about the counsellor's training, experience, and/or qualifications.

As authors, our relationship with you, the reader, is not the same as a client–counsellor relationship. However, just as clients want to know something about their counsellors, you may wish to know something about us, the authors. Much as we would in a counselling session, we will begin by introducing ourselves.

Firstly, I, Kathryn, will tell you something about myself and how I became a counsellor. I started my professional life not as a counsellor, but as an occupational therapist. However, my professional interests led me to train to work with young people in a psychiatric setting in the United States. As a consequence I became inevitably involved in psychotherapy and focused on working with children and young people who had behavioural and/or emotional problems. This interest led me to work with families and individual adults. As time progressed, I began to realise that my focus had shifted towards counselling, which led me to study for, and complete, a Master's degree in counselling. Perhaps the most important thing I have learnt is that theoretical knowledge on its own does not make a counsellor. For me the most significant attribute needed in counselling is the ability to build a trusting relationship. Now I will hand over to David, so that he can introduce himself.

Thank you Kathryn. I should start by explaining that when I was a young man I had ambitions to be a psychologist, but through lack of confidence I enrolled in another course which did not suit me. Much later in life, at a low point during which I had received counselling, I offered myself as a volunteer to the 'Meals On Wheels' organisation. My self-esteem received a dreadful blow when I was rejected by that organisation as a consequence of my inability to navigate around the neighbourhood in which I was delivering meals. I subsequently offered my services to Lifeline as a volunteer driver. To my surprise, instead of offering me a driver's position, Lifeline suggested that I might wish to train as a volunteer telephone counsellor. I took up this offer in trepidation, doubting whether I had the skills to be of help to anyone. After training and working as a volunteer telephone counsellor, I later trained as a face-to-face counsellor, studied psychology and in time graduated as a psychologist. As a counsellor, I initially focused on personal counselling, and later trained to work with couples, families, then children. I find counselling very satisfying as it encourages me to be creative and to use myself as a person. Generally it is stimulating and satisfying, but I must admit that at times it can be stressful and exhausting.

Why do you want to be a counsellor?

We hope you will enjoy reading this book and find it useful. Because you are reading it, we assume that you may be intending to train as a counsellor. Now that we have told you how we became counsellors, we will ask you to think about the question, 'Why do you want to be a counsellor?' As we write we remember how we felt when we first started our training. Our feelings and attitudes then were very different from those we have now. However, it was those feelings and attitudes which motivated us to go ahead. We wonder how you feel as you think about your decision to train as a counsellor. What are your motivations? Stop for a minute and think. As we have suggested, you might ask yourself the question, 'Why do I want to be a counsellor?' and, if you have the energy and inclination, write your answer on a sheet of paper so that you can refer to it later.

Your answer is, of course, individually yours, but it is quite probable that it fits into one of two moulds. It could be that you wrote a statement about your *own* needs. Maybe you have the idea that being a counsellor will give you status, power or satisfaction. Perhaps you think that counselling will add a new quality and richness to your life. It may be, though, that when you wrote your answer you were not thinking about your own needs at all. You may have decided to become a counsellor so that you can satisfy the needs of other people. You may have written down something like: 'I want to be a counsellor because I care about other people and want to help them.' Most counsellors are very caring people and helping others is an important part of their motivation. However it's important for all of us to remember that even if we become counsellors with the primary goal of satisfying other people's needs, we will *also* be satisfying some of our *own* needs. We will, for example, get satisfaction for ourselves out of caring for others. This discussion may not seem important right now, but it is, because if we are not careful, our motivations for becoming counsellors may negatively influence the way in which we will function as counsellors. While it probably doesn't matter greatly what our personal motivations are, it is important that we are aware of these motivations and of the needs of our own that we hope to satisfy. With this awareness we will be better able to avoid letting the satisfaction of our own needs interfere with the counselling process, and with our ability to meet the needs of clients.

Purposes and goals of counselling

As counsellors, if we are to meet the needs of clients we must have a clear understanding of the purposes and goals of the counselling process. Additionally, to be effective counsellors we need to have an understanding of what it means to be effective.

For most people it is not easy to make an appointment and then go to see a counsellor. Our society's value system holds that it's a sign of weakness if people are only able to handle their problems if they have outside help. This tends to make it difficult for those with heavy work responsibilities to come for counselling. Such people often believe that, if they admitted to seeking help from a counsellor, their colleagues would think that they were inadequate and not capable of taking responsibility. Consequently, many people are reluctant to seek counselling help unless they are in such a disturbed emotional state that their ability to carry out their normal daily tasks is significantly impaired, and they are no longer able to hide their pain and emotional distress from others.

If we remember that generally clients come to see us in a state of raised anxiety and a level of distress, then we must assume that the central purpose of counselling is to help clients to feel better. However, that is not sufficient. It is not going to be useful for clients if they feel better in the short term only to return to their previous uncomfortable emotional state within a short period of time. A major goal of the counselling process therefore needs to be to help clients change. If clients are unable to make changes either in the ways they think, or in the things they do, then it is likely that they will repeat patterns of thinking and behaving which are not adaptive, but return them to a state of discomfort.

Judging the effectiveness of counselling is usually subjective and there are clearly two different perspectives—the client's and the counsellor's. It may be that the client will perceive effectiveness in a different way from the counsellor, so we will ask you, the reader, to spend a few minutes considering first the client's expectations and then the counsellor's.

The client's perspective

Many clients, who are not used to the counselling process, go to counsellors expecting that the counsellor will give them direct advice and tell them exactly what they should do, so that at the end of the counselling session they can go away having been told how to solve their problems. This is generally not the case. Most experienced counsellors agree that it is usually, although not always, unhelpful to give advice. In fact, in many situations there may be real disadvantages for a client if a counsellor does try to give advice and provide solutions to problems.

There are several dangers inherent in giving advice. Firstly, human beings are remarkably resistant to advice. In fact, some counsellors have become so impressed by the way that clients resist advice, that in advanced counselling sessions they will use paradoxical methods to suggest that a client should do exactly the reverse of what the counsellor really believes is best! We need to say that we ourselves do not use paradoxical methods because we believe that they would compromise our authenticity.

Unfortunately, giving advice may be counterproductive even if the client follows the advice. If the advice turns out to be inappropriate, then quite clearly the counsellor has done the client a disservice and that client will not be impressed. On the other hand, if the advice has positive consequences then there may still be negative consequences in the long term. Instead of having worked things out for themselves, the client has accepted the counsellor's advice and may now regard the counsellor as a superior expert who needs to be consulted whenever major decisions are to be made. This is likely to compromise the client's ability to be self-reliant and to personally make use of adaptive decision-making processes.

We do need to make it clear that there are counselling situations where direct advice by the counsellor is required. For example, in medical emergencies, crisis situations, or situations where a person's safety is compromised, quick decisions may be required, and it may be imperative for counsellors to be directive.

If we as counsellors are generally not willing to give clients advice, then we do need to try to understand what the client is seeking when expecting advice. If we were to ask the client, as we sometimes do, 'What would you like to achieve by coming to counselling?', what do you think the answer would reflect? Generally, it seems to us, that clients want to feel better emotionally, and in order for this to happen they often believe that they need to find solutions to problems.

If we don't usually give clients advice, how can we help them feel better? Often, clients will feel better just because they have had an opportunity to share their problems with another person who is prepared to listen. This is the most important way in which a counsellor can meet the client's needs, by listening. Additionally, if clients are able to discover for themselves, during counselling sessions, better ways of responding to, dealing with, and managing their problems, then they are likely to feel better. They are also likely to feel satisfied with the outcome, even though they may not have received any advice.

The counsellor's perspective

If we are to be effective counsellors, we need to have a clear idea of our goals. A useful short-term goal is to help clients to feel better, or at least to feel more comfortable. In the long term, it is sensible to help clients to discover for themselves how to become more self-sufficient, and how to deal with ongoing and future life situations in a constructive way without requiring continual help. It is very much in both the client's and the counsellor's interests to promote enduring long-term change, rather than to engage in short-term problem-solving. A counsellor is clearly going to feel very frustrated if clients keep returning for counselling each time new problems are encountered. It is important, if counsellors are to feel a sense of satisfaction in their work, that clients change and grow in such a way that they learn to cope, as much as is realistically possible, on their own. Additionally, a counsellor might be seen to be more effective if change occurs more quickly. However, we need to be aware of the danger of producing short-term transitory change which is not sustainable, and which fails to enable the client to cope more effectively with future crises.

Encouraging self-reliance

It is not helpful for clients to perceive counsellors as superior experts who have the answers to other people's problems. Such perceptions are undesirable because they disempower clients instead of helping them to learn self-reliant ways of behaving. Thus, an important goal for a counsellor may be to help clients to discover for themselves how to become more self-reliant and how to feel confident about their own ability to make decisions. In the long term it is certainly not helpful for a client to become dependent on a counsellor's advice. It is far better for the client to become self-reliant, and capable of making and trusting his or her own decisions.

As we have discussed, in most situations, counsellors usually don't give direct advice, don't 'problem solve' for clients and don't seek to produce quick short-term solutions without long-term gain. Instead they do help clients sort out their own confusion, and by doing this enable them to discover for themselves solutions to their problems that fit for them. This is a process that is empowering for clients. Sometimes the counsellor may think that the client's solutions are not the most sensible or appropriate ones. However, it is important for clients to make decisions that are right for them. They can then test their decisions and learn from their own experiences, rather than learning to rely on the 'wisdom' of the counsellor.

Contracting with the client

From the previous discussion it is obvious that at times there may be a mismatch between the client's and the counsellor's expectations. One way of dealing with this mismatch when it occurs would be to ignore it and just to allow the counselling process to proceed. However, a more respectful approach is to discuss expectations openly with the client and to agree on a counselling contract that is mutually acceptable.

A counselling contract may include an agreement regarding issues such as those related to confidentiality, general and specific goals, the counselling process, the counselling methods to be used by the counsellor, and issues to be discussed. At the contracting stage we like to make it clear that the client's wishes will be respected with regard to what issues will and will not be discussed. This is very important for some clients who may fear that they will be pressured in subtle ways to discuss issues which they do not wish to explore.

Sometimes a contract will involve an agreement to attend counselling sessions at regular intervals; for example weekly or fortnightly for a particular number of sessions, with a review of the counselling process occurring at set times.

Learning summary

- A central feature of counselling is the client–counsellor relationship.
- Counsellors need to be aware of their motivation because this will influence their effectiveness.
- Client expectations may be at variance with counsellor goals.
- Clients often ask for direct advice and solutions to their problems.
- Counsellors generally try to empower clients so that they can become self-sufficient and discover their own solutions rather than be dependent on someone else's advice.
- Goals of the counselling process include working collaboratively with the client to help the client sort out their problems and

discover solutions, helping the client to change their thinking and/or behaviours, empowering the client to become self-sufficient, and helping the client to feel better.

Further reading

Brammer, L. M. 1999, *The Helping Relationship: Processes and Skills*, 7th edn, Allyn & Bacon, Boston.

Feltham, C. 1995, *What is Counselling? The Promise and Problems of the Talking Therapies*, Sage, London.

Kennedy, E. & Charles, S. C. 1990, *On Becoming a Counsellor: A Basic Guide for Non-Professional Counsellors*, Collins Dove, Melbourne.

McLeod, J. 1997, *An Introduction to Counselling*, Open University Press, Buckingham.

chapter **2**

The counselling relationship

Most counsellors would agree that the effectiveness of counselling is highly dependent on the quality of the relationship between the client and the counsellor. It needs to be recognised that there are many different models of counselling practice, and that the nature of the counselling relationship will depend on the preferred model of counselling practice selected by a particular counsellor. Even so, we believe that it is preferable for new counsellors to initially base their practice on ideas which were developed by Carl Rogers who wrote a book called *Client-Centered Therapy* many years ago, in 1955. Interestingly, some time after writing the book, Rogers preferred to call his approach '*person*-centred counselling', because he placed a very strong emphasis on the need for counsellors to think of their clients as people rather than impersonal entities. He saw the client–counsellor relationship as a person-to-person relationship where the person seeking help was respected and valued. Many of Rogers' ideas are still relevant today and in particular his concept of the counselling relationship is both powerful and useful, particularly for new counsellors. If you initially adopt a Rogerian counselling style, you can later learn skills from other counselling approaches and integrate these into the Rogerian base so that you have a style that suits you personally. A range of other counselling approaches will be discussed in later chapters.

Desirable qualities of the counselling relationship
Rogers identified three basic qualities that he believed are highly desirable for a counsellor, if counselling is to be effective. These qualities are *congru-*

ence, *empathy*, and *unconditional positive regard*. Additionally, we believe that it is very important for counsellors to have *respect for client competence*. David will discuss these qualities in the following paragraphs.

Congruence

To be congruent the counsellor must be genuinely themselves, a complete, integrated and whole person. Everything

What is good and what is not so good in this picture?

about the counsellor as a person must ring true. For example, there is only one David Geldard, even though I have a variety of roles. I am a husband, a father, a grandfather, a counsellor, a friend, a patient, a customer, a trainer, and have many other roles. It is clearly true that there are differences in the way that I behave in each of these roles, and in different situations. While I am playing with a child I am happy to romp around on the floor, and when I am attending a professional meeting of psychologists (which, frankly, I do not usually enjoy much) I prefer to dress more formally and sit upright on a chair. However, in both situations I have a choice. If I choose, I can be an actor playing a role or I can in the fullest sense really be me. I can either stay fully in contact with myself as a person and be genuine, without the need to change myself, or, if I choose, I can disown myself, wear a mask, and pretend to be different from who I really am. Similarly, as a counsellor I could pretend to be an expert who has all the answers and no vulnerabilities, or I can throw away my 'counsellor mask' and just be me, a real person complete with all my strengths and weaknesses. When a client comes to see me in my counsellor role, then two people meet. It is a person-to-person relationship. For the client to feel valued, I, the counsellor, need to be congruently myself, genuine in all regards. If this happens, then the relationship will be enhanced and the counselling process is likely to be more effective.

Each time I enter a counselling relationship I bring with me that part of me which is a parent, that part of me which is a professional psychologist, that part of me which is childlike and likes to have fun and play jokes on people, and the serious side of me. I am very much me and not just part of me. I am, within my own limitations, genuinely me and try to avoid pretending to be different from the real me. Naturally, when working as a counsellor I make use of those parts of me which are most relevant in the counselling relationship, and other parts of me may remain out of sight. These are not deliberately concealed from the client, but are available only if they can be appropriately used.

I ran a group some time ago, and in that group were two of my personal friends. These two people had never seen me as a counsellor before but had known me only as a friend. After the group, one of them said to me, 'I was really surprised because in the group you were the counsellor, but all I saw was the person that I had always known, and I expected to find someone different'.

A similar situation occurred when a lecturer friend of mine at our local university was teaching counselling skills. One of the students, early on in the course, said to the lecturer, 'How about you show us how you counsel by giving us a demonstration? You've been teaching us counselling micro-skills, but you've never actually sat down in front of us and demonstrated how to counsel'. The lecturer readily agreed, sat down and, as counsellor, helped a young student client to resolve a difficult and painful issue. After the session was over, the student who'd asked the lecturer to give the demonstration seemed to be amazed and delighted. She said to the lecturer, 'You know, I really can't believe it. It was just as though you were being yourself, and Irene [invented name] and you were talking together like friends.' Yes, that's how it was; the lecturer was being totally congruent and was relating to Irene as she related to other people in her daily life, as a real person. Of course, it wasn't quite the same, because in daily life we generally behave as though our own needs are equally as important as other people's needs, whereas in a counselling relationship the counsellor will generally focus on the client's needs rather than their own. After all, the counselling situation is not the appropriate place for a counsellor to work through their own problems; rather it's the place where the central focus is the client.

Self-disclosure

We believe that being congruent may sometimes require a counsellor to be willing to self-disclose a limited amount of personal information, as otherwise the client may experience an excessive lack of equality in the relationship. It must be acknowledged that in reality there is inevitably to some degree a lack of equality in a counselling relationship, because in the counselling situation the roles played by client and counsellor are different.

However, if the counsellor is able to respond openly and at times to disclose information which may be relevant to the counselling conversation, this can be helpful in enabling the client to feel at ease. As in every relationship, sensible boundaries need to be established. It would not be appropriate for a counsellor to disclose information of a highly personal nature. Additionally, self-disclosure needs to be used sparingly so that the focus is on the client's issues and to avoid the possibility that the client's issues might become contaminated by the counsellor's issues. It is essential for counsellors to ensure that they do not use counselling sessions with clients in order to work through their own issues. Excessive and inappropriate self-disclosure by a counsellor would be likely to move the focus onto the counsellor's issues rather than the client's.

Empathy

A good metaphor for the counselling process is for the counsellor to imagine that the client is walking along a path. Sometimes the client may wander away from the path, go into the woods, trip over, climb over rocks, wander through valleys, cross streams and generally explore. Sometimes they may go around in a circle and come back to the same point again. As a counsellor I am neither a follower nor a leader most of the time, although at times I will follow and at times I will lead. Most of the time, what I try to do is to walk alongside the client—to go where he or she chooses to go, to explore those things that the client chooses to explore, and to be warm, open, friendly, concerned, caring, real and genuine. This way, trust develops between the client and myself and I experience the world in almost the same way that the client experiences it. I try to think and feel the way the client does, so that I can share with the client what they are discovering about themselves. I go on a journey with them, listening to everything they say, matching their every move, and being right beside them. This is what is meant by empathy. Being empathic means having a togetherness with the client, and as a consequence creating a trusting environment in which the client feels cared for and safe. In such an environment clients can talk about their darkest secrets, their innermost feelings, and the things that seem to them to be so terrible, or so personal that they have not yet dared to talk to others about them.

Unconditional positive regard

The third counsellor characteristic which Rogers considered essential for effective counselling is unconditional positive regard. Unconditional positive regard involves accepting the client completely, in a non-judgmental way, as the person they are, with all their frailties and weaknesses, and with all their strengths and positive qualities. Having unconditional positive regard doesn't mean that I agree with or accept the values of the client for myself, but it does mean that I accept the client as he or she is now, that I value them as a person, am non-judgmental about their behaviour, and do not try to put my values onto them. I consequently enable them to feel free to be open in exploring their inner processes without censoring them for fear of criticism. This gives them the best opportunity for increased personal awareness and consequent personal growth.

Unconditional positive regard isn't always easy to achieve, and sometimes it is just not possible. However, attempting to achieve it is an excellent goal, as when it is achieved counselling outcomes are more likely to be effective. The first step in attempting to achieve unconditional positive regard is to try to see the world through the eyes of the client. By doing this I am better able to understand the client's motivations and to be more accepting of their behaviour. The longer I've been a counsellor, the more convinced I have become that even the most terrible behaviour is often understandable if I first understand the world that the client lives in and has lived in. I try to take the view that inside every person, behind the facade that the world sees, there is somebody who has the potential to be a good, creative, loving person. I am rarely disappointed by this expectation.

By caring for each person who talks with me in a similar way to the way in which I would like to be cared for myself, I am better able to be accepting and non-judgmental. I'm not going to pretend that this is easy, because sometimes it isn't. On occasions in counselling sessions clients will discuss their behaviours, beliefs or attitudes in ways which conflict with, or are offensive to, my own value system. At these times, it is really hard for me to be non-judgmental and also to remain congruent, but it is a goal that I strive for. I have found that if I am able to see the world from the client's perspective without judging, then the client is more likely to feel safe in being open and honest with me while exploring troubling issues. My belief is, that by being non-judgmental, I maximise the possibility that my client will feel free to fully disclose important information, and I increase the likelihood that the client will change. Only by being non-judgmental can I expect to earn the total trust of the client and to really see the world in the way the client does. Unfortunately, when I can't do this, and sometimes I can't, I may fail to facilitate change effectively because the client will not perceive me as understanding.

Clearly, being non-judgmental and accepting clients with unconditional positive regard is not easily achieved. Moreover it will be very difficult for me to create the relationship I need to have with a client and to be non-judgmental unless first I am very clear about who I am and what my own values are. If I have not sorted out my own value conflicts, then there is a risk that my own confusion will interfere with my ability to focus on the client's confusion, and I may inadvertently end up using the counselling session to resolve my own conflicts rather than the client's. To get a better understanding of my own values I have had to explore them, to scrutinise them and to question them. I have needed to carefully consider different values from my own and to understand where my feelings about those different values come from. This is an ongoing process that will never be finished. I have found that when I have had extremely polarised views, this has sometimes been because I have been afraid to look at the opposite point of view and to seek to understand it. Through sorting out my own value system, understanding myself better, and consequently being less threatened by views diametrically opposed to mine, I am better able to take a non-judgmental attitude towards clients who have very different values from mine.

Having respect for the client's competence

If a useful counselling relationship is to occur, the counsellor must respect and value the client as a person. It is also extremely important for a counsellor to respect the client's competence and to hold the belief that the client has the inner resources needed to deal with troubling issues, find solutions to problems, make decisions to change behaviour, and put desired changes into action. Some clients come to counselling believing that they do not have the inner resources and capability to do such things. Their expectation is that the counsellor will help them by finding solutions for them. Such clients are clearly lacking in a sense of personal power and the self-confidence which they require to enable them to be self-reliant. However, if the counsellor maintains the belief that the client does have the required inner strength and competence required for self-reliance, then the counsellor will be in a position to enable the client to get in touch with their own strengths and resources, to become self-reliant, and consequently to gain in self-esteem.

Importance of the counselling relationship

In this chapter we have discussed the counselling relationship, and have explained how that relationship is important in providing a trusting, caring environment in which the client will feel free to share with the counsellor in the most open way possible. The attributes of congruence, genuineness, warmth, empathy, unconditional positive regard, and trust in the client's competence, are extremely important if a counsellor is to be fully effective. A counsellor needs to walk alongside the client and to be with them in a very real sense so that the client experiences a togetherness. The precise words the counsellor uses are less important than their ability to form a meaningful relationship with the client and to listen intently to what the client is saying. An effective counsellor listens more than talks, and what they do say gives the client a sense of being heard and understood. The counsellor's role involves helping clients to explore their worlds and thus to make sense out of inner confusion. It is not the counsellor's role to choose the direction in which a client moves, but rather to provide the environment in which the client can best decide where to go. The counsellor then accompanies the client on their journey of exploration.

We suggest that as a counsellor, you allow your clients to go where their current energy is taking them rather than trying to lead them in particular directions. When a client has learnt to trust you, and to know that you will listen to what may appear trivial, then that client will feel safe enough to venture towards the real source of their pain. In other words, if you stay with what may appear trivial, the important will emerge.

You may by now have come to the conclusion that counselling is a terribly serious process. It often is. It is also a process which can give a great deal of satisfaction to the counsellor, and there are even times when counselling can be fun. Do you have a sense of fun? We certainly do, so we enjoy bringing our sense of humour into the therapeutic environment when that is appropriate. Don't fall into the trap of thinking that counselling is always a deadpan, heavy and serious process. It may not be. As counsellors we are real people and need to be congruent. Each of us needs to be able to bring all of ourselves into the counselling relationship, and to use those parts of our personalities that can add richness to the therapeutic encounter whenever possible.

Learning summary

- Important qualities in a counsellor are congruence, empathy, unconditional positive regard, and respect for the client's competence.
- Congruence means being genuine, integrated, and a whole person.
- Being empathic means joining with the client so that there is a feeling of togetherness.
- Unconditional positive regard involves accepting the client non-judgmentally as a person of value, regardless of strengths and weaknesses.
- Respecting the client's competence enables the client to become self-reliant.
- Counselling is usually a serious process but can legitimately involve humour.

Further reading

Hackney, H. & Cormier, L. S. 1996, *The Professional Counselor: A Process Guide to Helping*, 3rd edn, Allyn & Bacon, Boston.
Mearns, D. 1994, *Developing Person-Centred Counselling*, Sage, London.
Rogers, C. R. 1955, *Client-Centered Therapy*, Houghton Mifflin, Boston.
Thorne, B. 1992, *Carl Rogers*, Sage, London.

part **II**

Basic principles
and skills

Learning the necessary skills

When we came to revise this chapter for the latest edition of this book it was interesting for us to discover that we had some common ideas and beliefs about how to learn to be an effective counsellor, and we also had some differences in emphasis. We realised that it is important for us to recognise that we are all unique individuals and that we each have our own preferred ways of learning. For David, learning to become an effective counsellor was a long process during which he discovered and absorbed ideas about counselling from his participation in a practical training course, through contact with supervisors who supervised his counselling practice, through his own practical experience, and through contact with other counsellors, clients and friends. Additionally, he learnt through his own personal experiences as a client. Although he did read counselling textbooks he didn't find them particularly helpful and placed a much higher emphasis on experiential learning. Kathryn's learning process was similar in that it also included a considerable

amount of experiential learning. However, a major difference was that she placed a high value on information obtained through reading and recognised that information obtained in this way had significantly influenced her counselling style and effectiveness.

After discussing the issues, we recognise that some people will find it easiest to learn by reading, and others by experiential learning. We believe that a combination of both methods of learning is best. We think that it can be helpful to learn counselling skills for use in everyday life just by reading about them. However, we are both firmly of the opinion that to be an effective counsellor, as well as reading, trainees need to have practical training and supervision from an experienced counsellor. In fact, as counsellors ourselves, we both believe that ongoing supervision of our work by another counsellor is essential (see Chapter 37).

There are two components involved in learning to become a counsellor. One involves understanding what counselling is about and how you are going to use counselling skills and processes. This understanding can provide you with a theoretical framework from which you can operate. The other component is to obtain practical skills training under the supervision of a competent counsellor and trainer. We don't think that it is possible to learn to be a counsellor in any other way. Our assumption is that most readers are reading this book to gain an understanding of basic counselling principles, and will additionally undergo a practical course of training.

Enhancing natural counselling skills

Many people have the idea that counselling requires a great deal of skill and is something rather difficult and complicated to learn. If that is what you believe, then we suggest that you might stop and ask yourself some questions. Have you ever comforted a child who was crying? Have you ever spent time sitting quietly with a friend who was terribly upset? Have you ever listened to somebody who was faced with a dilemma, and who did not know what to do? My guess is that you have done all of these things many times. If so, you have on many occasions in your life acted in a natural way as a counsellor with a friend, a relative, a child or maybe even with someone you met casually.

What was the most important thing you did in these situations? Was it just to let the person know that you cared enough about them to listen to their problem and to be with them in their distress? If it was, then you were behaving like a counsellor. Counselling is an extension of what we all do naturally in our relationships with others when they are suffering emotional pain.

From your own experience you will know that some people are more gifted than others at counselling in a natural way. We all know people who are such good listeners that their friends frequently talk over problems with them. Such people are natural counsellors. The aim of counsellor training is to help you to improve your natural counselling skills, and so become more effective in helping others to deal with their pain.

Learning specific skills (micro-skills)

In Chapter 2 we considered the importance of the counselling relationship. Certainly the relationship is central in counselling, but also there are a number of individual skills that can be learnt which greatly enhance the quality and effectiveness of the counselling relationship. Techniques used by counsellors have been analysed and broken down into small elements of counselling behaviour known as micro-skills. Each of the micro-skills can be learnt individually. However, be warned: a trainee needs to remember that counselling competence seems initially to diminish after each input of micro-skill training. This is because the trainee inevitably concentrates on using the new skill, rather than on building and maintaining the relationship. Also, the trainee isn't able to behave naturally when using a new skill until that skill is fully mastered. Once the skill is fully mastered it becomes a natural part of the counsellor's way of relating, and counselling effectiveness is considerably increased.

Learning in triads

In the following chapters, each of the micro-skills will be explained. After reading each chapter, it will be best if you practise the relevant micro-skill in a group setting. The usual way to do this is in a triad or a group of three students. One student takes the role of counsellor, a second student takes the role of client and the third student takes the role of observer.

Here are some suggestions about how to work in triads. If you are training for face-to-face counselling, set the room up with the chairs facing each other as shown in Figure 3.1, so that the 'client' faces the 'counsellor' and the observer watches both.

Telephone counselling is rather different from face-to-face counselling

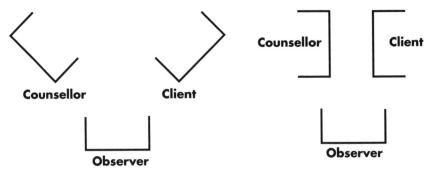

Figure 3.1 *Chair arrangement for face-to-face counselling practice*

Figure 3.2 *Chair arrangement for telephone counselling practice*

because the telephone counsellor can't see the caller who is their client. Consequently the counsellor doesn't have any visual indication of the client's non-verbal behaviour. For triad practice for trainee telephone counsellors, the chairs should therefore be set out with the 'counsellor' chair and the 'client' chair in a back-to-back arrangement as shown in Figure 3.2, so that the 'counsellor' and 'client' can't see each other. However the observer's chair should face the other two chairs so that the observer is aware of what is happening non-verbally, and can feed this back to the other two students at the end of each practice session.

The use of genuine personal problems

If counsellor training is to be most effective, then the 'client' in the triad needs to present a current and real personal problem of their own. Sometimes we have met students who have told us quite emphatically that they did not have such a thing as a personal problem, and we have found that difficult to believe. We doubt whether such people really exist. In our experience, whenever people have said to us that they don't have any personal problems, we have discovered later that there have been areas of their lives that they were unwilling to discuss, and that they had blocked off and were afraid to venture near. However, we can understand why many trainees worry about using real problems. There are a number of reasons for this, including the following:

1. The worry may be related to a lack of trust in other members of the triad, leading to feelings of vulnerability associated with self-disclosure. The trainee may think, 'They won't respect me if they find out about my problems'.

2. Unfortunately trainee counsellors frequently believe that they will not be accepted as counsellors if they disclose problems of their own. Our response to this is to say that as counsellor trainers we prefer to work with trainees who are able to own and address their problems. We are always worried by trainees who are not able to do this, because later, when they are trained, their disowned and unresolved issues may interfere with their ability to counsel effectively.
3. Trainees may be justifiably afraid that they may become distressed if they use a real problem.
4. Trainees may fear that if they do become distressed that they may not receive adequate counselling help from the trainee 'counsellor'. This is understandable. However, we believe that responsible trainers will inform trainees that follow-up counselling from experienced counsellors will always be available.

Trainees have often asked us whether they can use invented problems or other people's problems. Although this is better than not entering into a client role at all, in our view it is not very satisfactory. Most people who have been involved as trainers of counsellors would agree that it is much easier for the student counsellor to respond in a real and genuine way to what is being said if the problem is real, and not invented or borrowed from someone else. Whenever a make-believe problem is used, it is difficult for the trainee counsellor to accurately pick up the 'client's' feelings and to appropriately practise counselling skills.

Tasks of triad members

The 'counsellor' in a counselling triad should listen, and practise only those micro-skills that have been taught up to that point and should preferably try not to use any other type of response at all. This may seem to be very limiting, but in fact it is possible to carry out an effective counselling session by using only one or two micro-skills on their own. For example, Chapter 5 contains a transcript of a counselling session where only minimal responses and paraphrasing are used.

The observer's role in the triad is to take notes of anything significant they observe during the counselling practice session. The observer does not make judgments about what should have been done, but rather has the task of observing, as objectively as possible and without making interpretations, what actually happens during the practice session. For example, the observer may notice that when the 'counsellor' made a particular response, that there was a change in the 'client's' verbal or non-verbal behaviour. The observer may also notice tones of voice used, pace of speaking, silences, and the use of particular skills. The observer does not interrupt, but the information noticed by the observer is fed back to the 'counsellor' and 'client' at the end of the session.

Length of triad practice sessions

Practice counselling sessions should typically be short, of about 10 minutes' length, and at the end of each session the observer should share their observations with the other two members of the triad. After that, the 'client' should be given the opportunity to talk about how they felt during the counselling session, and finally the 'counsellor' should explore their own feelings, and share with the group how the session was for them. Preferably, in addition to the student observer there should be an experienced trainer observing the triad throughout. Unfortunately, in large group counsellor training, it frequently happens that trainers have to go from triad to triad and are able to spend only a short time with each small group.

Learning through observation

Before practising micro-skills in a triad, the relevant micro-skill should be modelled by a competent counsellor. There are two ways in which this can be done. Either the demonstration can be performed live, or a video-recording may be used. Our favoured option is the video-recorded demonstration. Too often live demonstrations, even with competent counsellors, include segments of inappropriate modelling or long sections of client material where it is not appropriate to use the relevant micro-skill.

Modelling of the counselling process

In addition to learning by practising micro-skills in triads, and by observing those micro-skills being modelled by an experienced counsellor, it is very valuable for trainee counsellors to have the opportunity to observe experienced counsellors in real life counselling sessions. There are three ways in which this can happen:

1. An experienced counsellor can counsel a trainee who has volunteered to discuss a real problem in front of the training group.
2. An experienced counsellor may counsel a client with the trainee observing while sitting in the same room, watching over a video link, or observing

through a one-way mirror equipped with sound system. For this to occur, the permission of the client is clearly required.

3. The trainee may watch a videotape of a real counselling session where the client has given permission for this to happen.

Ongoing training

This chapter has dealt with an overview of skills training for beginners with no previous counselling experience. Once basic skills have been learnt, the trainee counsellor needs to have ongoing training with real clients under supervision as discussed in Chapter 37.

The following chapters on micro-skills have been deliberately arranged in the most suitable sequence for training. By learning the skills in this sequence, the trainee can practise counselling by using only one or two micro-skills initially, and can then gradually incorporate additional skills into their repertoire. The sequence given is such that the most important basic skills are learnt first, with the consequence that more practice will be obtained in using these skills and the trainee counsellor will begin to rely on them as being the ones that are most appropriate for frequent use.

Learning summary

- Learning to be a counsellor must involve practical training and supervision as well as theoretical knowledge.
- Some people are natural counsellors; however counsellor training can improve their effectiveness.
- A micro-skill is a small element of counsellor behaviour which can be learnt and practised.

Further reading

Dryden, W., Horton, I. & Mearns, D. 1995, *Issues in Professional Counsellor Training*, Cassell, London.

Dryden, W. & Thorne, B. (eds) 1991, *Training and Supervision for Counselling in Action*, Sage, London.

chapter

Joining and listening

This chapter deals with both joining and listening because these two processes are interrelated. If we are to join with our clients we need to listen to them and attend to what they are saying. We also need to use a range of behaviours to help them to feel at ease.

The first meeting

The initial meeting with a client is extremely important. The client's first impressions of the counsellor will influence their willingness to share openly. First impressions can be enduring and even if they aren't, they are likely to influence the early part of the relationship. It is therefore very important that the climate of the relationship is established right from the beginning. However, it needs to be recognised that joining doesn't just occur at the initial meeting with the client but is an ongoing process. Throughout the counselling process the client needs to feel comfortable with their relationship with the counsellor.

Some counsellors work in a face-to-face situation, and others work on the telephone. In this chapter we will discuss the initial contact in the face-to-face counselling situation. We will discuss the initial contact in telephone counselling later, in Chapter 30.

Greeting the client

Imagine that you are meeting a client for the first time in your waiting room. What you do, as you move towards the client to greet them, will in some way affect their feelings towards you, and their confidence in you. It's important that the person you meet feels valued and at ease with you. As you meet the client, you need to be true to yourself rather than putting on an act. Remember that you are a person, like everybody else, so try to meet the client in a person-to-person encounter where you aren't intimidating, are neither expert nor inferior, but friendly, open and informal. Most importantly, help the client to feel at ease and welcome.

Be aware of cultural considerations when greeting clients. In some cultures hand-shaking is seen as an intimate act so offering your hand may be excessively intrusive for some people (see Chapter 34).

Observing the client

As you greet the client you can, if you are observant, pick up a lot of information without asking any questions. Notice the way they are sitting or standing. The client's non-verbal behaviour will tell you something about the way they feel. Look at the clothes they are wearing, and how they are worn. By doing this you will learn something about how the client sees themselves, and how they want to be seen. Don't jump to unverified conclusions, but use the information gleaned from your first meeting so that you can gradually build up a picture of the client's world and of their view of that world.

Putting the client at ease

When one of us meets a client for the first time, we introduce ourself and usually chat to the client as we walk to the counselling room. This helps the client to feel at ease. When we meet the client prior to subsequent interviews we may be generally less chatty, and sometimes silent. This enables the client to stay with any troubling thoughts rather than to be taken away from them. Be aware that as a client leaves the waiting room and walks to the counselling room, they may well be putting their thoughts together, and may be experiencing the beginnings of heavy emotion as they get nearer to the issues they want to discuss. If the client is doing that, then it isn't helpful to be chatting about unimportant matters. It's better to be silent.

Notice that we have differentiated between the first and subsequent sessions. We try to help the client to feel very much at ease during the first session, and are happy to use the first few minutes during that meeting to allow the client to settle in and feel comfortable. We allow the client to sit down, to look around, and maybe to comment on the pot-plants in the room or some other aspect of the room or the agency. We may even talk about some other casual topic like how the client travelled to the agency, and what the traffic was like, or we may share something of ourselves and our day with them. As a result we start to establish a relationship before moving forward into working on issues.

The invitation to talk

Clients sometimes find it difficult to know how to start to talk about their problems. There are obviously many different ways of inviting a client to talk about their problems. Here are some suggestions:

> 'Would you like to tell me what made you decide to come to see me today?'
> 'I'm wondering what is troubling you.'
> 'What is it that you would like to talk to me about?'

Some clients may feel pressured to respond to your invitation by talking quickly and concisely so that they don't take up too much of your time. Reassure them that it is OK to take time. Other clients may find it difficult to start to talk and may say that they don't know how to begin. When this happens, you might say something like:

> 'Just relax and take time. Then if you can, tell me whatever it is that comes into your head even if it's unimportant.'

This invitation is good for enabling a nervous client to start talking. Once the client has started to talk it is important for them to know that you are listening and attending to what they are saying.

Tuning in

Have you ever talked about being on the same 'wavelength' as someone? Maybe you have sometimes noticed that a person has really 'tuned in' to what you are saying. Joining is about 'tuning in', or 'being on the same wavelength' as someone else. Thus, a harmonious connection is established between the person who is talking and the person who is listening. This is what we need to achieve as counsellors.

Whenever we listen to someone, we give out very subtle clues. These clues give an indication of how we are responding to what is being said, and give an indication of our feelings towards the person who is speaking. As helpers we therefore need to be careful to give out the right messages.

Listening with interest

People usually go to counsellors because they are troubled and don't know what to do to cope with their emotions. They will often expect that the counsellor will give them advice to enable them to change their situation. Because of this it is easy for new counsellors to feel pressured into trying, even early in the counselling process, to find solutions for clients. As a new counsellor, try to remember that the counsellor's primary task is to *listen to the client* and to use strategies which will enable them to find their own solutions. These solutions are likely to suit them because they have discovered them for themselves. The client will have also discovered that they are capable of making their own decisions.

In our experience, before looking for solutions, the first thing most people want to do when they seek counselling help is to *talk about* the things that trouble them. They want to get things off their chests, to vent their feelings, and to say things which might be very difficult or maybe impossible to say to friends or family.

When you are with a client, try to remember that the client has come to talk to you and wants to feel free to unload the stuff that is troubling them. To do this they need an invitation and opportunity to talk without unnecessary interruption. If you do a lot of talking, then you are likely to interfere with their ability to talk freely and the counselling process is likely to be less useful.

A counsellor is primarily a listener. By listening to what the client says, the counsellor is able to help them to sort through their confusion, identify their dilemmas, explore their options, and come away from the counselling session feeling that something useful has occurred. The counsellor therefore needs to attend very carefully to everything that the client is saying and to remember, as far as is possible, the details of the conversation. If you want to convince your client that you really are listening, then focus your concentration on the client and on what they are telling you. Try to remember, for example, the names of relatives, what happened five years ago in their relationships, and those things which are briefly mentioned.

The first skill for the new counsellor to learn is to put deliberate effort into *listening with interest*. This needs to be done in such a way that the client recognises that you are totally focusing your attention on what is being said, and are comprehending and understanding it. Listening with interest involves the use of the following:

1. minimal responses
2. brief invitations to continue
3. non-verbal behaviour
4. voice
5. silence

We will now discuss each of these.

Use of minimal responses

A good way to let a client know that they have your full attention and that you are listening to what they are saying is by use of minimal responses. The minimal response is something we naturally do in conversation when we are predominantly listening rather than talking. Minimal responses are sometimes non-verbal and include just a nod of the head. Also included among minimal responses are expressions like:

'Mm', 'Mm-hmm', 'Ah-ha', 'I see', 'Yes', 'OK', 'Sure', 'Right', 'Oh' *and* 'Really'

These expressions let clients know that they have been heard and also encourage them to continue talking. Some longer responses serve a similar function to the minimal response. For example, the counsellor might say:

'I hear what you say' *or* 'I understand'

While the client is talking continuously, the counsellor needs from time to time to reaffirm that they are listening to what the client is saying, and this can be done by inserting minimal responses at regular intervals. Space your minimal responses appropriately. If they are given too frequently, then they will become intrusive and will be distracting. Conversely, if they are not included frequently enough the client may believe that you are not really attending to what is being said.

Using the minimal response to convey a message

The minimal response is not just an acknowledgment that the client is being heard. It can also be a way, sometimes subtle, of communicating other messages. It may be used to signify that the counsellor agrees with the client, or to emphasise the importance of a client statement, to express surprise, or even to query what the client is saying. The way in which a minimal response is given—the tone and intensity of voice used, the accompanying non-verbal behaviour such as eye movements, facial expressions and body posture—all combine to convey a message to the client.

Counsellors need to be careful in giving out messages of agreement or disagreement. Sometimes with the best of intentions showing agreement with a client may be counterproductive. David remembers being told by an acquaintance that she had discontinued going to see a counsellor because that counsellor had strongly agreed with her criticisms of her husband. Presumably the counsellor thought that by doing this he would join with the client. Unfortunately the counsellor's behaviour prevented the person concerned from talking further because she felt that by doing this she would be being disloyal to her husband. By agreeing with her, the counsellor also blocked her from talking through her own feelings of guilt about her relationship with her husband. She wanted to be heard, understood, and valued, but did not want a stranger who didn't know her husband to be critical of him.

Being *empathic* involves hearing, understanding, and valuing the client. Can you see how this is different from *agreeing* with the client? Although there are times when agreeing with the client may be useful, generally it is more helpful to listen and understand without judgment.

Use of brief invitations to continue

Sometimes, a client will pause and it is important for the counsellor to allow the client time to think. However, once the client has finished thinking it may be useful to give a brief invitation to the client to continue. This can be done by using one of the following responses:

'Then . . .', 'And . . .', 'Tell me more', 'Can you tell me more?', 'Would you like to tell me more?' *or* 'Would you like to continue?'

Counselling involves the art of listening constructively, so appropriate use of minimal responses and brief invitations to continue is essential.

Use of non-verbal behaviour

There are a number of ways in which a counsellor can use non-verbal behaviour to join with the client and enhance the counselling process. These include:

- matching non-verbal behaviour
- physical closeness
- the use of movement
- facial expression
- eye contact

Matching non-verbal behaviour

Along with the use of minimal responses, another way in which counsellors can help clients to feel that they are really being listened to is to match their non-verbal behaviour. If a client is sitting on the edge of the seat, with their arms on their knees looking forward, then it may be useful for the counsellor to sit in the same way and in effect to mirror the client's posture. By doing this, the client is likely to feel as though there is some intimacy between themself and the counsellor, rather than seeing the counsellor as a superior expert sitting back, listening and judging what is being said. Similarly, if the client leans back in their chair with legs crossed, and the counsellor casually matches that posture, the client may well feel more at ease. Clearly, matching needs to be done appropriately so that the counsellor is seen to be acting naturally rather than mimicking the client.

If a counsellor matches a client's non-verbal behaviour and posture for a while, then more often than not the client will match the counsellor's behaviour when the counsellor makes a change. In this way the counsellor can sometimes bring about some change in the client's emotional state. For example, a client may be so tense that they are sitting on the edge of the chair and are unable to relax into a more comfortable sitting position. If the counsellor matches this position initially and then moves back to sit more comfortably, the client is likely to follow the counsellor's example and consequently to experience a reduction in level of tension.

Physical closeness

We all have different personal comfort levels with regard to physical closeness. Also, we need to recognise that there are major differences in comfort levels related to physical closeness for people from different cultures (see Chapter 34).

Think about how you would feel personally if someone you were talking to was to stand a long way from you, or was to move further away while you were talking. You might get the message that that person wasn't interested in what you were saying, or that they thought that you weren't a very nice person so didn't want to be close to you. Also, consider what it's like when someone stands too close to you for your comfort. How does that feel?

Clearly, as a counsellor, it is best to sit at an appropriate distance from the person you are helping, so that they feel comfortable. Knowing the correct distance is a matter of judgment. Remember, you need to sense what is comfortable for the other person and to be careful not to intrude on their personal space.

The use of movement

Sometimes, at significant times in the counselling process or when a client is experiencing a high level of emotional distress it can be useful for the counsellor to lean forward. This can help the client to recognise that the counsellor is joining with them in an empathic way. However, a counsellor should be careful not to move too quickly during a counselling session, as this can distract the client and interrupt their train of thought. However, a counsellor does need to feel as relaxed as possible and should feel free to move position in a natural way whenever that is more comfortable, but this should preferably be done slowly and not suddenly.

Facial expression

Facial expression usually has a significant impact on the joining process. Our facial expressions give very obvious clues about what we are thinking, and about our attitudes. Clearly, we want to show an expression of interest, care, and concern. Also, we want to try to avoid giving the impression that we are making negative judgments about the person, or what the person is saying.

Eye contact

Eye contact is an important way in which we human beings make contact and join with each other. Not only do we use our eyes to make contact, but we also convey subtle messages by the way in which we use our eyes. I wonder what impression you would get if somebody was looking away from you while you were talking to them? My guess is that you might believe that they weren't interested in what you were saying. However, if that person were to look at you directly, eye to eye, you might feel uncomfortable and think that their eyes were 'boring into you'. What is required is an appropriate level of eye contact where your eyes meet with the other person's eyes in a socially and culturally acceptable way. It is important to remember that different cultures have different social norms with regard to appropriate levels of eye contact. However, if your client is to believe that you are listening to what is being said, then eye contact at an appropriate level will give a clear message that you are attending to, and interested in, what is being said.

Use of voice

When we speak, it is not only the words that convey a message. Additionally, a message is conveyed through the way in which we use our voices. If we want to create an empathic relationship with our clients and to make it clear to them that we are concentrating on, and listening to, what they are saying, then we need to attend to our voice quality and be aware of the effects of:

- clarity and volume
- speed of speaking
- tone of voice

Over an extended period I, David, sought counselling help from a very capable and skilled counsellor. He helped me to address many painful issues and to experience satisfaction through personal growth. I very much appreciate the help he gave me. However, he had one annoying fault. Sometimes, I couldn't hear what he was saying because he mumbled. He didn't articulate words clearly and didn't talk loudly enough. At times this interfered with the counselling process by distracting me. At other times it enabled me to deflect away from issues which I needed to address. It was also embarrassing for me to have to tell him from time to time that I couldn't hear him.

When you are counselling, be careful to talk clearly and at a comfortable volume. Make sure that your tone of voice is one which will help to create an empathic relationship. Generally, it can be helpful if you match the speed of talking and tone of voice of your client. When the client talks rapidly respond similarly, and when they slow up be more leisurely yourself. If you match, to an appropriate degree, the speed and tone of speaking, and also the speed of breathing of an agitated client, you will be likely to join with them. Then, if you slow down your breathing and your speaking speed, and sit back comfortably in your chair, the client may follow your example, slow down and adopt a more relaxed posture.

Use of silence

When I, David, was a new counsellor, I remember often not focusing fully on what the client was saying because I was too concerned with trying to decide what my next counselling response would be. This was really destructive to the counselling process. It was due to my nervousness and desire to appear to be professional and competent rather than friendly and real. At that time, I was uncomfortable with silence and felt that I had a responsibility to fill gaps in the conversation. Now I am more comfortable with silence so there is little pressure on me to give a response the instant the client stops talking. Instead I feel relaxed enough to allow the client, if they want, to think in silence. Often a client who has just finished making a very powerful and personal statement will need time to sit silently and process what has been said.

When a client is silent, match that silence while continuing to pay attention by using appropriate eye contact, so that you are seen to be listening with a high level of interest. If you observe the client's eye movements and focusing, you may be able to tell when they are thinking and need to be left to think rather than be interrupted.

Learning summary

- Joining is an ongoing process.
- A counsellor's primary function is to deliberately and intentionally listen.
- Deliberate listening with interest involves use of minimal responses, brief invitations to continue, non-verbal behaviour, voice and silence.
- Minimal responses can be verbal or non-verbal.
- Minimal responses let the client know that you are attending, and help create an empathic relationship. They can also give messages.
- Joining with the client is enhanced by matching non-verbal behaviour such as posture, matching verbal tone and speed, and making appropriate eye contact.
- Rapid movements by a counsellor can distract a client.
- Silence is important in giving the client time to think and process what has been said.
- A client's eyes may give you an indication of when they have stopped thinking.

chapter **5**

Reflection of content (paraphrasing)

As explained in the previous chapter, the primary function of a counsellor is to deliberately listen with interest so that clients believe with confidence that they are being both heard and understood. However, it's obvious that just attending to a client by matching non-verbal behaviour and giving minimal responses is not sufficient. The counsellor also needs to respond more actively, and by doing so to draw out the really important details of what the client is saying and to clarify those for the client. The most common and generally most effective way of doing this is by using the skill called *paraphrasing* or *reflection of content*. Using this skill the counsellor reflects back to the client what the client has said to the counsellor. The counsellor does not just parrot or repeat word for word what the client has said but instead paraphrases it. This means that the counsellor picks out the most important content details of what the client has said and re-expresses them in a clearer way, if that is possible, and in the counsellor's own words rather than in the client's. The following are some examples of paraphrasing to illustrate how the skill is used.

Examples of paraphrasing or reflection of content

Example 1

Client Statement: *I'm fighting with my daughter, my husband's not speaking to me, at work the boss keeps picking on me, and what's more my best friend doesn't seem to understand me any more.*
Counsellor Response: You're having a lot of relationship problems.

Example 2

Client Statement: *I spent all day Saturday cleaning up my girlfriend's yard but she was annoyed because she said I'd cut the shrubs too short, I'd over-pruned them. Then I went to a great deal of trouble repainting the back door. Once again she didn't like the colour. Finally I suggested that she might go out to eat with me and would you believe when she got to the restaurant she decided that she really didn't like that restaurant at all. I keep trying to think of things that she would like but whatever I do she never seems to be happy.*
Counsellor Response: It seems as though you just can't please your girlfriend.

Example 3

Client Statement: *Yesterday I rushed around, I seemed to have no time to myself, I went from one place to another and it was really hard to fit everything in.*
Counsellor Response: You had a very full day yesterday.

What the counsellor does when paraphrasing or reflecting content is literally to tell the client, in a clear, brief way, in the counsellor's own words, the most important things that the client has just told the counsellor. The counsellor tries to capture the essential ingredients of what the client is saying and reflect these back. This method alone, together with minimal responses, can be used successfully throughout a complete counselling session, if it is carried out by a skilful person who is capable of accurately and clearly reflecting content.

The following transcript of a short counselling session (using invented names) demonstrates the way in which paraphrasing alone can be used to bring a client to a sense of resolution.

Transcript of a counselling session using minimal responses and paraphrasing

Mary: Susan, you said that you would like to talk something over with me. Can you tell me what's troubling you? [Mary gives Susan an invitation to talk.]

Susan: *Yes. I'm worried about what's happening at work. I'm getting very stressed when I'm there.*

Mary: Mm-hmm.

Susan: *It seems as though I am continually at odds with some of the other workers and with my boss. I just don't seem to be on the same wavelength as them.*

Mary: You're not fitting in.

Susan: *No, I'm not. I don't agree with the policies which are being adopted by the top management because they don't fit in with the way I learnt to deal with customers. Over the years I've developed ways of working which I think work . . .*

Mary: Right.

Susan: *And now I'm being expected to change my whole style of working.*

Mary: They want you to work in a way which doesn't suit you.

Susan: *Yes they do, and I'm beginning to think that I'll either have to resign or compromise my principles. I'm just not sure what to do.*

Mary: You have a difficult choice to make.

Susan: *Yes, I have . . . [pause]*

Mary: [silent but attending]

Susan: *. . . but you know I don't see why I should resign. I need the job, it's convenient, the money's good and there aren't many other jobs I could do that would suit me. They will just have to put up with me.*

Mary: You sound as though you've made a decision to stay.

Susan: *Yes, I have, but I'll need to think about the implications.*

Mary: Mm-hmm.

Susan: *I suppose that if I continue to work in the way I think is best I'll still get the outcomes the boss wants but she'll get annoyed because I'm not following policy . . . Somehow, I've got to compromise so that I can satisfy the boss and still feel OK about what I'm doing myself.*

Mary: You'd like to please the boss and still feel OK yourself.

Susan: *Yes, I would. I would like to please the boss so that the atmosphere at work is more relaxed. I suppose I've been a bit stubborn in resisting change.*

Mary: Mmm.

Susan: *That's probably the issue. I don't like change. But then nobody does. I'd rather change and continue working where I am than move somewhere else.*

Mary: Accepting change is difficult for you.

Susan: *Yes it is. But that's what I need to do. I suppose that if I agreed to do some in-service training I'd feel more confident about the new methods but I don't like other people believing that I need further training after all these years.*

Mary: Ah-ha.

Susan: *I suppose that the truth is that I do need further training and it's hard for me to accept that fact.*

Mary: You want other people to respect you as an experienced worker.

Susan: *Yes, and at the moment they see me as a dinosaur. Out of date and inflexible.*

Mary: Ah-ha, they don't see you as able to adapt.

Susan: *Well, I am out of date but I'm not inflexible. I can learn new ways of working. I'll show them that an old magician can learn new tricks!*

Mary: You're going to accept the challenge.

Susan: *Yes, I am. I don't want to be seen as an old fossil, because I'm not.*

Mary: You seem to have reached a firm conclusion.

Susan: *Yes, I have. Thank you for listening.*

If you look through the transcript above, you will notice that Mary has used no other responses except minimal responses and reflection of content. Once she combined a minimal response with paraphrasing by saying, 'Ah-ha, they don't see you as able to adapt'.

Did you notice as you read the transcript that there was a natural flow in the conversation? Each time Susan made a statement and Mary paraphrased it, her reflection of Susan's statement set off a train of thoughts for Susan so that she continued with the conversation in a natural way. Consequently, it would have seemed to Susan that Mary really was understanding what she was saying. Mary wasn't intruding on Susan's thoughts by adding in her own ideas.

By reflecting back what Susan said, Mary was able to help her think clearly about what she had said. This enabled her to continue talking about the same issue, in a constructive way. It was as though she was walking along a path, in her thoughts, with Mary walking alongside her.

You may have noticed that even though the conversation between Susan and Mary was short, Susan resolved her issue without Mary asking questions, putting in suggestions or giving advice. All she did was to skilfully reflect back to Susan what she was saying.

It's important for you to learn how to paraphrase. In order to help you to do this we have provided some more examples of paraphrasing below. In each case we suggest that you might like to cover up the counsellor response with a sheet of paper, read the client statement and see whether you can work out a suitable counsellor response to the client's statement. Good paraphrasing doesn't intrude. It doesn't distract the client from the real issues which they are trying to resolve.

Further examples of paraphrasing

Example 4

Client Statement: *Within a week I've had a rates notice, an electricity bill, my car broke down and I've had to spend $300 having it fixed, there was a big dinner I had to attend as part of my work and it was very expensive, and in addition I've had to fork out money for my son's trip overseas and for my daughter's school fees.*

Counsellor Response: You've had a lot of expenses to meet in a very short time.

Example 5

Client Statement: *Now that my father has died I can't help thinking about him. I think about the good times I had with him when I was young and about the way he showed so much interest in me in the early days of my marriage. I remember the way he played with my children, his grandchildren. He always seemed to be enjoying himself.*

Counsellor Response: You have some good memories of your father.

Example 6

Client Statement: *The house is old and ramshackle, the rooms are very large, there isn't much in it and it needs redecorating. Parts of it are starting to fall down. Where you walk there are bare floorboards and they creak. It doesn't sound very much like home because it is such a big, open, old, barren sort of a place, but you know I really like living there.*

Counsellor Response: Even though the house is in poor condition it's home to you.

Example 7

Client Statement: *I used to have a very bad drinking problem so I stopped drinking for a couple of years. Well last night I had a drink and now I'm just wondering how that's going to affect me in the future. I'm really surprised though because I was able to have just one drink and stop, whereas in the past I always used to carry on drinking once I'd started.*

Counsellor Response: Although you surprised yourself, you're not too sure how you'll cope with alcohol from now on.

Example 8

Client Statement: *My daughter's a very attractive girl, she's good looking and vivacious, she dresses very nicely and she is a good-natured person. She often smiles and seems to be very happy.*

Counsellor Response: Your daughter has many positive qualities.

Please remember that individual counsellors may paraphrase the same client statement differently. They may not pick up on the same detail as each other. The model answers which we have been given above are not necessarily the best responses. We believe that we are good counsellors, but do not consider ourselves to be perfect in any of the micro-skills. We have yet to find someone who is. It's really important to remember that it doesn't matter how perfect your responses are. What does matter is that you create a real, trusting, caring, empathic relationship with the client in which you are genuinely yourself. This may mean sometimes being a bungler, and occasionally saying something inappropriate. Both of us have at times given inappropriate responses. Although we try not to do that, there will always be times when we do.

Using inappropriate responses

I, David, used to think that it was a disaster to give an inappropriate response until an artist friend of mine talked to me about pencil sketching. I told her how it was that when I tried to sketch I very often had the sketch three-quarters complete and then ruined it by putting in a dark line in an inappropriate place. My artist friend laughed and said, 'You never draw lines in the wrong place, because whenever you put in a line you can use it to create something different'. I learnt a lesson from what she said, and applied it to my counselling. When I make an inappropriate response, I use that response. It will generate an interaction between the client and myself, and I am able to encourage the client to explore the effect that the inappropriate response had on her. By doing this I am using the immediacy of the relationship between the client and myself. This will be discussed more fully in Chapter 20.

Parroting

Parroting is not the same as paraphrasing. Parroting involves repeating word for word what the client has said to you. Occasionally it can be useful to parrot the client's last few words to draw attention to the importance of those words, or to enable the client to continue a half-finished statement. As a general rule, paraphrasing is a much more helpful process. This is because paraphrasing picks out the most important and salient parts of the content rather than just repeating the words the client has used. Continually repeating part or all of what the client has said would be likely to annoy the client rather then create a good rela-tionship. Skilful reflection of content in the counsellor's own words does the reverse. It makes the client feel valued, listened to, and heard, and is useful in helping the client to move forward in their exploration.

In conclusion

In this chapter we have discussed paraphrasing or reflection of content. Paraphrasing is a very useful basic skill to use. To paraphrase you have to listen carefully and to repeat back in your own words the essence of what the client has said. By doing this the client believes that you have heard them and also becomes more fully aware of what they have said. They are then able to really savour the importance of what they are talking about and to sort out their confusion.

Learning summary

- Paraphrasing involves reflecting back to the client the important content of what the client has said but in a clearer way and using the counsellor's words.
- Parroting involves repetition of some of the client's words.
- Occasional parroting can be useful either to emphasise the importance of what the client has said or to help a client to complete a half-finished statement.
- Paraphrasing, together with the use of minimal responses, helps the client to follow through on a train of thoughts and continue talking.

Examples of client statements for use by trainers in teaching paraphrasing

1. *'My brother has had a serious motorbike accident and it looks as though he may be permanently crippled. He's a builder by trade and now he may never be able to walk again. I don't know how he'll be able to work.'*

2. *'The cancer is malignant and now I only have six months to live at the most. There is so much that I want to do and I can't decide what to do first. I am certainly going to have to do things in a hurry.'*

3. *'The law is very unjust. He discovered where I live, followed me, deliberately aimed the gun, and fired several shots directly at me to try to kill me. He even asked the police if I was dead, and then he's given a light sentence on so-called psychiatric grounds. It's not fair.'*

4. *'I've never stayed in one place for more than a couple of years. In the last few months I've lived in five different houses. It's hardly worth unpacking when I move now because I know I'll move on again. I just can't settle.'*

5. *'The pain starts in my head and moves down into my back. Sometimes my whole body aches. The pain never stops and is overwhelming.'*

6. *'I think my father is a hypocrite. He's a preacher who preaches love and forgiveness and is charming to everybody except his own family. In the family he's a tyrant who bullies everyone and is unforgiving. I'm rapidly losing my respect for him.'*

chapter **6**

Reflection of feelings

As explained in the previous chapter, one of the best ways to help clients to feel as though you are listening to them is to reflect back to them the content of what they are saying. Reflection of feelings is similarly useful. We ourselves think that it may be the most useful micro-skill of all.

Reflection of feelings is at the same time similar to and different from paraphrasing. It is similar because it involves reflecting back to the client information provided by the client. However it is different because it deals with emotional feelings, whereas paraphrasing generally deals with the information and thoughts that make up the content of what the client is saying.

Are feelings different from thoughts?

Feelings are quite different from thoughts. Thoughts mill around in our brains. They are at a 'head' level, whereas feelings are to do with emotions. Feelings are at a gut level, not a head level, and they tie into our physiological sensations. For example, a person who is feeling tense emotionally may experience the tension in their muscles, often in the neck or shoulders, and an anxious person may have sweaty palms, an increased heart rate or the sensation of 'butterflies in the stomach'.

Avoiding feelings

Frequently clients try to avoid exploring their feelings because they want to avoid the pain associated with strong emotions such as sadness, despair, anger, and anxiety. We both recognise that it's much less painful for us to philosophise about our problems, and to discuss them as though they were 'out there' and don't really belong to us, than for us to get in touch with the related emotions. Unfortunately when we avoid our feelings, philosophise, and talk in a general way about our problems rather than fully experiencing the effect they have on us emotionally, we rarely feel better or reach a resolution. Instead, we tend to go around in circles and get nowhere. However, if we get in touch with our feelings, own them, and experience them fully, then we usually move forward, to feel better emotionally and maybe then to make sensible decisions.

Experiencing feelings

It may be tempting for a new counsellor to help the client to avoid painful feelings rather than to face them. Many of us learn from childhood to comfort people by encouraging them to run away from their feelings. We are taught to say, 'Don't cry, it'll be all right', when it quite probably won't be all right, and the person really needs to cry to release their emotional pain. To be an effective counsellor you will need to unlearn some of what you learnt as a child. You will generally need to encourage your clients to experience their emotions, to be sad, to cry, to be angry and to shout, to be overwhelmed, to be amused, to be frightened or whatever. By doing this you will help them to gain from emotional release and to move forward. This healing process of emotional release is called *catharsis*.

There are exceptions to this approach. A small minority of people are so continually in touch with, and overwhelmed by their emotions, that to encourage them to do more of the same is unlikely to be useful. These people may find it more helpful to make use of their thinking processes in order to control their emotions. For them a more cognitive behavioural approach may be preferred (see Chapter 11).

Distinguishing between thoughts and feelings

New counsellors often have problems in distinguishing between thoughts and feelings because people often use the word 'feel' when they are describing a thought. For example if someone were to say, 'I feel angry', then they would be expressing a feeling, but if they were to say, 'I feel that counsellors learn best through practical experience', they would not be expressing a feeling, they would be describing a thought. It would have been more accurate to say, 'I think that counsellors learn best through practical experience'. The words 'feel that' followed by a string of words generally mean that a thought is being expressed and not a feeling. Feelings are usually expressed by one word. For example, a person can feel 'angry', 'sad', 'depressed', 'frustrated', 'miserable', 'tense', 'relaxed', 'happy' or 'frantic'. Each of these feelings is expressed by one word, whereas thoughts can only be expressed by using a string of words.

Reflecting back feelings

When a counsellor reflects back a feeling to a client it is not essential to use the word 'feel'. Here are some options for reflecting feelings of anger and hapiness:

'You're feeling angry' *or* 'You feel angry' *or* 'You're angry'
'You're feeling happy' *or* 'You feel happy' *or* 'You're happy'

An experienced counsellor continually identifies the client's feelings and reflects them back at appropriate times. Sometimes a client will tell you directly how they are feeling and at other times you will need to be able to assess what they are feeling by listening to the content of what they are saying or by noting their non-verbal behaviour or by listening to their tone of voice.

Feeling words

Table 6.1 provides a list of commonly used 'feeling' words. Notice that all of the words in the table could be used as counsellor responses by prefacing them with 'You're feeling . . .', or 'You feel . . .', or 'You're . . .' In some cases we have to use our personal judgment in deciding which option to use. For example 'You're grieving' sounds empathic, whereas 'You're feeling grief' sounds awkward.

The words in Table 6.1 have been arranged so that the words on each line relate to each other over a continuum from strong feelings to mild feelings. Some of the cells in the table are white and contain question marks. You may wish to choose suitable words for insertion in these white cells and then look at Table 6.2 at the end of this chapter for our suggestions. Can you see how if we choose our words carefully we may be able to accurately describe the client's feelings?

With practice it becomes easier to identify feelings such as tension, distress and sadness from a person's body posture, facial expressions and movements. Tears starting to well up in your client's eyes might let you know about their sadness.

Table 6.1 *Some commonly used feeling words*

Line	Strong feelings	Medium level feelings	Mild feelings
1	honoured cherished treasured	valued appreciated	accepted
2	powerful energetic	strong determined	positive certain
3	powerless	weak	tired
4	thrilled	very pleased	pleased
5	???	loved	liked respected
6	optimistic confident	???	uncertain
7	paranoid	suspicious	curious
8	hated	alienated	disliked
9	proud	self-satisfied	contented
10	perplexed	puzzled confused	uncertain doubtful
11	frantic agitated	???	concerned
12	relaxed	calm	indifferent
13	jealous	envious	discontented
14	???	surprised	pleased
15	terrified	???	worried anxious
16	distraught	distressed miserable	unhappy

continued ...

Table 6.1 *continued*

Line	Strong feelings	Medium level feelings	Mild feelings
17	secure	safe	OK
18	vulnerable	???	uncertain
19	appalled	dismayed	disappointed
20	humiliated ashamed	embarrassed	stupid
21	???	worn out	tired
22	intolerant	impatient	uneasy
23	betrayed	cheated	misled
24	ready to snap	tense	???
25	bewildered	puzzled	uncertain
26	horrified appalled shocked	dismayed taken aback	surprised
27	???	delighted	happy
28	devastated shattered broken-hearted	sad miserable depressed	disappointed troubled
29	grieving	shocked lost empty	alone
30	furious mad	angry resentful	???
31	abused victimised attacked	threatened	blamed

Permission to cry

Sometimes people need permission to cry because in our culture crying, particularly by men, is often considered to be unacceptable. If you say to a client, 'I can see the tears in your eyes' or 'For me, it's OK if you cry' or just 'It's OK to cry' in a gentle, accepting tone of voice, then the tears may start to flow. If this happens, allow your client to cry. If you hand the client tissues or comfort them before the emotion subsides naturally, you may well intrude on their internal processes. The client may then withdraw from fully experiencing their feelings, and the healing effects of emotional release may be diminished.

Response to reflection of feelings

If you reflect feelings accurately it is likely that the client will get more fully in touch with their emotional feelings. As a counsellor you do need to be prepared for a variety of possible responses when you reflect feelings. Sometimes a new counsellor will experience high levels of anxiety or heightened emotional feelings themselves, as a consequence of a client's response to reflection of feelings. For example, if you correctly say to your client, 'I get the impression that you are really hurting inside', then the client may get in touch with their painful feelings and start to cry. In this case, you will need to deal with your own emotional feelings that have been generated by being in the presence of someone who is crying.

Counsellors also will need to be prepared for other possible responses to reflection of feelings. For example, you may correctly reflect back anger by saying, 'You're angry' or perhaps 'You sound very angry'. Instead of owning the anger and recognising its true source, the client may respond by angrily snapping back with, 'I'm not angry' followed by an angry tirade, sometimes directed at the counsellor. If this happens, allow yourself to feel good, because you have enabled the client to express anger which they do not wish to own openly. They have been able to discharge some of their anger on you, and it may be that they will feel better for that. However, dealing with angry clients can have its dangers, so be careful. A full chapter has been devoted to this topic (Chapter 25).

Another way in which an angry client may disown feelings of anger is to say, 'I'm not angry, I'm just frustrated'. In this case it may be helpful for the counsellor to respond by saying, 'My guess is that if I were you, I would feel angry'. By saying this, the counsellor effectively gives the client permission to get more fully in touch with angry feelings.

Ready to burst!

Human beings can be likened in some ways to party balloons. When we are functioning effectively, we have sufficient emotional energy inside us to keep us motivated to live our daily lives functionally and creatively: the balloon has sufficient air inside it to be robust and float through the air. At crisis times in our lives, the emotional pressure builds up until we are ready to burst. In this state our thought processes are often blocked or distorted and we are unable to cope. We feel out of control of ourselves. To regain control we first need to release some of the emotional pressure. This may be difficult as many of us have been taught from childhood to hold our emotions in, not to cry, and not to be angry.

An effective counsellor can help a client to fully experience their emotions and thus to feel better as a result of releasing those emotions. With cathartic release the pressure in the balloon drops back to normal. Rational thinking can start to take place again so that constructive decision making can occur.

Reflection of feelings is therefore, as stated previously, one of the most important, perhaps *the* most important, counselling skill. The following are examples of client statements, followed by suitable reflections of feeling. Before reading the suggested counsellor response for each example, you may wish to think about the response you would give.

Examples of reflection of feelings

Example 1

Client Statement: *I keep expecting my mother to show more interest in me. Time and again I've asked her to come over to see me but she never does. Yesterday it was my birthday and she did come to visit me, but do you know she didn't even remember that it was my birthday. I just don't think she cares about me at all. [Said slowly in a flat tone of voice.]*
Counsellor Response: You're disappointed *or* You feel hurt.

Example 2

Client Statement: *First of all, my brother broke my electric drill. He didn't bother to tell me that he'd broken it, he just left it lying there. Then what do you think he did, he borrowed my motorbike without asking me. I feel like thumping him.*

Counsellor Response: You're very angry *or* You're furious.

Example 3

Client Statement: *I got a new job recently. It's quite different from the old one. The boss is nice to me, I've got a good office to work in, the whole atmosphere in the firm is really positive. I can't believe that I'm so lucky.*
Counsellor Response: You feel really happy *or* You're really happy.

Example 4

Client Statement: *Young people nowadays aren't like they used to be in my day, dressed smartly; they're dirty, they're rude, they don't stand for you in buses, I don't know what's become of the new generation!*
Counsellor Response: You're disgusted.

Example 5

Client Statement: *My boyfriend just rang me from his hotel overseas. He's a reporter and is in a real trouble spot. While I was talking to him on the phone I could hear angry voices in the background, and then there was an incredible crash, and the line went dead, and I don't know what's happened to him! [Said very quickly and breathlessly.]*
Counsellor Response: You're terribly worried *or* You're panicking.

These examples probably gave you an idea of how difficult it is to assess the feelings underlying a client statement when non-verbal cues including facial expression and body posture are not available. When you are actively engaged in a counselling interaction with a client, it will be easier for you to identify what the client is feeling because you will have the use of all your senses. If you are attending closely to your client your own feelings may start to match theirs. When they are hurting, you may experience something of the hurt, at a less intense level, and this will be useful in helping you to reflect feelings accurately.

With experience at reflecting feelings you will be able to use a variety of expressions so that your responses sound natural rather than stereotyped and somewhat mechanical. Sometimes a short response such as 'You're hurting' is appropriate. But at other times you might use expressions such as the following:

'I get the impression that you are really hurting now.'

'From what you are saying my guess is that you are hurting deep down.'

'Right now you're hurting.'

As a general rule try to keep your counselling responses short. Remember that it is desirable for the client to do most of the talking and that your job is to listen and hear. Long counsellor responses intrude on the client's own inner processes and prevent the client from freely and openly exploring their issues.

When you have fully mastered reflection of feelings move ahead to the next chapter to discover how to combine reflection of *content* with reflection of *feelings*.

Learning summary

- Feelings are emotions, not thoughts. They are experienced at a gut level and not at a head level.
- Feelings are usually expressed by one word, for example, 'sad', 'happy', 'lonely' or 'bewildered'.
- Reflecting feelings back to clients is helpful in promoting emotional release with consequent healing.
- Clients sometimes need permission to cry.

Examples of client statements for use by trainers in teaching reflection of feelings

1. *'I don't know how I'm going to do it all. I have to go to work, pay the bills, look after the children, do the washing, and clean the house, all before Wednesday. I just can't do it!'*

2. *'I know he's got a gun and he could come round to the house at any time. The police say they can't do anything because he hasn't done anything yet. It'll be too late when they do come to help. I'll be dead.'*

3. 'He's a good boy and I love him but he does get into trouble. I never know what he's going to get up to next. Every day I wonder who is going to come knocking at the door to tell me something terrible.'

4. 'We won. We won the big prize, the new car!'

5. 'My brother died last week. I miss him dreadfully. I wish I hadn't criticised him so much recently because he was really a very good person.'

6. 'My mother treats me like dirt. She never praises me for anything. Colleen gets all the praise. All I get is black looks.'

Table 6.2 *Suggested solutions for Table 6.1*

Line	Suggested solutions	Line	Suggested solutions
5	adored worshipped idolised	18	insecure
6	hopeful	21	exhausted
11	worried	24	nervous worried
14	amazed astonished	27	ecstatic
15	frightened scared	30	annoyed

chapter **7**

Reflection of content and feeling

In previous chapters we have discussed the skills involved in listening, using minimal responses and encouragers, in reflecting content and in reflecting feelings. These skills are known as Rogerian counselling skills because they were initially identified and extensively used by Carl Rogers. We believe that these skills are the most basic and important ones, because they provide a foundation onto which other skills can be added. In addition to using reflection of content and reflection of feelings as separate skills, Rogers also combined these skills to reflect content and feeling in single counsellor responses.

In this chapter we will consider ways to combine reflection of content and feelings. With experience you will find that it is often convenient to combine these two types of reflection. For example, the statement 'You feel disappointed because your brother didn't do as he promised' includes both feeling and content. The feeling is disappointment, the content is to do with the reasons for being disappointed—because the brother didn't do as he promised. So that the idea of combining reflection of feeling and content becomes clearer, let us look at a few examples. First, we will take another look at the examples given in Chapter 6, but this time the counsellor responses will include reflection of both feeling and content, whereas in Chapter 6 reflection of feeling alone was used. Notice that the responses are short and not wordy.

Examples of reflection of content and feeling

Example 1

Client Statement: *I keep expecting my mother to show more interest in me. Time and again I've asked her to come over to see me but she never does. Yesterday it was my birthday and she did come to visit me, but do you know she didn't even remember that it was my birthday. I just don't think she cares about me at all. [Said slowly in a flat tone of voice.]*
Counsellor Response: You're disappointed by your mother's behaviour *or* You feel hurt by your mother's apparent lack of caring.

Example 2

Client Statement: *First of all, my brother broke my electric drill. He didn't bother to tell me that he'd broken it, he just left it lying there. Then what do you think he did, he went and borrowed my motorbike without telling me. I feel like thumping him.*
Counsellor Response: You're very angry with your brother because he doesn't respect your possessions *or* You're furious with your brother because he doesn't respect your possessions.

Example 3

Client Statement: *I got a new job recently. It's quite different from the old one. The boss is nice to me, I've got a good office to work in, the whole atmosphere in the firm is really positive. I can't believe that I'm so lucky.*
Counsellor Response: You feel really happy with your new job *or* You're delighted to have a pleasant work environment.

Example 4

Client Statement: *Young people nowadays aren't like they used to be in my day, dressed smartly; they're dirty, they're rude, they don't stand for you in buses, I don't know what's become of the new generation!*
Counsellor Response: Young people disgust you *or* You feel disgusted by the younger generation's behaviour.

Example 5

Client Statement: *My boyfriend just rang me from his hotel overseas. He's a reporter and is in a real trouble spot. While I was talking to him on the phone I could hear angry voices in the background, and then there was an incredible crash, and the line went dead, and I don't know what's happened to him! [Said very quickly and breathlessly.]*
Counsellor Response: You sound really worried about what might have happened to your boyfriend.

Further examples of reflection of feeling and content

Here are some more client statements for you to use for practice if you wish. In each case, you might like to invent a suitable counsellor response and then compare your response with the one supplied at the end of this chapter.

Example 6A

Client Statement: *I'm getting very worn out, whenever anything goes wrong I get blamed. I spend my time running around looking after other people's needs and in return I get no thanks and lots of criticism. It's just not fair. The more I do the less I'm appreciated.*

Example 7A

Client Statement: *You just wouldn't believe the dishwasher has broken down, the washing machine still hasn't been fixed, my husband ran the car into a post, my daughter's bike has a puncture, I just can't believe it, so much is going wrong. What's going to go wrong next? I just can't take any more.*

Example 8A

Client Statement: *I just can't understand my son and daughter. They always want to be together, but whenever they are together they fight. It doesn't seem to matter what I suggest they do when they're together, they start an argument. It's incessant, it never stops and now I'm starting to get like them, I'm starting to get angry and irritable too. Sometimes I'm so angry that I could knock their heads together.*

Example 9A

Client Statement: *I've done everything I can to get her back. I've given her presents, I've phoned her, I've written her letters, sent messages through her friends, I've said I'm sorry, and I've even offered to go and get counselling with her, but whatever I do I just can't get through to her and she just won't come back to me. I just can't live without her!*

Example 10A

Client Statement: *I can't understand why my landlord won't give me my bond back but he won't. I cleaned the flat, I left it in good condition, I know he doesn't like me and he just won't give me the bond back. I know I really ought to go and confront him and say to him that this isn't fair. It's not fair. I even got my friends to come round and help me clean up. I spent two days trying to make the place decent, and it was beautiful when I walked out, but he still won't give me the money back. I really ought to go and confront him, but he's a big man and he tends to get very angry at times and you never know—if there was an argument he might hit me!*

Example 11A

Client Statement: *I went next door to ask my neighbour if he would drive me over to my boyfriend's place because I'm worried about him. I know it's a long way, but I'm sure my neighbour could do it. All he said was, 'No, I can't afford the petrol, and in any case I don't want to go out in this bad weather'. I can't understand how he can be so callous because my boyfriend could be seriously ill for all I know. I just can't understand how my neighbour can sit and do nothing, and I'm sure that if it was one of his friends, someone he cared about, that he would go out tonight.*

The use of short responses

As stated previously, it's desirable for a counsellor to keep responses short so as not to intrude on the client's inner processes. The problem with using long statements is that they may take the client away from what they are currently experiencing and may bring them out of their own world and into the counsellor's world.

Deciding whether to reflect content or feeling or both

We have just been explaining how it is easy to combine the skills of reflection of content and reflection of feelings. There are times when it is appropriate to use this combined type of response. However, at other times it will be more appropriate, in the interests of brevity, to use either reflection of content, or reflection of feeling, but not both. This is particularly true when using reflection of feeling. Sometimes reflecting the feeling alone, without mention of content, can be more powerful in helping the client to own a feeling that they may be trying to avoid owning. If a counsellor says, 'You're really hurting' the statement focuses on the client's pain rather than encouraging the client to escape from experiencing pain by latching onto 'content' words and moving into a cognitive rather than a feeling level of experiencing.

Generally, it is desirable for counsellors to help clients to experience their emotional feelings rather than to suppress feelings by working at a head or cognitive level. Experiencing feelings fully is often painful, but is cathartic and consequently therapeutically desirable for most clients. However, as discussed in Chapter 6, there are a minority of clients who have difficulty living adaptive lives because they are not able to deal with and control continually high levels of emotional expression. For such clients, it may be more useful to focus on content rather than feelings.

The use of lead-in words when reflecting

Generally, it is sufficient to use the reflection statements as given in the previous examples in this chapter and in Chapters 5 and 6. However, sometimes it can be helpful to preface a reflection statement by using words such as those suggested below.

When reflecting content

> 'I've heard you say . . .'
> 'What I've heard you say is . . .'
> 'I get the impression that . . .'
> 'I'm getting the idea that . . .'

When reflecting feelings or content and feelings

> 'If I'm hearing you correctly you are (disappointed etc.) . . .'
> 'I'm sensing that you feel . . .'
> 'I get the impression that you feel . . .'

These suggestions should be used sparingly otherwise they are likely to sound repetitive and trite. Usually, a reflection such as 'You're angry because . . .' is sufficient.

Learning the skills

We have now discussed the use of the basic skills of *listening, the use of minimal responses and encouragers, reflection of content, reflection of feelings* and *reflection of both content and feelings.* We believe that it is sensible to practise these skills until they are fully mastered before proceeding to learn any of the other micro-skills. This is because, in our view, these skills provide a foundation onto which other skills can be added. Use of these skills is also extremely helpful in enhancing the quality of the counselling relationship.

Initially, during the learning process, you may feel awkward in using counselling skills. This is normal, because it is always difficult to learn new ways of relating. However we suggest that you keep practising until you can use the skills in a natural way which does not seem to be contrived or artificial. Once this has been achieved, the counselling interaction will flow smoothly and you will not feel pressured to think of 'smart' responses. Instead your listening skills will be enhanced and you will feel more relaxed and spontaneous. Interestingly, if the skills are used competently, the client will not realise that you are primarily using reflection, but will feel as though you are listening and commenting in a sensible way on what is being said. Many experienced counsellors use the basic skills which we have already discussed more frequently than any other skills, because these skills enable the client to explore their world fully in their own way without interference by the counsellor, but with the certain knowledge that the counsellor is actively listening.

Focusing on the counselling relationship

Remember that counselling is about walking alongside a person as they explore their world. Some people say that a counsellor should, metaphorically speaking, walk in the shoes of the other person. Certainly it is important that the counsellor attempts to see the world in the way the client sees the world. Thus, at times, an experienced counsellor will almost get into the client's shoes, so that they can better understand what it feels like to be the client, and how it might be to look at the world from the client's viewpoint. By doing this a trusting relationship is developed which enables the client to risk exploring the most painful issues of their life, and so to move forward out of confusion.

Suggested counsellor responses for further examples of reflection of content and feeling

Example 6B

'You feel resentful because other people don't appreciate your efforts.'

Example 7B

'You're feeling overwhelmed by so many negative experiences' *or* 'So many things have gone wrong that you're starting to feel pressured and unable to cope'.

Example 8B

'The continual fighting between your son and daughter infuriates you.'

Example 9B

'You're despairing because you can't get your wife to come back to you.'

Example 10B

'Even though you believe the landlord is being unfair you're too scared to confront him.'

Example 11B

'You're disgusted by your neighbour's unwillingness to help.'

Learning summary

- Reflection of feeling and content can be combined into one statement.
- There are times when it is more effective to reflect back only feelings, or only content, and not both.
- Effective counsellors try to see the world as their client sees it.

Examples of client statements for use by trainers in teaching reflection of content and feelings

1. *'My children are able to use computers without worrying. They learnt to use them at school. Unfortunately I haven't been able to keep up with the times and as a result, I don't think that my children respect me. I feel quite stupid.'*

2. *'Every time my father comes to visit me I dread the time when he'll leave to go home because he lives such a long way away and he's so old now. He's going back this weekend and I can't stop thinking that maybe I'll never see him again.'*

3. *'My son is driving me crazy. He never stops doing silly things. I have to watch him all the time. Yesterday he climbed onto the roof and then fell out of a tree. I'm starting to lose patience with him.'*

4. *'I can't make sense of what Freda wants. Firstly, she asks me to go to visit her on Friday and then she tells me that if I do she'll feel overwhelmed. I just don't know what to do.'*

5. *'Some very strange things are happening. A disreputable looking person keeps hanging around my house and I'm not sure but I think that some things have disappeared. I think I'll have to be careful to check that the house is kept locked.'*

6. *'My partner has left and I can't track him down. I wish I could find him and tell him that I still love him and want him back. I know that I've hurt him badly by having the affair. Now it's me that's suffering.'*

Use of questions

You may be surprised that the chapter on asking questions should come so late in this book, after you have already learnt several other skills. Well, surprisingly, it is not necessary to ask many questions at all in most counselling interviews. Certainly this is true for interviews concerned with counselling people for emotional problems. Most of the information the counsellor needs to know will emerge naturally without asking questions if the counsellor actively listens to the client, uses the skills which have already been learnt, and skilfully reflects back the content and feeling of what the client is saying.

Asking too many questions

It is very tempting for new counsellors to ask lots of questions. If you find yourself repeatedly asking questions, it's important for you to ask yourself what your goal is in asking these questions. If your goal is to stimulate the client into talking, then you may well be using the wrong approach. More often than not, simply reflecting back what has already been said will stimulate the client into further sharing of important and relevant personal information without the need for you to ask a question. If a counsellor asks too many questions the counselling session become

Interrogating is NOT counselling

more like an interrogation and the client is likely to be less open and less communicative. The counsellor then ends up controlling the direction in which the interview will go. This is, as a general rule, unfortunate, because it is desirable for the client to go in whatever direction their energy leads them. It is important for the client to fully explore the area in which their problem lies. Often a client won't zero in on their real problem until they have spent some time meandering around the general problem area. If the counsellor tries to find out what is really troubling a person by predominantly asking questions, the client may never move towards the most painful things that are causing trouble, but may in fact just go off at a tangent in a direction of the counsellor's choosing.

Another problem with the excessive asking of questions is that the client may quickly learn to expect questions, and may consequently wait for the counsellor to ask another question instead of thinking out for herself what is important. There is therefore a real danger in asking unnecessary questions and it is our view that asking questions should be limited to those situations in which there is little alternative but to ask a question. When you do ask a question be clear about what it is that you hope to achieve by asking the question.

Before considering the goals that can be achieved through asking questions it is helpful to think about the types of questions counsellors can ask. Questions broadly fall into two categories: open questions and closed questions. Additionally, there are a number of types of question which are useful for specific purposes.

Open and closed questions

Some questions are called 'open questions' and other questions are called 'closed questions'. Both categories of question can be useful in the counselling process and it is necessary for you to fully understand the difference between the two types. It will be clear when it is more appropriate to use closed questions and when it is more appropriate to use open questions.

Closed questions

Closed questions are questions that lead to a specific answer. Usually the answer to a closed question is very short. It may be an answer like 'Yes' or 'No'. Consider for example the closed question, 'Did you come here by bus today?' Obviously the most probable answer is either 'Yes' or 'No'. The client may choose to expand on the answer but is unlikely to do so. Closed questions such as 'Do you love your wife?' and 'Are you angry?' usually lead to the answer 'Yes' or 'No'. If I ask the closed question, 'How many years have you lived in Queensland?' the answer might be 'Twenty-four', and it is a specific answer.

There are times in a counselling session when you will need to ask closed questions because you require a specific answer to a very definite question. There are also other important reasons for asking closed questions as we shall see later. However, there are some problems with asking closed questions and these will probably be apparent to you already. If you ask a closed question, it is possible that the client may continue to talk to you and to enlarge on the answer given, but it is not necessary for the client to do that. Moreover, you have limited the client in the sense that the sort of answer they can give, if they directly answer your question, is restricted. Another problem is that closed questions can be leading questions and sometimes suggest to the client that the counsellor has a specific agenda or point of view. The client may then feel constrained with regard to what they may say, and may believe that it is important for them to respect the perceived agenda or point of view of the counsellor. For example, if a counsellor were to ask the question, 'Do you think that you did that because your mother is a domineering person?', the client might feel restricted in what they would be able to say believing that the counsellor sees their mother as domineering and their behaviour as a result of that. Thus, the counsellor's implied suggestion might constrain the client from thinking and talking freely. Lawyers in a court like to ask closed questions so that witnesses are restricted in the range of answers that can be given. Counsellors are not lawyers, and generally the counsellor's intention is to free the client up so they can speak more freely.

Open questions

The open question is very different in its effect from the closed question. It gives the client lots of scope, allows the client to explore any relevant area, and in fact encourages the client to freely divulge additional material. If I ask the closed question, 'Did you come here by bus?', the answer is likely to be 'Yes' or 'No'. Contrast this with the open question, 'How did you travel here?' The client is freer to answer the open question and the answer is likely to be richer in information. For example, the client might explain the difficulties involved in the journey, might describe the type of transport used, might talk about having travelled with someone else, or might talk about experiences during the journey.

Examples of open and closed questions

Examples to illustrate the difference between closed and open questions are presented below. In each case we suggest that you might like to read the closed question and try to replace it by an equivalent open question yourself before reading the suggested alternative.

Example 1

Closed Question: *Do you feel angry?*
Open Question: How do you feel?

Example 2

Closed Question: *How many children do you have?*
Open Question: What can you tell me about your children?
(An alternative to this open question is to use a statement requesting information such as: 'Tell me about your children'.)

Example 3

Closed Question: *Do you argue with your wife often?*
Open Question: What is your relationship like with your wife?

Example 4

Closed Question: *Did you punish your son when he misbehaved?*
Open Question: What did you do when your son misbehaved?

Example 5

Closed Question: *Do you love your husband?*
Open Question: Can you tell me about your feelings towards your husband?

Example 6

Closed Question: *Is the atmosphere tense at home?*
Open Question: What's the atmosphere like at home?

The closed questions above give the client little room to use their own imagination when giving an answer. The sort of answer given to a closed question will usually be direct and probably short. A closed question doesn't encourage the client to be creative and share new information, but tends to confine the client to a limited response.

The open question is quite different as you can see from the above examples. In each case, by asking an open question, the counsellor might get unexpected additional information. If you look at the open question, 'What can you tell me about your children?', you will realise that the client could give a number of quite different answers. For example, the client might say, 'My children are beautiful and very happy' or 'I have two sons and a daughter' or 'My children are all grown up and my husband and I live happily together on our own'. It is clear from this example that by asking an open question the counsellor may get a variety of answers and may get an answer quite different to the one which might have been expected. This is an advantage, because counsellors are not mind-readers, and cannot know what the client is thinking unless the client verbalises their thoughts. Also, it is sensible for counsellors to use questions that will encourage the client to bring out those things that are of most interest to the client, rather than those things that are of most interest to the counsellor.

When to use closed questions

As explained previously, it is generally preferable to use open questions rather than closed questions. Exceptions are when helping a client to be more specific, or when specific information is required. In these latter cases closed questions are very appropriate. In order to make sense of the client's story a counsellor may need to know whether the client is married, whether they have children, how old they are. If a counsellor needs to know this information, then it may be appropriate to ask directly by using closed questions.

Practice examples

Below are some more examples of closed questions. You may wish to practise framing open questions to replace them. Suggested open questions for each example are given at the end of this chapter.

Example 7A

Would you like fish for dinner tonight?

Example 8A

Do you like it when your husband praises you?

Example 9A

Was your mother a dominating person?

Example 10A

Did your father make you come to see me?

Example 11A

Did the change disrupt your life?

Questions for specific purposes

In the previous discussion we have strongly suggested that questions are best used sparingly. However, it is important to recognise that when questions are used creatively and appropriately, they can be extremely powerful in achieving specific purposes. Next, a number of questions which are useful for specific purposes will be discussed. Additionally, questions which are extremely useful when using solution-focused counselling methods and narrative therapy will be discussed in Chapters 23 and 24.

General information-seeking questions

We use general information-seeking questions in everyday conversation in order to find out information which may be useful, or of interest to us. In counselling, when such questions are framed in a way which indicates the counsellor's genuine curiosity and interest, the client is likely to feel valued and to respond positively. Requests for information should be made with caution. As a counsellor, before you ask for information, ask yourself whether you really need it. If you didn't have the information would you still be able to help the client? If the answer to that question is 'Yes', then asking a question may be unnecessary, and the desire to ask a question may stem from your own needs and/or curiosity. In our opinion, there is no justification for a counsellor seeking information in order to satisfy their own curiosity. To do so would be to pry unnecessarily into the client's affairs. Such prying is likely to intrude into the counselling process and interrupt the natural flow of the counselling interaction.

Questions which clarify what the client has said, or help the client to be more specific

Clients frequently make very general, vague statements, and this is unhelpful to both the client and the counsellor because it is impossible to think clearly about a problem if it is expressed in vague, woolly, non-specific language. Consequently, and when clients make such statements, it is often useful for the counsellor to ask a question to help the client be more specific and to focus on the real issue. This is likely to help the client to clarify their thinking. For instance, if a client makes a vague statement like, 'That sort of thing always makes me annoyed', it may not be at all clear to either the client or the counsellor what is really meant by the words 'that sort of thing'. It is then appropriate for the counsellor to ask the client, 'What sort of thing?'. Similarly, a client might say, 'I just can't stand it any more'. The word 'it' is non-specific and to help the client to be more specific the counsellor might ask, 'What is it that you can't stand any more?' Similarly, consider the client statement, 'I'm fed up with him'. This is a very general statement and may need clarification, in which case the counsellor might well respond by saying, 'Tell me in what ways you are fed up with him'.

Questions to heighten the client's awareness

These questions are commonly used in Gestalt therapy (Clarkson 2000). The aim of these questions is to help the client to become more fully aware of what is happening within them, either somatically or emotionally, so that they can intensify those bodily or emotional feelings, deal with them, and move on to discussing associated thoughts. Typical questions in this category are:

'What are you feeling emotionally right now?'
'Where in your body do you experience that emotional feeling?'
'Can you tell me what's happening inside you right now? '
'What's happening inside you right now?'

If a client is starting to cry, the counsellor might ask, 'Can you put words to your tears?'. This may enable the person to verbalise thoughts related to the internal experience. By doing this, these thoughts can be processed, the counsellor is aware of them, and can achieve empathic joining and help the client move ahead. Similarly, if a client seems to be stuck and unable to speak, the counsellor might ask, 'Can you tell me what is happening inside you right now? What are you experiencing in your body?'

Transitional questions

Generally, as we have discussed previously, it is important to allow the client to travel in their own direction in the counselling conversation. However, sometimes the client will deflect away from discussing important issues which are troubling them. One way of addressing this is to give them feedback about the process that you have noticed. An alternative is to use a transitional question. The transitional question effectively returns the focus to an earlier part of the discussion. Transitional questions generally start with a statement about an earlier part of the conversation, and then raise a question about that earlier discussion. Examples of transitional questions are:

> 'Earlier you talked about the option of leaving your job. I'm wondering about how you're feeling about that option now?'
> 'A few minutes ago you mentioned the possibility that you might consider killing yourself. I'm wondering how you're feeling about the possibility right now?'
> 'Earlier today you mentioned that you are extremely troubled by your relationship with your neighbour. Would you like to spend some time talking about the relationship now?'
> 'I've noticed that several times you've alluded to your fear of the future. Would you like to tell me more about that fear?'

When using transitional questions the counsellor makes a clear decision to be an active participant in the conversation, and to take responsibility for introducing a possible change in the direction of the counselling process. Transitional questions do need to be used with some caution. They should only be introduced at points where the client is not likely to be deflected away from discussion of important and/or painful material.

Choice questions

Choice questions have their origin in Reality therapy (Glasser & Wubbolding 2000). In the past, they have been popular for use by counsellors who work with young people. These questions provided a way for a counsellor to indirectly suggest that the client has choice about the way they think and behave. Additionally, choice questions specifically invite the client to think about and consider alternative choices. Examples of choice questions are:

'What would have been a better choice for you to have made at that time?'

'In what other ways could you respond to that?'

'If the same situation arises during the coming weeks, what do you think you will do? (Will you do this, or will you do that?)'

'What would you like to do now, would you like to continue talking about this issue or would you like to leave it there for now?'

Such questions about the past, present, or future, enable the client to look at the likely consequences of different behaviours. By exploring choices and consequences, the adolescent is better prepared for future situations.

The Guru question

Guru questions have their origin in Gestalt therapy (Clarkson 2000). When using this type of question, the counsellor first invites the client to imagine that they can stand aside and look at themselves from a distance, and to give themselves some advice. For example, the counsellor might say, 'Imagine for a minute that you were a guru and that you could give advice to someone just like you. What advice would you give them?'

Career questions

Career questions are questions which exaggerate and extrapolate beyond the client's present behaviour. They help the client to recognise that they have choice about the direction in which they are heading and that this choice might lead to extremes of lifestyle. An example of a career question is:

'What would it be like for you to make a career out of being an extremely high achiever who set an example for everybody else by giving up everything except hard work?'

This question raises the client's awareness of a path or journey along which they can progress, if they wish. It enhances their ability to make choices to bring about change, at the current point in time, which might have long-term consequences for them.

Career questions have a level of paradoxical intent, in that hopefully ensuing discussion will result in satisfying behaviours that are not extreme.

We need to be careful to use these questions with discretion or they may become self-fulfilling prophecies. Consider the question:

> 'Would you like to continue your shoplifting behaviour, take more risks, and move on to becoming a career criminal?'

While this question might be useful for some clients, for others it might encourage them to follow the 'suggested' career.

Circular questions

Circular questions come from the Milan model of family therapy (Palazzoli et al. 1980). They are most useful when working with couples or families. However circular questions can also be useful when working with individual clients who are having difficulty in getting in touch with their own feelings, attitudes, thoughts, or beliefs. Instead of asking the client directly about how they feel or what they think, or what their attitude is, the counsellor asks them how someone else feels or thinks, or asks what their attitude might be. Examples of circular questions are:

> 'I wonder how your brother feels now that your father has gone to jail?'
> 'If your wife was here what do you think she would say about your need to come for counselling?'
> 'How do think your colleague feels about the possibility that you might both be retrenched?'
> 'If you had to guess, what do think your wife's attitude is to your loss of mobility?'

By asking circular questions such as these, the counsellor effectively invites the client to speculate about someone else's feelings, thoughts, beliefs or attitudes. This can be less threatening than asking the client to talk directly about themselves. Often, having answered a circular question, the client will continue by talking about their own feelings, beliefs or thoughts, because they want to make it clear whether they agree or disagree with the person who was mentioned in the circular question.

A question to avoid

There is one particular type of question that we recommend that counsellors try to avoid asking unless absolutely necessary. Try to avoid asking questions beginning with 'Why'. The problem with asking 'Why' questions is that in response to such questions clients tend to look for an intellectually thought-out responses, rather than centring on what is happening to them internally. 'Why' questions tend to generate answers that are 'out there'—answers that don't seem to come from inside the client and often aren't convincing. They frequently fall into the category of 'excuses' or 'rationalisations'.

In comparison to 'Why' questions, questions beginning with 'What', 'How', and 'When' are generally more useful. Open questions often begin with these words.

In conclusion

In this chapter we have looked at the usefulness of closed and open questions and have discussed the differences between the two. We have also considered the use of a number of questions that are useful for particular purposes. Now is the time for you to practise using questions. There is a risk that through practising asking questions, you may quickly become reliant on using them excessively. If that were to happen it would be unfortunate because instead of clients feeling that you were travelling beside them as they explored their thoughts and feelings, they would feel more as though they were being interrogated. This would greatly diminish the quality of the counselling relationship and would inhibit clients from opening up freely. When a person is continually questioned, that person tends to withdraw rather than to open up.

Remember that paraphrasing and reflection of feelings are more likely to motivate the client to talk freely than asking questions. Because of this, we suggest that when you are practising asking questions you try to ask only one question in every three or four responses, with the other responses being reflection of content or feelings or minimal responses. There is no need to be rigid when doing this, because counselling needs to be a natural free-flowing process rather conforming to rigid rules. However, if you use fewer questions than other responses in practice sessions, then your continued practice of the most important basic reflective responses will be ensured. Consequently, when you start counselling real clients you will be skilled in reflection of feelings and content, and will use questions only when it is advantageous to do so because reflection is not appropriate.

Suggested open questions to replace closed questions in practice examples

Example 7B

What would you like for dinner tonight?

Example 8B

How do you feel when your husband praises you?

Example 9B

What was your mother like? *or* How did your mother behave in her relationships with other people?

Example 10B

What brought you here?

Example 11B

How did the change affect your life?

Learning summary

- Dangers in asking too many questions:
  - The counselling session may become more like an interrogation.
  - The counsellor may deflect the client from the real issue by controlling the direction of the session.
  - The client may stop exploring their own world and instead wait for the counsellor to ask more questions.
- Closed questions:
  - lead to a specific answer
  - confine the client to a limited response
  - help the client to be more precise
  - are useful in eliciting specific information.

- Open questions encourage the client:
  - to share new information
  - to speak freely and openly
  - to bring out those things that are of most importance.
- Questions which are useful for specific purposes include general information seeking questions, questions to heighten the client's awareness, transitional questions, choice questions, guru questions, career questions, and circular questions, as well as those questions used in solution-focused therapy (see Chapter 23) and narrative therapy (see Chapter 24).
- Counsellors are not justified in asking questions merely to satisfy their own curiosity.

Further reading

Questions to raise awareness
Clarkson, P. 2000, *Gestalt Counselling in Action*, 2nd edn, Sage, London.

Choice questions
Glasser, W. & Wubbolding, R. 2000, 'Reality therapy', in R. Corsini & D. Wedding (eds), *Current Psychotherapies*, 6th edn, Peacock, Itasca, IL, pp. 293–321.

Circular questions
Boscolo, L., Cecchin, G., Hoffman, L. & Penn, P. 1987, *Milan Systemic Family Therapy: Conversations in Theory and Practice*, Basic Books, New York.
Jones, E. 1993, *Family Systems Therapy: Developments in Milan-Systemic Therapies*, Wiley, Chichester.
Palazzoli, S. N., Boscolo, L., Cecchin, F. G. & Prata, G. 1980, 'Hypothesising circularity and neutrality: three quidelines for the conductor of the session', *Family Process*, vol. 19, pp. 3–12.

Examples of closed questions for use by trainers for conversion to open questions

1. 'Do you intend to arrive at 2 p.m.?'

2. 'Are you disappointed?'

3. 'Do you have two children?'

4. 'Is your household always tense?'

5. 'Will you achieve your goals by writing to him?'

6. 'Did that happen on Thursday?'

Summarising

The skills we have previously discussed have been those designed to create a good counselling relationship so that the client will feel free to talk openly, sharing with the counsellor issues that are causing emotional distress. If we use the analogy of the counsellor walking alongside the client on a journey, then the skills we have described encourage the client to continue exploring. As this journey of exploration occurs, the client moves in a direction of their own choice with the counsellor walking alongside. From time to time it is important for the client to stop and review the ground that has recently been traversed. This review can be encouraged if the counsellor uses the skill of *summarising*.

Summarising is rather like paraphrasing. When a counsellor paraphrases, they reflect back whatever has been said in a single client statement. Similarly, when a counsellor summarises, what the counsellor does is to reflect back to the client what has been said in a number of client statements. The summary draws together the main points from the content, and may also take into account the feelings the client has described. A summary does not involve a complete re-run of the ground covered, but rather picks out the salient points, the important things that the client has been talking about, and presents them in such a way that the client is provided with an overview of what they have been discussing. By doing this, the counsellor enables the client to absorb and to ponder on what they have been sharing. Summarising clarifies what the client has been saying and puts it into an organised format so that the client is better able to see a clear picture of the situation.

Frequently when a client comes to counselling they are confused. It is as though they are walking through a forest and can see nothing clearly. They are lost in a confusing jungle of overgrowth and trees. By summarising, the counsellor assists the client to see the trees more clearly and to find a path between them.

The following is a short transcript of part of a practice counselling session to illustrate the use of summarising.

Transcript to illustrate summarising

Client: *You know . . . [pause] . . . I really believe in people taking responsibility for themselves . . . [pause] . . . and so I can't really understand why it is that I do so much worrying about my brothers.*

Counsellor: You sound puzzled by your concern for your brothers. (Reflection of feeling and content.)

Client: *Yes, I am concerned. I'm not too sure what it's all about because I even seem to be worrying about them when I'm at work and yet I know that they are adults and are quite capable of looking after themselves.*

Counsellor: Even though you know they're adults, you still worry. (Reflection of content and feeling.)

Client: *Yes, I do. Incessantly. I'm always thinking the worst, you know. That maybe Bill has had an accident in that crazy car which he will insist on driving around, and I'm afraid that as far as Sidney is concerned, he's just not in very good health and I'd hate anything to happen to either of them.*

Counsellor: Even as you speak now you sound anxious. (Reflection of feeling.)

Client: *Yes, I am anxious, I'm really anxious . . . [pause]*

Counsellor: As you experience that anxiety can you tell me more about it? (Open question.)

Client: *Yes, yes I think I can, I'm just, uh-mm, becoming aware of some very painful memories that I have of my elder sister. [Said slowly and with hesitation.]*

Counsellor: I get the impression that you're finding it difficult to talk about your memories. (Reflection of feeling.)

Client: *Yes, it's really painful for me to remember what happened to her. I was really very fond of her and I hurt a great deal when I think about the way she finished her life. [Voice quivering.]*

Counsellor: It distresses you to think about her death. (Reflection of feeling and content.)

Client: *Yes, it does. You see she killed herself. She took an overdose and it was too late when we found her.*

Counsellor: I can understand you feeling very sad. (Joining statement, bringing closeness between client and counsellor.)

Client: *[Sobs] . . . yeah, it was very sad for me and it still is. I just wished I could have done something to have changed the way she saw her life.*

Counsellor: You wish that you could have helped her. (Reflection of feeling and content.)

Client: *Yes, I do. I would love to have been able to put my arms around her and to tell her that I really loved her. I couldn't have told her that her life was good because it wasn't, but I could have told her that she mattered to me.*

Counsellor: You'd have liked to have told her how much you cared about her. (Reflection of content.)

Client: *Yes I would, and that I guess would have made me feel a lot better even if she had still killed herself. I suppose it would have been much better for me if I could have told her how I felt when she was alive and now it's too late.*

Counsellor: You're sad because you missed an opportunity. (Reflection of feeling and content.)

Client: *Yes, I did, and I suppose I'm starting to realise something about the way I feel anxious when I think about my two brothers. You see, I would really like to be able to tell them how much I care about them, but somehow I just can't.*

Counsellor: You've told me how you worry about your brothers and how your sister killed herself. It seems as though you're really sad because you weren't able to tell your sister that you really cared for her when she was alive and now you'd like to be able to tell your brothers that you care about them, but somehow you can't. (Summary.)

Client: *You're right. That's what my problem is. I think what I need to do is to go and talk to them, and then maybe I'll stop worrying about them.*

What the summary does

If you look at the above transcript you will see that in summarising, the counsellor tied together the elements of what the client had said during the previous statements. This enabled the client to put the whole package together and, as a result, to get some resolution. The resolution was the client's own and as such was fitting for the client. It wasn't suggested by the counsellor.

When to summarise

Summarising is something that needs to be done from time to time during a counselling session so that the client is able to clarify their ideas and combine the various elements of what they are saying into an understandable form. In particular, towards the end of the counselling session it is often sensible for the counsellor to summarise the main issues that were dealt with during the session. By doing this, the counsellor ties together the thoughts, ideas and feelings that were expressed in the session, leaving the client feeling less confused and better able to deal with their life situation. This tying together enables the counsellor to move towards terminating the session as explained in Chapter 10.

Learning summary

Summarising does the following:

- picks out salient points;
- draws these together; and
- presents them to the client in a clear and precise way.

Transcript for use by trainers in teaching summarising

Students can be asked to identify the types of counsellor responses used and to add a summary to complete the transcript.

Client: *My anxiety rises when I think about going to work. I almost start to panic . . . I wonder how I am going to cope with another day at that place.*

Counsellor: You're really worried. (Counselling skill used: _____)

Client: *Worried? I feel as though I'm going crazy. I despair. The new boss is putting in place policies which infuriate me. They disadvantage our customers and are frankly disrespectful. She doesn't seem to understand the basics of modern commercial practice and if I comply with her wishes I will compromise my own standards. I just don't know what to do.*

Counsellor: You are faced with a dilemma. (Counselling skill used: _____)

Client: *Yes I am. If I continue to work there I either have to compromise my ideals or I will be in continual conflict with my boss. I'd like to leave, but the pay is excellent, and in the present economic climate good jobs in my line are difficult to find.*

Counsellor: You're stuck in a frustrating situation because finding a new job wouldn't be easy. (Counselling skill used: _____)

Client: *It wouldn't. There aren't many jobs being advertised right now. But I'll keep looking because I do want to leave and eventually a new opportunity is sure to turn up. I suppose in the meantime I'll have to make the best of the present situation. That's where my difficulty lies.*

Counsellor: What ideas do you have about ways of responding to your current work situation? (Counselling skill used: _____)

Client: *Well I suppose that I could avoid conflict by following the new policy but interpreting it fairly loosely whenever I can. Also, I could be clear with customers that I don't have any alternative but to follow company policy. That way, I would be making it clear that I wasn't being personally unco-operative. I'd need to be careful how I did that though, because I do have some loyalty towards the firm.*

Counsellor: I am getting the impression that you believe that you could accept some compromise without too much difficulty. (Counselling skill used: _____)

Client: *Yes, there are ways to alter the way I work without feeling personally compromised, particularly if I remember that I intend to leave as soon as I can . . . mm . . . Yes I know what to do.*

chapter **10**

Creating comfortable closure

It is often very hard for new counsellors to know when to terminate a counselling session or when to terminate a series of counselling sessions. In this chapter we will discuss the following aspects of termination:
1. the termination of an individual counselling session
2. the need for ongoing appointments
3. client and counsellor dependency
4. the termination of a series of counselling sessions
5. the termination of a telephone counselling call.

The termination of an individual counselling session

Most counselling agencies and private practitioners schedule a particular length of time for each counselling session, and it is fairly common for this to be one hour. In our experience, this is a suitable time for most individual counselling sessions although a longer time may be required for marital or family counselling. Of course, there are exceptions. Sometimes it will be clear after a shorter time that an interview can be terminated because the client has resolved their issues and there is little point in sitting around chatting unnecessarily. At other times it may be apparent that a client is in a highly distressed emotional state at the end of a one-hour session and it may be necessary to continue the interview for longer.

Work to be done between sessions

Between counselling sessions, the counsellor may need to make another appointment for the client who is leaving, to show the client out, and to write up notes on the interview. They may also need to debrief, as otherwise there may be emotional consequences for them as a result of listening to the client's painful story. When a counsellor is not able to do this, they may not be emotionally ready to meet a new client and are setting themselves up for burnout (see Chapter 38 entitled 'Looking after yourself'). Debriefing can sometimes be achieved just by writing up case notes, or having a cup of tea, or by chatting informally with someone. However, in cases where a counselling session has been particularly stressful for the counsellor it may be necessary for them to talk through their issues with a supervisor or another counsellor. After debriefing the counsellor needs to prepare for the next client by reading case notes, if they are available.

Because of the counsellor's own needs and the work that is preferably done between appointments, we believe that it is wise for agencies to schedule in a quarter of an hour between the end of one counselling session and the beginning of the next, particularly where counsellors are dealing with very distressed clients.

Keeping the counselling experience dynamic

In our experience clients often deal with important issues in the first three-quarters of an hour of a counselling session, and then begin to lose energy. It is important that each counselling session is dynamic and that the client is working actively throughout the session. Once a client becomes used to sessions being of fixed length, they will tend to work comfortably within that time frame. During a one-hour interview a client will be likely to have raised important issues and to have explored them. The client then needs time in which to process the work done. It may therefore be appropriate to terminate the session at that point and to leave a few days, or maybe a week or two, before making another appointment, if that is needed.

Client anxiety about time constraints

If the matter is raised, let the client know that you, the counsellor, are in control of the length of the counselling session. Frequently clients show anxiety by looking at a clock in the room, because they are worried about taking up too much of a counsellor's time. In such cases it is important for the counsellor to say that they will control the length of the session, and that the session will probably last about 60 minutes, or whatever is appropriate. If a client is told this, their anxiety regarding timekeeping is likely to be reduced.

Preparing for the end of a session

Where a counsellor is working within a set time frame, and knows that there is a time limit to the counselling session, the counsellor needs to prepare for terminating the session. This preparation should be commenced about ten minutes before the end of the session. If the counselling session is to last an hour, then after about 50 minutes it is sensible for the counsellor to assess the progress of the session. The counsellor can then

decide how to use the remaining time in order to close the session in a way that is satisfactory for the client. It may be advisable for the counsellor to say to the client: 'I am conscious of the need for us to finish the session in about 10 minutes time and it seems to me that you may wish to explore . . . (a particular area) . . . that we have been talking about.' By giving the client some warning that the counselling session must end within a few minutes, the client is given an opportunity to deal with, or at least mention, any pressing unfinished business.

Closing the session

Near the finishing time, it is sometimes appropriate for the counsellor to provide a summary of the material discussed by the client during the session. Whenever possible it's useful to give the client some positive feedback, especially as clients usually come to see counsellors at times when their self-esteem is low. The counsellor might also add a statement regarding goals for the future and the possibility or probability of future counselling sessions being required.

The counsellor should take control of the termination of the session. With some clients who want to linger on and chat rather than do useful work, a counsellor may need to be assertive. In such a case, be direct. You may even find it necessary to interrupt and say something like: 'We do need to finish the session right now.' Then stand up and lead the way firmly out of the room without stopping to linger, even if the client wishes to do so. Many counsellors find this difficult to do, because it is hard to do politely and respectfully. However if you are direct and firm, you will still be able to give your client a positive message by saying, 'Goodbye Sam' (or whatever their name is) in a friendly way as you turn away to leave their company.

The need for ongoing appointments

Inexperienced counsellors are often apprehensive about asking clients to come back for further appointments. If you feel apprehensive about doing this, explore your feelings. You may be afraid that the client will not want to come back and will reject your offer of another appointment. If the client does do that, would it be a disaster? If you think that it would, then you need to discuss the issue with your supervisor. Remember that it is hard for clients to make appointments. It is much easier for them to cancel. If you don't make another appointment for the client, then they are likely to assume that you don't think that it is necessary for them to come back. They may wonder whether you would consider it to be a nuisance if they were to do so. It is therefore important, if you do not make another appointment, that you say to your client: 'I won't make another appointment for you now, because I am not sure that it's necessary for you to come back to see me as your issues seem to be reasonably well resolved. However, I would like you to know that if you decide that it would be useful for you to come back, then you are welcome to ring up and make an appointment.'

Making a contract for ongoing appointments

For clients who need ongoing appointments, it may be desirable for the counsellor to spell out an ongoing contract. It may be sufficient to say, 'I think it would be useful for you to come back to see me again next week—would you like to do this?' Alternatively, it may be appropriate to say: 'It seems to me that you have a number of issues which need to be resolved, and this is likely to take several counselling sessions. Would you like to come to see me on a weekly basis for the next three or four weeks and then review the situation?' In this way, the client can be made aware of the counsellor's willingness to continue seeing them.

Clients often feel insecure about the counselling relationship and are afraid that the counsellor will terminate the counselling process before important issues have been explored. It is therefore important to ensure that the client has some clear expectation regarding the possible duration of the counselling relationship.

Client and counsellor dependency

Sometimes it's desirable to terminate a series of counselling sessions sooner than the client would wish. This raises the issue of dependency. It's very easy, in fact probably inevitable, that dependency will occur in ongoing counselling relationships.

Dependency on the relationship

It is easy for clients to become dependent on counsellors for a number of reasons. Firstly, it is inevitable that a meaningful relationship will develop if the counsellor is genuine, warm and accepting. Of course, there are necessary and appropriate limits to the counselling relationship (see Chapter 36 regarding ethical issues). However, the quality of a counselling relationship is such that it is natural for some clients to wish that the counselling relationship could continue after its usefulness for legitimate counselling purposes has ended.

Clients tell counsellors their innermost secrets, whereas generally, from childhood, people learn to share such private material only with someone they love. There can be almost an expectation by the client, from previous life learnings, that intimate personal sharing will result in an ongoing relationship.

Some people who come to counsellors are very alone in the world, and do not have a close relative or friend with whom to share the problems and stressors which arise in their daily lives. There is good reason for such people to want to become dependent on the counselling relationship. We all have a need for some degree of closeness and affection, and the counselling relationship may provide this for the lonely, who may then become dependent on the relationship.

Dependency on the counselling process

After the initial trauma of a crisis has passed, it is often very comfortable for a client to be able to continue to discuss and work through less important life issues in the caring counselling environment. Most of us like comfort, but to continue to provide counselling to clients who no longer need it does them a disservice. It effectively interferes with the natural and desirable tendency of people to become self-sufficient. Effective counselling teaches clients how to work through most troubling issues on their own, and how to recognise when counselling help is really needed.

Counsellors can become dependent too

Dependency can occur in two directions. The client may become dependent on the counsellor, and equally the counsellor may become dependent on the client. Counsellors are not emotionless robots, but are human beings with emotions and needs. As described above and in Chapter 36, the counselling relationship often involves an unusual degree of intimate sharing, and by its very nature involves a degree of closeness. Consequently, it is easy to understand how a counsellor can get hooked into a dependency relationship. Clearly, a counsellor needs to stay vigilant to ensure that they do not encourage their clients to continue with counselling merely to satisfy their own needs.

It is inevitable that dependency issues will arise from time to time for counsellors. Sometimes counsellors will be unaware that such dependency is occurring. It is here that regular supervision is essential to help counsellors identify dependency issues and to reduce the likelihood of inappropriate transgression of professional boundaries (see Chapter 37).

The termination of a series of counselling sessions

The decision about when to terminate a series of counselling sessions is often fairly clear, and will frequently be made by the client in discussion with the counsellor. However, there will be times when the decision is more difficult, particularly if either client or counsellor dependency is occurring. Counsellors therefore need to regularly review the progress that is being made in counselling sessions, and the goals that are being achieved, to ensure that counselling is continuing for the client's wellbeing, rather than for satisfying dependency needs. Where progress is not being made and goals are not being achieved, it is essential for the counsellor to discuss the case with their supervisor in order to make a sensible decision about what action to take. It may be that as a consequence of supervision the counsellor will be able to identify why the counselling process is failing to enable the client to change. This might be as a consequence of the counsellor's own unresolved personal issues interfering with the counselling process. Alternatively it may be because the counsellor lacks the required skills to help the client in question. We do need to recognise, of course, that all clients will not change. As a consequence of supervision, the counsellor may be able to use a different strategy, or approach, with a client who appears to be stuck and is unable to change. Another possibility is that the client concerned may require a different approach which is not within the counsellor's current repertoire of skills. In this case the counsellor might say to the client, 'I've noticed that although you have been coming to talk with me for several weeks, you still seem to be experiencing the same difficulties. This makes me wonder whether it might be more useful for you to seek help in some other way.' The counsellor might then invite the client to think of possible alternatives, and/or may make some suggestions of alternatives which might be useful.

Confronting dependency

If client dependency is identified, then the issue needs to be brought into the open to let the client know what the counsellor believes is happening. This needs to be done with sensitivity, because it would be easy for a client to feel hurt and rejected as a consequence of inept confrontation regarding dependency. However, if the dependency is reframed positively, as a normal occurrence which involves both counsellor and client, then progress can be made towards termination.

Dealing with the loss of the relationship

With clients who are terminating a long counselling relationship, there will be some grief associated with the loss of that relationship. Particularly where a long relationship has been established, counsellors need to help their clients prepare for the feelings of loss that will occur when the relationship ends. In order to minimise this pain, it may be advisable for a counsellor to make one or two appointments at long intervals at the end of a series of counselling sessions. For example, when we have seen clients on a weekly basis for several weeks, we have often made remaining appointments at fortnightly and monthly intervals.

With some clients it can be useful to have a follow-up session at the end of three months. A three-monthly follow-up session serves three purposes. First, it helps the client to adjust to the idea of being independent and not dependent on the counsellor; second, it enables the client to deal with the loss of the counselling relationship in a gentle way; and third, it enables the counsellor to review the progress that the client continues to make after regular counselling has ceased. Also, it sometimes happens that after a series of counselling sessions has been completed, a three-monthly follow-up session will reveal that there is a 'loose end' that needs to be tied up before final termination.

Termination of both single sessions and a series of sessions is often slightly painful. It is usually difficult to say 'Goodbye', and accept the loss of a meaningful relationship. As a counsellor, be aware of this, both for the client and for yourself. As discussed previously, it is important to address this issue openly and to help the client to adjust to termination. Termination needs to be done sensitively and caringly.

The termination of a telephone counselling call

Terminating a telephone counselling call is an art and if it is carried out expertly the caller will feel comfortable about hanging up, recognising that the call has come to a natural end. In order to achieve this result, the termination stage needs to be integrated with the total process of the call so that it occurs smoothly and is expected.

Generally, the termination process for a counselling call of average or longer length will follow a sequence of steps that prepare the caller for the end of the call. Naturally, each call is different and what is appropriate for one call will not fit another. Here are some commonly used steps that can be used when ending a call:

1. Decide when to finish a call.
2. Warn the caller that the time to finish is approaching.
3. Summarise the call.
4. Give the caller some positive feedback.
5. Take control.
6. Tell the caller that you are going to finish the call.
7. Invite the caller to phone back if appropriate.
8. Say 'Goodbye' and hang up.

We will now discuss these steps in detail so that you can use them as a guide if you wish. However, remember that you are a unique individual and will need to develop your own way of ending calls.

Decide when to finish a call

As you know, there can be no standard rule about how long a telephone counselling call should be. However, we don't believe that it's useful to let calls continue after useful work has finished. If the call is losing energy, or not making constructive progress for the caller, then it is time to prepare for termination or alternatively to look for different strategies so that the call regains its usefulness. Generally, we find that it is not helpful to allow calls to continue for longer than one hour at the most, although there are naturally exceptions to the rule.

We think that it is worth mentally evaluating what is happening in a call if it is still continuing after about 45 minutes. A decision can then be made about how to influence the process of the call so that the remaining minutes are useful to the caller.

Warn the caller that the time to finish is approaching

As with face-to-face counselling, it's a good idea to warn your client or caller, in advance, that the counselling session or call is nearing its end. When you sense that it is appropriate, you may wish to say to the caller something like this: 'I realise that we have been talking for a while now and hope that we have covered some useful ground together. I would like to finish our call within the next few minutes, and wonder whether there are some important things that you would like to say before we finish talking together.' This statement gives the caller an opportunity to deal with anything pressing that has been omitted. The caller is also prepared for the impending closure. Notice that the statement is clear and owned by the counsellor: 'I would like to finish our call.' You may not be comfortable using this style and that is OK, because you are different from us. Personally, we like to let the caller know our expectations rather than be indirect. The message is then clear and the caller can deal with it in any way they think fit.

Having warned the caller that the call is nearing its end, the caller may take the opportunity to bring in new material. A judgment is then needed as to whether to deal with that material in the current call or whether to say to the caller something like: 'You have now raised some important new issues and I think that they need to be considered carefully. Maybe you would like to phone back another time to talk through those issues. However, today I think that we should try to summarise those things that we have talked about and then finish our conversation.'

Summarise the call and give positive feedback

If the caller doesn't raise new issues, then you, the counsellor, have the opportunity to move into summarising the content and possibly the process of the call. An example of a process statement included in a summary might be: 'I notice that you seemed to be very distressed at the start of this call when you were discussing . . . and I get the impression that you are now more confident of your ability to handle the situation.' Notice that in this statement the caller receives positive feedback. Wherever possible give your caller positive feedback because people in crisis often do not feel good about themselves and may not be getting positive feedback from others. Sometimes it is hard to think of something positive to say, but it is rare not to be able to find something if you join with your client effectively. Be careful, however, to ensure that the feedback you give is credible. Here are some examples of positive feedback:

> 'I am impressed by the way that you have been able to think through the issues and come to some decisions.'
>
> 'I have heard how you have struggled on your own against many difficulties. You strike me as a fighter; someone who doesn't give in easily.'
>
> 'I think that you are remarkable to have done as well as you have when I take into account the negative messages you have received from your family. You must have a lot of internal strength.'
>
> 'In spite of the personal setbacks you have suffered you have persisted in your efforts to do the best you can. I think that you've done well.'

We do need to recognise that there will be times when a caller will still be experiencing a level of painful emotions at the end of a call. For example, it is not reasonable to expect that the counselling process will take away the sadness of a person who has lost a loved one. In a case like this, the counsellor might close the call by summarising and inviting the caller to call back: 'You are going through a difficult time having suffered a terrible loss. My guess is that you will need to talk to someone from time to time, so please feel welcome to call back.'

Take control

Having given your caller some positive feedback, or having invited them to call back, it is now time for you to take control so that termination occurs. Terminating a telephone counselling call can often be quite difficult and is often more difficult than terminating a face-to-face counselling session. In the face-to-face session, as discussed previously, it's possible for the counsellor to stand up and to move out of the room, giving clear signals that the session is over. These non-verbal signals are not available to the telephone counsellor. Moreover, we human beings are conditioned to believe that it is bad manners to assertively break off a conversation, particularly if the other person would really like to continue.

Some clients love to talk and would happily keep you on the phone for hours. Others just do not know how to close off a conversation. With both types of clients it is important to be clear and assertive.

Closing the call

Take control! Tell the caller that you intend to finish the call now and at the same time reassure them with regard to the possibility that they may want to phone back. It is very important to do this because some callers feel guilty about taking up a telephone counsellor's time and say things such as: 'There must be other people with much more important problems who need your help.' Such people need to be reassured that it is OK for them to ring up again.

Here are some suitable termination statements:

> 'Thank you for sharing your personal difficulties with me. I have appreciated the way you have trusted me enough to be able to share so much. Please feel welcome to phone back if you think that I can be of help. Goodbye.'
>
> 'It has been good to talk with you about the issues that have been troubling you. I hope that you will feel free to call back another day. Goodbye.'
>
> 'I think that you were sensible to phone; everyone needs to talk about personal matters privately at times. Please call again when you need to. Goodbye.'

Notice that the statements are clear and end with 'Goodbye'.

Regular callers

Crisis telephone counselling agencies usually have some callers who phone in regularly, enjoy talking and do not want to finish their calls at an appropriate time. With these callers the telephone counsellor needs to be very firm in making a termination statement similar to one of the examples above. If the caller then tries to restart the conversation, the counsellor is, in our view, justified in saying: 'I know that you would like to continue talking but I am going to hang up now because I want to finish here. Goodbye.' Then regardless of what the caller is saying the phone can be gently replaced on the hook. You may have noticed that in the example given the client is given a clear statement about the counsellor's intention before the hang-up occurs.

The three 'don'ts'

To terminate this chapter, here are three 'don'ts'. At the end of a face-to-face counselling session or telephone call:

DON'T ask the client a question.
DON'T reflect back content.
DON'T reflect back feelings.

If you do any of these things the session or call is certain to continue because the client or caller has an implied invitation to respond!

Learning summary

- Let the client know that you are in control of the length of the session.
- Warn the client when the session is coming to an end.
- Negotiate a contract with the client with regard to future appointments.
- Finish each session by summarising, outlining future goals if appropriate, and giving some positive feedback where possible.
- Take control when finishing a session.
- During a series of ongoing counselling sessions, review progress and be aware of dependency.
- Deal with dependency by openly discussing it.
- If necessary, deal with grief associated with closure of a series of sessions.
- Remember that terminating telephone calls may require considerable firmness.
- When terminating, don't ask questions or reflect content or feelings.

part III

Promoting change

chapter 11

Various approaches to counselling

There are many different styles of counselling in use today. Additionally, many counsellors do not limit themselves to the use of one style, but instead draw on ideas from a number of different counselling frameworks. They use what some writers (such as Culley 1991) call an 'integrated' approach because it involves integrating skills from different theoretical and practical sources.

In this book we will start by using as a base the non-directive counselling style originated by Carl Rogers, and will then build on that Rogerian foundation to incorporate techniques from other more active counselling methods.

The counselling style which you eventually adopt yourself will probably be one which suits your personality best. You may be surprised to know that it doesn't matter much what that style is, because most counsellors agree, as we suggested in Chapter 2, that the key to helping clients work effectively through their problems to feel better lies in the client–counsellor relationship. What is important is that the relationship between the client and counsellor is appropriate for producing therapeutic change.

In this chapter we will take a brief look at a selection of the differing counselling philosophies and methods which many counsellors find useful. We will begin by going back in history to look at the work of Sigmund Freud, who developed psychoanalysis in the 1930s. We will then consider the work of some other major contributors who have developed other styles of counselling since then.

Contributors to counselling theory and practice

Listed below is a selection of contributors to counselling theory and practice.

Psychoanalytic psychotherapy

- Sigmund Freud

Humanistic/existentialist counselling

- Carl Rogers
- Frederick (Fritz) Perls
- Richard Bandler and John Grinder

Cognitive behavioural counselling

- Albert Ellis

Narrative therapy

- Michael White
- David Epston

Solution-focused therapy

- Steve de Shazer

There have been, and are, many other important contributors to counselling theory and practice. In this book we will predominantly use ideas which were originated and developed by the people listed above. We ask you to remember that this is an introductory book which deals only with individual counselling for adults who are emotionally distressed.

Many counsellors believe that working with individual adults is the best way to learn basic counselling skills. Once basic counselling skills have been mastered, readers can, if they wish, build on these by learning additional skills for working with couples, families and children. Readers who wish to work with children or adolescents, rather than adults, might like to read our books *Counselling Children* (1997), *Counselling Adolescents* (1999) or *Working With Children In Groups* (2001). For readers who want to counsel families there are many books available on family therapy.

We will now briefly discuss the work of each of the people listed previously, starting with Freud. In each case we will consider only aspects of the person's work which, in some way, relate to the counselling methods discussed in this book. Readers who wish to learn more about the work of these major contributors may wish to select books from the 'further reading' list at the end of this chapter.

Psychoanalytic psychotherapy

Sigmund Freud was the originator of psychoanalytic psychotherapy. Although some counsellors still use a psychoanalytic approach, most contemporary counsellors do not. Even so, many of Freud's theories have significantly influenced contemporary approaches to counselling. It is therefore useful for a new counsellor to have some understanding of Freud's ideas.

Sigmund Freud

Sigmund Freud made a major and profound contribution to the understanding of human personality. Although some of his ideas are contentious he was a radical thinker whose individual contribution to psychology has been of great significance in shaping the way modern counsellors think about people and understand the underlying origins of their problems. Freud originated and developed the theory and methods of psychoanalysis. Although, as suggested previously, only a minority of counsellors work psychoanalytically nowadays, many contemporary counsellors use psychodynamic concepts to underpin their work.

Freud was a psychiatrist who saw his work as psychotherapy. Interestingly, Rogers later saw psychotherapy and counselling as synonymous. Freud made a major contribution to the recognition that counselling (or psychotherapy) was a valid and necessary process if we are to help people to overcome emotional problems. Films and TV programs often lampoon the Freudian psychoanalyst's couch on which the patient lies to talk about current and past anxieties while the psychiatrist listens. Although many people find such a situation amusing, this underlying concept is a forerunner to modern counselling methods where the counsellor gives undivided attention to the client while the client talks about troubling issues.

Freud introduced the idea of the 'unconscious' and proposed that our disturbed behaviours have their origins in unconscious processes that occur within the individual. As counsellors today, we need to be aware of the reality that often a person's attitudes, beliefs, thoughts, emotions and behaviours have their origins in unconscious processes that are suppressed.

Freud believed in what he called 'free association' where one idea triggers off another. He believed that by allowing the client to talk freely, free association would occur and the client would inevitably reveal ideas that were suppressed into the subconscious. Similarly, as contemporary counsellors we need to recognise the need to allow the client to travel without interruption along their own path, so that we do not interfere unnecessarily with a process which may result in the client dealing with the underlying source of painful current and past experiences.

Freud placed a great emphasis on the influence of past and childhood experiences. Frequently in counselling we find that a person's current problems have their origin in some earlier experience. Freud also identified a number of what he called 'defence mechanisms'. These defence mechanisms provide some protection for a person against current pain but block the person from dealing with underlying causes of distress. He described the way that the therapist (counsellor) would meet with what he called 'resistance' as the person avoided, deflected away from or suppressed painful material during psychotherapy (counselling).

Other ideas of Freud's which are important for the contemporary counsellor are 'transference' and 'counter-transference'. These will be discussed in Chapter 20. Freud had many other useful ideas, including his definitions of id, ego and super-ego. As this is not a book about Freud's work, if you are interested in this, you may wish to read Burton and Davey (1996).

If Freud had so many good ideas, you may be wondering why we don't teach all counsellors to use the psychoanalytic method. Well, there are several very important reasons, two of which are as follows:

1. Psychoanalysis, as originated by Freud, is a very slow process. Some psychoanalysts work with their clients over a period of several years in order to help their clients gain insight into the underlying causes of their behaviour. Psychoanalysts themselves undergo lengthy training. Most counsellors today would agree that rather than using lengthy counselling methods, it is generally more useful to provide clients with brief interventions which will quickly enable them to overcome emotional pain and function adaptively. We do need to recognise, however, that some clients will require long-term help.

2. Freud believed that the psychoanalyst was an expert who could help the client gain insight by interpreting the material the client disclosed. Many, if not most, modern counsellors do not see themselves as experts who are able to interpret what is meaningful for another person. Rather, they try to encourage and facilitate the client's own interpretation of their

inner processes and outward behaviours. As discussed in Chapter 1, the contemporary counsellor's goals include helping the client to feel more self-sufficient rather than dependent on the counsellor.

Around Freud's time counselling theory was influenced by the psychological theories of people such as Adler and Jung. However, major advances in counselling methods did not occur until the 1950s when the existential humanistic counselling methods emerged.

Humanistic/existentialist counselling

Two of the major contributors in this field were Carl Rogers and Fritz Perls. They believed that each individual had within himself the natural ability and resources to achieve personal growth. The counsellor, therefore, did not need to be an expert but merely a facilitator to enable the client to access their own resources to bring about change. Ideas developed by Richard Bandler and John Grinder can also be usefully incorporated into existential humanistic counselling.

Carl Rogers

Rogers originated and developed 'client-centred counselling' which he later renamed 'person-centred counselling'. In Chapter 2 we discussed some of Rogers' ideas. He radically differed from the psychoanalytic approach by suggesting that people have the ability within themselves to solve their own problems. He saw the counsellor as a facilitator who listened to clients with empathy and without judgment, and thus enabled them to work through their issues. His ideas are respectful of people. He did not see himself as a superior expert but as another person, different from his clients, but of equal value.

As discussed previously, Rogers placed great emphasis on the counselling skills of reflection (see Chapters 5, 6 and 7). He reflected back to clients what they were feeling emotionally. Also, he reflected back the content of what the client had said, but in the counsellor's own words.

Rogers' ideas are extremely useful to the modern counsellor, especially during the early parts of the counselling process where relationship building is paramount. Some counsellors still predominantly use a Rogerian approach. However, the problem with doing this is that the Rogerian approach, although very effective with some clients, tends to be slow in achieving results by comparison with other methods of counselling which are less time-consuming. Our personal experience suggests that integrating the Rogerian approach with other methods, as described in this book, is most effective.

Frederick (Fritz) Perls

Fritz Perls was initially trained as a psychoanalyst but moved away from psychoanalysis to develop Gestalt therapy. Gestalt therapy makes use of, or modifies, many psychoanalytic ideas. In contrast to psychoanalysis which placed emphasis on the client's past experiences, Perls placed strong emphasis on the present 'here and now' experience of the client. Perls encouraged clients to take personal responsibility for their current experience rather than blaming either the past or others.

Perls concentrated on raising the client's awareness of current bodily sensations, emotional feelings and related thoughts. By encouraging clients to become fully aware of their current experience in the here and now, he believed that he could enable them to work through 'unfinished business', sort out their emotional confusion, achieve what he called a 'Gestalt', or 'Ah-ha' experience, and thus feel more integrated.

Fritz Perls' counselling style was quite different from Carl Rogers' warm and caring style. Perls challenged and frustrated the client during the counselling process in order to move the client into a clearer understanding of troubling issues, thoughts, emotions and behaviours. At times, when counselling some clients, and at particular stages in the counselling process, it can be very advantageous to use Gestalt therapy techniques. However, we personally strongly contend that when using Gestalt therapy techniques the counselling relationship should retain the qualities suggested by Rogers so that clients are not threatened by the process.

Gestalt therapy counselling techniques include:

1. giving the client immediate feedback about non-verbal behaviour as it is observed during the counselling process. This is particularly useful in drawing the client's attention to feelings that are being suppressed;
2. inviting the client to get in touch with and describe bodily sensations and relate these to emotional feelings and thoughts;
3. encouraging clients to make 'I' statements and to take responsibility for their actions;
4. challenging and confronting what the counsellor sees as 'neurotic' behaviour, for example, confronting clients when they deflect away from talking about troubling issues;

5. encouraging clients to role play different parts of themselves and to create a dialogue between those parts; and
6. encouraging clients to role-play both themselves and someone else with whom they have a problem and to create a dialogue between themselves and the other person.

Ideas from Gestalt therapy are particularly useful when helping a client to explore options, and to move forward to take action. Examples of the use of Gestalt therapy will be given in a number of chapters but particularly in Chapters 19, 20, 21 and 22. Readers who would like to learn more about Gestalt therapy might like to read Clarkson (2000).

Richard Bandler and John Grinder

Richard Bandler and John Grinder were the originators of neuro-linguistic programming, commonly known as NLP. Readers who would like to learn about this method of helping people might like to read Bandler (1989 and 1990). In this book we will make use of two very useful concepts from NLP. These are:

1. the need for a counsellor to match the way people relate to their world through the use of differing senses such as seeing, hearing, feeling etc.; and
2. the concept of reframing.

These concepts will be discussed in Chapters 14 and 15.

Cognitive behavioural counselling

Starting in the 1960s Albert Ellis and other workers moved away from the humanistic existentialist approaches, which placed considerable importance on dealing with emotional feelings in the counselling process. Instead of focusing on feelings, they focused on thoughts (cognitions), and developed what are now referred to as *cognitive behavioural* counselling methods. Cognitive behavioural counsellors target the client's thinking (cognitive) processes and their behaviours rather than their emotions. They believe that a person's emotional feelings depend on the way they think and behave. Consequently, they believe that the best way to help someone to feel better emotionally is by helping them to change their thoughts and behaviours. These methods are popular for a number of reasons including the following:

1. They are believed to be useful in changing undesirable behaviours (consequently many counsellors who work with young people choose cognitive behavioural methods).

2. They tend to be less stressful for the counsellor who does not encourage clients to express strong emotions (being in the presence of a client who is expressing strong emotions can be emotionally draining for a counsellor).

Albert Ellis

Albert Ellis developed rational emotive therapy which is now known as 'rational emotive behaviour therapy'. A central idea in rational emotive behaviour therapy is that emotionally disturbed people are disturbed because they are making assumptions which are based on irrational beliefs. Ellis believes that the counsellor's job is to identify and challenge these irrational beliefs and to encourage the client to replace them by what he believes are rational beliefs. In Chapter 17 we will make use of Ellis's ideas to look at ways to help clients to challenge what we call 'self-destructive beliefs'.

Ellis's counselling style is different from both Rogers and Perls. Ellis does not place emphasis on joining with the client but uses questions to identify irrational beliefs. He then works enthusiastically to convince the client that these irrational beliefs are causing the problem and need to be replaced by other beliefs. Although we do not work with clients in the way he does, we find that at particular stages in the counselling process his ideas can be very useful for helping people to feel better. Further, we believe that it is possible to use his ideas and still retain the important qualities of the counselling relationship which we described in Chapter 2.

Readers who would like to learn more about rational emotive therapy may wish to read Dryden (1995).

Narrative therapy

In 1974, Lewis and Butler practised what they called 'life-review therapy'. Their approach helped clients restructure their past into a positive and integrated story. This concept was later developed into narrative therapy. Important contributors to the development of narrative therapy were, and are, David Epston and Michael White. Narrative therapy is based on the concept of 'storying'. Using 'storying', the client is invited to tell the story of how the problem has influenced their life. They are then encouraged to create a new and preferred alternative story in which the problem does not dominate their life. Narrative therapists help the client recognise that the problem is the problem, as opposed to the person being the problem. A more detailed description of narrative therapy is given in Chapter 24.

Solution-focused therapy

Solution-focused therapy grew out of ideas proposed by Milton Erickson who placed emphasis on turning perceived deficits into resources. A major contributor to the development of solution-focused therapy was Steve de Shazer (1988). Solution-focused therapists think in terms of solutions, resources and competency, rather than problems, deficits and limitations. They amplify what is already working, look for times when the client has been successful in the past and for times when the client has used coping skills successfully. They look for exceptions in the client's behaviour—the exceptions being times when the client has engaged in successful and adaptive behaviours. Solution-focused therapy is time-effective with the client generally being engaged in the counselling process for a brief period. A more detailed description of solution-focused therapy is given in Chapter 23.

An eclectic approach

As discussed at the beginning of this chapter, the counselling style described in this book is eclectic, that is, it draws ideas from all the counselling methods described in this chapter. Our eclectic approach relies on Rogerian ideas for relationship building and enabling the client to talk freely. It recognises the importance of understanding the psychodynamic approach as described previously. Additionally it draws on Gestalt therapy philosophy and techniques, and uses ideas from rational emotive therapy, neuro-linguistic programming, solution-focused therapy and narrative therapy.

Learning summary

- Many counsellors use an eclectic or integrative approach, drawing ideas from various therapies to suit the current needs of the client and to fit with their own personalities.
- It doesn't matter too much what style of counselling is used as the key to producing therapeutic change lies in the client–counsellor relationship.
- Freud encouraged the client to talk freely while he gave his undivided attention. He placed great emphasis on the past and on childhood experiences. The counsellor (or psychoanalyst) was the expert who interpreted for the client (patient) so that the client could gain insight and thus change.

- Existentialist humanistic counsellors such as Rogers and Perls believe that the client has the potential to solve their own problems. The counsellor (therapist) is a facilitator of change. The client is the expert.
- Rogers, in client-centred counselling, placed emphasis on the relationship and on reflecting back to the client what the client had said.
- Perls' goal in Gestalt therapy was to bring about increased client awareness through helping the client to integrate information from bodily sensations, thoughts and emotional feelings. He placed great emphasis on encouraging the client to take personal responsibility by using 'I' statements and staying in the 'here and now'.
- Bandler and Grinder in neuro-linguistic programming recognised the need for a counsellor to match the client's way of experiencing the world through the use of particular senses. They also introduced the concept of reframing.
- Cognitive behavioural counsellors believe that our thoughts and behaviours control our emotions. Consequently they focus on changing thoughts and behaviours in order to help people to feel better and behave more adaptively.
- Albert Ellis originated rational emotive behaviour therapy. He believes that people become emotionally distressed because of irrational beliefs and that the counsellor should convince the client to replace these beliefs with rational beliefs.
- Narrative therapy places emphasis on separating the problem from the person. It encourages the person to reconstruct their story so that the problem does not dominate their life.
- Solution-focused therapy is a brief therapy which focuses on strengths, resources and competencies rather than on problems, deficits and limitations.

Further reading

Historical perspectives
Dryden, W. 1996, *Developments in Psychotherapy: Historical Perspectives*, Sage, London.

An integrated approach to counselling
Culley, S. 1991, *Integrative Counselling Skills in Action*, Sage, London.

Psychodynamic counselling
Burton, M. & Davey, T. 1996, 'The Psychodynamic Paradigm', *Handbook of Counselling Psychology*, Woolfe, R. & Dryden, W. (eds), Sage, London.
Jacobs, M. 1989, *Psychodynamic Counselling in Action*, 2nd edn, Sage, London.

Person-centred counselling (Rogers)
Mearns, D. 1994, *Developing Person-Centred Counselling*, Sage, London.
Rogers, C. R. 1955, *Client-Centered Therapy*, Houghton Mifflin, Boston.
Thorne, B. 1992, *Carl Rogers*, Sage, London.

Gestalt therapy (Perls)
Clarkson, P. 2000, *Gestalt Counselling in Action*, 2nd edn, Sage, London.
Clarkson, P. & Mackewn, J. 1993, *Fritz Perls*, Sage, London.
O'Leary, E. 1992, *Gestalt Therapy, Theory, Practice and Research*, Chapman & Hall, London,

Neuro-linguistic programming (Bandler and Grinder)
Bandler, R. & Grinder, J. 1990, *The Structure of Magic: A Book about Language and Therapy*, Science and Behavior Books, Palo Alto.
Bandler, R., Grinder, J. & Andreas, C. 1989, *Reframing: Neurolinguistic Programming and the Transformation of Meaning*, Real People Press, Moab.

Rational emotive therapy (Ellis)
Dryden, W. 1995, *Brief Rational Emotive Behaviour Therapy*, Wiley, London.
Ellis, A. 1995, *Better, Deeper, and More Enduring Brief Therapy: The Rational Emotive Behavior Therapy Approach*, Bruner/Mazel, New York.

Narrative therapy
Morgan, A. 2000, *What is Narrative Therapy: An Easy to Read Introduction*, Dulwich Centre, Adelaide.

White, M. & Epston, D. 1990, *Narrative Means to Therapeutic Ends*, Norton, New York.

Solution-focused therapy
de Shazer, S. 1988, *Clues: Investigating Solutions in Brief Therapy*, Norton, New York.
de Shazer, S. 1991, *Putting Difference to Work*, Norton, New York.
Walter, J. L. & Peller, J. E. 1992, *Becoming Solution-Focused in Brief Therapy*, Brunner/Mazel, New York.

Counselling children
Geldard, K. & Geldard, D. 1997, *Counselling Children: A Practical Introduction*, Sage, London.
Geldard, K. & Geldard, D. 2001, *Working with Children in Groups: A Handbook for Counsellors, Educators, and Community Workers*, Palgrave, London.

Counselling adolescents
Geldard, K. & Geldard, D. 1999, *Counselling Adolescents: The Pro-active Approach*, Sage, London.

chapter 12

Helping people change

As we have stated previously, a major goal of counselling is to help people change. People come to counsellors at times of crisis and are usually emotionally distressed and do not know how to change so that they can feel better and be able to live more comfortable, satisfying and adaptive lives. If we are to be effective as counsellors in helping our clients to change, then we need to have some understanding of the change processes which can occur as a consequence of counselling.

James Prochaska (1999) points out that positive change occurs regardless of the model of counselling used. It is clear that the relationship between the client and counsellor is a more important factor in producing change than the model of counselling. Prochaska's claim is certainly correct as it is based on research findings. However, in our experience, the extent of change can be maximised if we recognise differences in the ways in which changes in the client's emotional state, thinking processes and behaviours can be achieved. Some counsellors pay attention to the way the client feels emotionally, thinks, and behaves, by directly addressing emotions, thoughts, and behaviours. This is particularly the case for those counsellors who use an eclectic approach. Other counsellors primarily focus on either emotional feelings, or thinking processes (cognitions), or behavioural change, believing that if change occurs in one of these, then change will automatically occur in the others.

In order to help in the understanding of change processes we will discuss the use of catharsis in producing emotional change, the use of awareness raising or insight development in producing emotional, cognitive and sometimes behavioural change, and the use of cognitive behavioural methods which directly target thoughts and behaviours.

Emotional release

As we know, most clients come for counselling help when they are experiencing a level of emotional distress. For some clients, their emotions are clearly expressed, either verbally or non-verbally. For other clients, although they may exhibit levels of anxiety or confusion, their emotional expression is more contained. Many clients are unable to identify with clarity the emotions they are experiencing. Sometimes a client's emotions are so repressed that in the early stages of counselling it may be impossible for the client to get in touch with them.

As human beings our experience is that when we release our emotions we tend to feel better and to enter into a calmer state. For example, if a client is grieving, and very sad, our experience is that if they let their emotions out by crying, afterwards they will feel better. They may not feel happy, but they are likely to be less disturbed and more comfortable. Similarly, if they are very angry, they may need to release their anger in some way. This may be by shouting, punching a pillow or engaging in a symbolic ritual. Clearly, one way in which a counsellor may help a client to feel better is to help the client to achieve catharsis through emotional release.

Some forms of counselling directly aim to produce emotional release. For example, Mark Pearson and Patricia Nolan have written a book containing emotional release exercises for children (Pearson & Nolan 1991).

Many counsellors who use Carl Rogers's approach place an emphasis on reflection of emotional feelings. As a consequence, clients tend to get in touch with strong emotions. Most Rogerian counsellors allow their clients to fully experience any emotions which emerge (subject to safety when dealing with clients who are very angry). Generally, if a client starts to cry, the counsellor will allow the crying to continue until it naturally abates. Consequently emotions are released and catharsis occurs. With regard to other emotions, such as frustration, anger, and despair, the Rogerian counsellor encourages the client, through reflection of content and feelings, to verbally express the emotions rather than to avoid dealing with them. It needs to be recognised that in addition to dealing with emotions, Rogerian counselling helps the client to sort out troubled thoughts and to make decisions about new behaviours.

Gestalt therapy directly seeks to achieve catharsis. In the counselling process, the counsellor will encourage the client to act out emotional feelings, thereby achieving emotional release. As will be discussed, Gestalt therapy is also useful in addressing thoughts and behaviours.

You might ask, 'Is emotional release sufficient in itself?' Pierce, Nichols and Du Brin (1983) in their book, *Emotional Expression in Psychotherapy*, are clear in their belief that when feelings are expressed fully they lead to new ways for clients to view themselves and the world. In other words their thinking changes. They go on to say that the new ways of thinking and viewing the world then lead to more satisfying behaviours. However, they do recognise that this process does not happen automatically.

We ourselves believe that emotional release is an important component of the healing process, but we do not believe that it is sufficient in itself. In our experience many clients who release emotions in counselling are unable to make significant changes to their thinking and behaviour without receiving help to deal directly with their thoughts and behaviours. Unfortunately, clients who are unable to make changes in their thinking and behaviours are quite likely to re-experience ongoing problems in the future as troubling situations arise.

Insight development, awareness raising and the discovery of possibilities

Other ways in which counselling can be useful in helping clients move to more comfortable and satisfying life positions, is through the development of insight (when a psychoanalytic counselling model is used), through the raising of awareness (when a Gestalt therapy approach is used), and by discovering solutions and possibilities (when solution-focused counselling or narrative therapy is used).

The psychoanalytic approach to counselling relies heavily on the development of insight which enables clients to understand themselves more fully, and to make sense of their current and past experiences, thoughts, behaviours and feelings.

Gestalt therapy, which grew out of psychoanalysis, puts the emphasis on awareness raising as distinct from insight development. Awareness raising involves helping the client to get in touch with their current experience involving somatic or bodily sensations, emotional feelings, and thoughts. As a consequence of awareness raising, the client has the opportunity to get in touch with strong emotions with possible cathartic release, and additionally is likely to experience what Fritz Perls called an 'Ah-ha' experience, suddenly seeing with clarity instead of staying confused, as though a light had been switched on in their brain. Perls believed that as a consequence the client would feel better, think differently, and start to engage in more adaptive behaviours (Clarkson 2000). It also needs to be recognised that Gestalt therapy is useful in directly targeting behaviours.

When using solution-focused or narrative therapy a process of inquiry by the counsellor helps the client to recognise future possibilities and so to change their thinking and behaviours. These two approaches do not directly target emotional feelings by promoting emotional release, but use a process called externalising. The externalising process claims to give the client control over the relevant emotion rather than releasing it.

It can be seen that the psychoanalytic, Gestalt therapy, solution-focused and narrative therapy approaches are useful in helping clients in a process of self-discovery.

A good model to illustrate the usefulness of this process of self-discovery is the Johari window. The Johari window, as devised by Joseph Luft and Harry Ingham at a workshop in 1955 (Luft 1969), is shown in Figure 12.1.

	Known to self	Unknown to self
Known to others	Open	Blind
Unknown to others	Hidden	Unknown

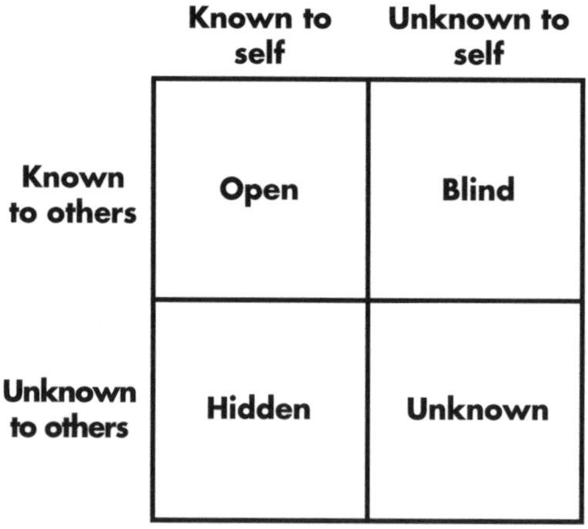

Figure 12.1 *The Johari window*
(From: Group Processes: An Introduction to Group Dynamics, *3rd edn, by Joseph Luft © 1984, 1970, 1963. Reprinted by permission of Mayfield Publishing Company.)*

According to Luft the name 'Johari' is pronounced as if it were 'Joe' and 'Harry', which is where the name comes from: Joe–Harry. The window has four panes as shown. Each pane in the window contains information about the person represented by the window. The two panes on the left-hand side contain information which is known to the person, whereas the two panes on the right-hand side contain information which is unknown to the person. The two panes at the top contain information which is known to others and the two panes at the bottom contain information which is unknown to others.

Information in the top left-hand pane (the *open* pane) is openly recognised by both the person and other people. If I, David, use my own personal window as an example, I know that I get satisfaction from writing textbooks and other people are aware of this information. Consequently this information is in my *open* pane. Information in the bottom left-hand pane, labelled *hidden*, is known to me and unknown to others. I can think of some characteristics and beliefs of mine which fit into that pane, but I won't let you know what they are or they would no longer be in that pane. Information in the top right-hand pane labelled *blind* is known to others but not to me. For example, other people may know that I am arrogant but I may not recognise this. Information in the bottom right-hand pane labelled *unknown* is totally unseen and is locked in my subconscious.

The influence of counselling on the Johari window

The likely influence of successful counselling on the Johari window is shown in Figure 12.2. When a person comes to talk with a counsellor it is quite likely that at first they will talk about information in the *open* pane. However, if a trusting relationship develops the person may take the counsellor into their confidence and self-disclose information from the *hidden* pane, thus enlarging the open pane.

Additionally, as counselling proceeds the counsellor may give the client feedback or ask questions. As a result of the feedback and questioning the client may discover information which was unknown to them but may, or may not, have been recognised by the counsellor. Once again the open pane is enlarged. As a consequence of the counselling process the client may gain in insight (to use a psychoanalytic term), or gain in awareness (to use a

Figure 12.2 *The effect of counselling on the Johari window*

Gestalt therapy term), or discover previously unknown possibilities (to use a solution-focused or narrative therapy description). As shown in Figure 12.2 the person's self-knowledge is likely to increase during an effective counselling process, allowing for personal growth and change to occur.

Changing behaviours

Up to now, we have discussed ways of helping a client by using methods which involve emotional release and changes in thinking. For some clients, this may be sufficient to produce behavioural change but for others the counselling process needs to be more strongly directed towards behaviours.

As explained in the previous section, Gestalt therapy awareness-raising processes can be useful in helping a client to deal with emotions, thoughts and behaviour. Gestalt therapy deals with behavioural problems by using an experiential approach which involves experiencing practical experiments related to behavioural change (see Chapters 21 and 22). Additionally solution-focused counselling and narrative therapy help the client to discover possible alternative behaviours.

Another useful way of addressing behaviours is to use a cognitive behavioural counselling approach. To illustrate this we will briefly describe some aspects of rational emotive behaviour therapy as a method of promoting changes in behaviours. Additionally, we will briefly discuss the use of behaviour therapy.

Rational emotive behaviour therapy (REBT)

Central to rational emotive behaviour therapy (REBT) is the ABCDE model as described by Dryden (1995). A diagrammatic representation of this model is shown in Figure 12.3.

A	**A**ctivating event
B	**B**eliefs—rational or irrational
C	**C**onsequences—emotional or behavioural response
D	**D**isputing irrational beliefs
E	**E**ffects of disputing irrational beliefs

Figure 12.3 *The ABCDE model in rational emotive behaviour therapy*

This model is dependent on the notion of irrational beliefs (see Chapter 17 regarding challenging self-destructive beliefs). It is assumed that a sequence of events, as described in Figure 12.3, occurs which leads the client to experience uncomfortable emotions and/or to engage in maladaptive behaviours. The letters ABCDE are the first letters of words which describe the sequence. The letter A represents the first stage of the sequence, which is an *activating event*. According to REBT theory the activating event triggers off an irrational *belief* represented by the B. The *consequence* (C) of this irrational belief is the person's response involving unhelpful emotions and/or behaviours. The D represents the stage where the counsellor *disputes* the irrational belief, helping the client to replace the irrational belief with a more constructive belief. Finally, E represents the *effects* of disputing as a result of which the client will hopefully experience more helpful emotions and/or behaviours.

Once an irrational belief has been disputed and replaced by a more useful belief, it is expected that similar activating events in the future will result in more positive consequences as the client moves through the A, B and C stages.

It can be seen that the REBT approach does not encourage the client to express emotions but instead encourages them to focus on their beliefs and behaviours.

Behaviour therapy

When counselling parents some counsellors make use of behavioural methods in order to help the parents in the management of their children's behaviours. These methods rely on the use of consequences for behaviours. Thus, the parent is encouraged to use negative consequences in response to undesirable behaviour and positive consequences in response to desirable behaviour. Additionally, star charts, where a reward is given after a set number of stars is received, may be used. We ourselves are counsellors who frequently work with children, young people and their families and have some reservations about the indiscriminate use of behaviour therapy. We are uncomfortable with the use of behaviour therapy unless earlier work has been done to address the emotional and cognitive problems of the child or young person. After that, if it is needed, we think that behaviour therapy can be useful.

In conclusion

It can be seen from the discussion in this chapter that if we are to be effective in helping clients, it is important for us, as counsellors, to enable them to make changes. If we help them to release emotions they will feel better in the short-term. However, if our counselling help is to be of long-term value, after emotions have been released we also need to help clients to change their thoughts and behaviours. If we do this it is more likely that they will be able to deal with future problems in more adaptive ways.

Rogerian counselling methods are useful in helping clients to release emotions, and can also be of use in helping clients to change the way they think and choose different behaviours. However, the Rogerian approach does not address thoughts and behaviours as directly as some other approaches. Gestalt therapy awareness-raising techniques can be used to help the client release emotions, and change thoughts and behaviours. Thus, Gestalt therapy tends to be holistic. The cognitive behavioural methods such as rational emotive behaviour therapy are very powerful in addressing self-destructive thoughts and behaviours. REBT also addresses emotions, although indirectly and not through emotional release. Solution-focused and narrative therapy are powerful in helping the client to look at future options and choices. As a consequence the client's behaviours are directly targeted. As a result their emotional feelings may also change, even though these have not been directly addressed.

Learning summary

- Clients will generally feel better if they are able to talk about and express their emotions.
- Emotional release alone may not result in long-term benefit. Changes to thoughts and behaviours are also required to promote long-term change.
- Human beings naturally have information about themselves, some of which is hidden from others and some of which is hidden from themselves, as described by the Johari window.
- If clients can accept the hidden parts of themselves, then they are likely to be better able to deal with these parts, and consequently to be able to lead more adaptive and satisfying lives.

- The counselling process may increase insight, raise self-awareness, or help the client discover future possibilities (depending on the model of counselling used), resulting in personal growth and enabling the client to change and feel better.

Further reading

Clarkson, P. 2000, *Gestalt Counselling in Action*, 2nd edn, Sage, London.

Dryden, W. 1995, *Brief Rational Emotive Behaviour Therapy*, Sage, London.

Luft, J. 1969, *Of Human Interaction*, Mayfield, California.

Morgan, A. 2000, *What is Narrative Therapy: An Easy to Read Introduction*, Dulwich Centre, Adelaide.

O'Leary, E. 1992, *Gestalt Therapy, Theory, Practice and Research*, Chapman & Hall, London.

Pearson, M. & Nolan, P. 1991, *Emotional First-Aid for Children: Emotional Release Exercises and Inner-Life Skills*, Butterfly, Springwood, Australia.

Pierce, R. A., Nichols, M. P. & Du Brin, M. A. 1983, *Emotional Expression In Psychotherapy*, Gardner, New York.

Prochaska, J. O. 1999, 'How do people change, and how can we change to help many more people?', in *The Heart & Soul of Change: What Works in Therapy*, M. A. Hubble, B. L. Duncan & S. D. Miller (eds), American Psychological Association, Washington, DC.

Walter, J. L. & Peller, J. E. 1992, *Becoming Solution-Focused in Brief Therapy*, Brunner/Mazel, New York.

chapter 13

Combining skills to facilitate the change process

In this chapter we will look at the way in which we can combine the counselling skills learnt so far into a sequential process which optimises the possibility of producing change. In looking at this process we do need to recognise that each counselling session will be different from every other session. No two interventions are going to be the same. However, after counselling for a long time, many counsellors recognise a common pattern in the processes that occur during counselling sessions. The flow chart in Figure 13.1 illustrates this pattern in diagrammatic form. Although this flow chart is useful in creating a general understanding of the sequence of counselling processes which commonly occur in a counselling session, please be aware that the various stages described by the chart will often overlap each other, repeat themselves and occur in a different order from that shown. The flow chart will be discussed in some detail in the following paragraphs under the headings shown on the left-hand side of the chart.

Preparation
The counselling process starts even before the client and counsellor meet. Clients on the way to counselling sessions will often rehearse what they intend to say. They are likely to bring with them preconceived ideas about what's going to happen in the counselling session. They will have not only expectations, but probably considerable apprehension too. Coming to a counselling session can be quite difficult for a client because it is painful to

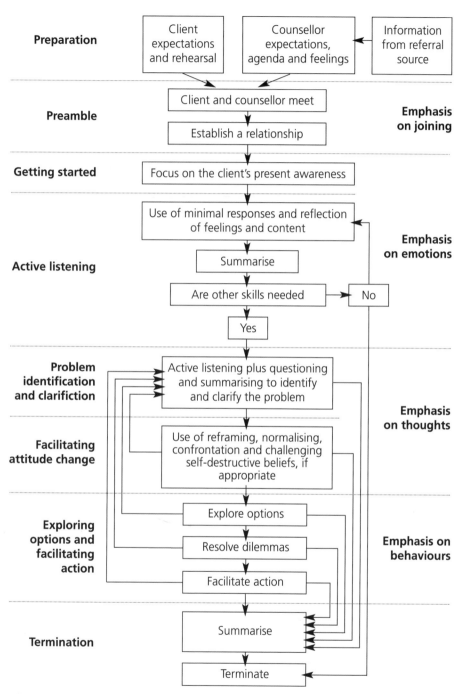

Figure 13.1 *Process of a counselling session*

talk about deep inner feelings, and it can be quite threatening to do this with a stranger.

The counsellor's own experience

Counsellors also bring their own expectations, agendas and personal feelings to counselling sessions. The counsellor's expectations and agenda may be inappropriate for the client, and the counsellor's personal feelings may intrude on the counselling process to the detriment of the client. The counsellor's own attitudes, beliefs and feelings are certain to influence what happens in the session. If counsellors have personal problems of their own that are unresolved and currently troubling them, these are certain to affect their counselling. Obviously, it is very important for counsellors to try to minimise the intrusion of their own issues into the counselling process. One of the best ways for counsellors to achieve this is for them to become as aware as possible of their own personal troubling issues, and as aware as possible of what they are experiencing internally during each counselling session. We believe that if when counselling, you deliberately try to stay aware of what is happening within yourself, then you will be better able to deal appropriately with what is yours, and to separate that from what is the client's. In this way your own issues will be less likely to intrude on the counselling process.

Information gained prior to counselling

Before a counsellor has met with the client, it is possible for them to have some preconceived ideas about the client. Often the counsellor will have information about a client before the session starts. This information may have come from the person or agency that referred the client for counselling. As a new counsellor, I, David, believed that such material often distorted my own understanding of the client. Consequently I went through a stage of trying not to listen to what referral sources told me, and of making an appointment and saying to the referral source: 'I'll find it all out from the client.' I have changed that approach because I have discovered that quite often a referral source will have factual information which may take time to come out in the counselling session, and which is useful in enabling me to understand the client better. Additionally, some clients may have an expectation that a referral source will have given me information.

Preamble

This is the joining stage where the client and counsellor meet and a relationship is established as discussed in Chapter 4, so that the client feels at ease. Also, at this time, the counsellor may be able to check out and adjust some of their initial ideas about the client.

Getting started

After the initial settling-in period, it can be useful to start the working part of the session by asking the client how they are feeling emotionally, right now. This brings the focus onto the client's current awareness and enables the client to get in touch with their own anxiety or tension about coming for counselling. By getting in touch with these feelings, a change usually occurs, and this makes it easier for the client to move on to talking about troubling issues. Sometimes a client will come with a 'shopping list' of things which they wish to talk about, and may even produce lengthy handwritten notes. If a client has done this, try to help them feel that what they have done is useful and valuable preparation. However, avoid getting trapped into working through the shopping list item by item, but instead use the list to generate energy in the client. For example, you might say, 'This list is really important. When you think about it, what do you think about first?' Thus the client finds a starting point from which to proceed naturally, in whatever direction their energy takes them. More often than not the shopping list will become irrelevant as more important underlying issues emerge.

Clarifying the counsellor's role

Unfortunately clients often perceive counsellors as 'experts', with almost magical skills, who are capable of using clever psychological techniques to solve other people's problems. Consequently, there may need to be a re-education process, where you, the counsellor, spell out to the client exactly how you *do* see yourself. It may be necessary for you to say to the client:

'Look, I don't see myself as an expert who can solve your problems for you. In fact, I believe that you will always know and understand yourself better than I will know and understand you. However, I hope that in this session you and I together can explore what's troubling you so that you can make some progress towards feeling more comfortable.'

Alternatively, you might say something like:

> 'It would be great if I were a magician who could wave a wand over you to solve your problems. I can't do that, but I can offer you the opportunity to come here and explore your problems with me in a safe and confidential setting. Hopefully, by doing that, you will start to feel more comfortable.'

Active listening

During the early parts of a session, as the client starts to talk about their issues, the counsellor is able to make use of minimal responses, and to reflect content and feelings. By doing this the client is encouraged to disclose what is troubling them, in their own way and at their own pace, and without unnecessary intrusion into that process by the counsellor. Consequently the client's story unfolds and the relationship between client and counsellor develops as the client feels valued by the counsellor's active listening. During this stage of the counselling process it is likely that clients who are experiencing high levels of distress will get in touch with, and express, their emotional feelings.

Respecting the client's pace

In the early stages of counselling it is common for clients to be unable to recognise and talk about their emotional feelings. Clients often want to talk about things 'out there' rather than get in touch with their inner experiences. They want to talk about other people's behaviour, and about other people's fears. They want to focus on what happened in the past rather than on the present, and to focus on events, instead of on their own inner feelings. It is useful to encourage a client, in this situation, to focus on their inner feelings and thoughts, as they are, in the present. However, it is also important not to pressure the client, but to allow them to move at their own pace. At first, allow your client to talk about the 'out there' things, if it is too painful for them to focus on their own inner processes. With time, as they deal with the 'out there' problems, and with the 'out there' situations, they are likely to move slowly towards recognising and talking about their own feelings from the past. This is because past feelings will probably not be as threatening as present feelings. Later, the client may feel more able to own current feelings and move towards experiencing them. Take time in helping the client to experience their own thoughts and feelings in the present. It is important to do this sensitively because the client needs to be able to gradually approach the painful parts of their life, rather than to be pushed too quickly, and then to run away from looking at the issues that are troubling them. The counsellor who pushes too hard too early does the client a disservice, because the client may close the lid on a box of uncomfortable feelings and thoughts, and not come back to another counselling session.

The counsellor's behaviour

During the active listening phase, while keeping a check on their own inner experiences, counsellors need to focus their energy by concentrating as fully as they can on what is happening inside the counselling room. In particular they need to fully attend to the client, to concentrate on listening to and observing the client, and to sense what the client is experiencing. This is not always easy and there will inevitably be occasions when a counsellor's attention does wander through an intrusion in the counselling environment, the presence of intrusive thoughts, over-tiredness, or for some other reason. If this does happen it may be best to be open and honest with the client and then to re-focus on the counselling process. Remember that no-one is perfect. If you are starting to become over-tired read Chapter 38 entitled 'Looking after yourself'.

Problem identification and clarification

At times, the counsellor will need to draw together the important parts of what the client has said, and to help the client to focus more clearly by summarising these. As the client's trust develops, the counsellor will be able to ask appropriate questions where necessary, in order to help the client move forward and identify the most pressing problem.

Facilitating attitude change

Often the focus at this point in the counselling process will tend to move away from an emphasis on emotions towards an emphasis on attitudes, beliefs and thoughts. At this stage in the process it is still of considerable value to continue using the skills which have been learnt from previous chapters. There are however some additional skills that are particularly useful in promoting change. These are the skills of reframing, confrontation, challenging self-destructive beliefs and normalising, which will be discussed in Chapters 15, 16, 17 and 18. Additionally, the counsellor may find it useful to explore polarities and make use of the 'here and now' experience, as will be discussed in Chapters 19 and 20. Thus, a range of skills can be selected and used to encourage the client to choose more constructive attitudes and beliefs.

Exploring options and facilitating action

The counsellor may now be able to assist the client to move forward into exploring options, resolving dilemmas and planning for action as will be discussed in Chapters 21 and 22. However it is important to ensure, as stated previously, that the client does not feel pressured. It is important to focus on raising the client's awareness rather than pushing for choice or action (see Chapters 21 and 22). To encourage a client to make a choice prematurely will pressure them and will make it harder for them to reach a decision. If the client is not ready to make a choice, they must be allowed to feel that it is OK to be unable to make a decision, and to feel that it is OK to remain stuck for the present.

Termination

A good way to terminate a counselling session is to summarise important personal discoveries for the client that have emerged during the session. Generally, it is better to pick out what was important in a session rather than to attempt to summarise everything covered in the session. At the close of a session you might wish to imagine when the session began the client brought into the room an awkward bundle of thoughts and feelings. The client then dropped the bundle onto the floor and started to examine the contents one at a time. After examining each item, some were retained, some were thrown away and others were exchanged. After that the client needed help to tie up the bundle into a neater, more manageable package. This help can be provided by using a summary to tie together important themes which have emerged during the counselling process. It is important to remember, using the metaphor of the bundle, that the bundle belongs to the client, so it must be their decision about how and when they complete their repackaging.

Respecting the client's process

Sometimes a client will not be ready to tie up the package. Sometimes the client will be left in a very uncomfortable space, either feeling stuck or fairly unhappy or distressed about what they have discovered during the counselling process. Many counsellors, especially new ones, want clients to leave sessions feeling happy. It is important to remember that often it is useful for a client to be able to spend time mulling over what has been discussed in the counselling session so that they can absorb and make sense of it before coming back again if they need to.

It can be distressing for a new counsellor when a client who arrived for a counselling session looking composed, leaves the session showing signs of emotion. This will inevitably happen at times because if a counsellor is effective, the client may move into areas that previously had not been openly explored. Consequently, the client may feel the pain of experiencing emotions that had been suppressed and leave the counselling session exhausted and sad. Sometimes allowing the client to do this can be therapeutic and the positive results of this process may be seen when the client returns for a subsequent session. However, if the counsellor suspects that the client may engage in self-harming behaviour as a consequence of raised emotions, then appropriate action needs to be taken (see Chapter 28).

In conclusion

The process of a counselling session described in this chapter gives an overview of the process as it might occur. However, as a counsellor, do not attempt to follow this process, but rather let it emerge naturally. Do as described in Chapter 2: allow the client to go at their own pace, in their own direction and to feel as though they are going on a journey with you, the counsellor, walking alongside. If you do this, the counselling process will occur naturally, smoothly and without great effort on your part. Most importantly, the client will be undergoing a process of growth which may enable them to lead a more fulfilling and less painful life.

Learning summary

- A typical process for a counselling session is described schematically in Figure 13.1, 'Process of a counselling session'.
- Client and counsellor expectations, agenda and personal feelings will affect the helpfulness of a counselling intervention.
- The client's first impressions are important.
- Special relationship-building time is needed in the first session.

- Counsellors don't pretend to have magic wands!
- Initially clients often want to talk about things 'out there', other people and past events.
- When clients are ready, encourage them to move towards focusing on their own feelings and thoughts, as they are in the immediate present.
- When appropriate, move from active listening to problem identification and clarification, facilitating attitude change, exploring options, taking action, and termination.

Further reading

Corey, G. 1996, *Theory and Practice of Counseling and Psychotherapy*, 5th edn, Brooks/Cole, Pacific Grove.

Egan, G. 1998, *The Skilled Helper: A Problem Management Approach to Helping*, 6th edn, Brooks/Cole, Pacific Grove.

Hackney, H. & Cormier, L. S. 2000, *The Professional Counselor: A Process Guide to Helping*, 4th edn, Allyn & Bacon, Boston.

part **IV**

Additional skills for promoting change

Matching the client's language

The joining, listening, reflection and summarising skills covered in Chapters 4 to 8, are Rogerian counselling skills developed by Carl Rogers. In this chapter, and in Chapter 15, we will consider skills which derive from neuro-linguistic programming as developed by Bandler and Grinder.

Different ways of experiencing the world

You are unique because you are a human being. I, David, am unique, as all human beings are. Being unique is important to me—I'm not quite the same as you, and you're not quite the same as me. All of us in the world are a bit different from each other. The ways in which we do things are different, and most importantly, the ways in which we experience and think about the world are different. An important difference in the way individuals experience the world has to do with the senses we all use for maintaining contact with our environment.

As you know, there are a number of different senses that we use to experience our world. We can smell, taste, touch, see and hear.

The feeling (or kinaesthetic) mode

By smelling, tasting and touching we make contact with things that are present in the environment surrounding us. Additionally, we have sensations within our bodies that are a response to our external environment. For example, when we are anxious, our bodies may tense up or we may get 'butterflies in the stomach'. When we are excited our adrenalin flows faster and our metabolism speeds up.

The senses of smelling, tasting and touching, together with our internal bodily sensations, link up with our emotional feelings. These sensations and feelings combine to contribute to our awareness of the world. Together, they make up what is generally referred to as the *feeling* or *kinaesthetic* mode of awareness.

The seeing and hearing modes of awareness

We may also be aware of our world by using either the seeing mode or the hearing mode of awareness. By using either of these modes we experience the world in which we live.

Three important modes of awareness

Hence, we can describe three important ways in which we can experience the world by using our senses. These are:
1. the *feeling* or *kinaesthetic mode*
2. the *seeing* or *visual mode*
3. the *hearing* or *auditory mode*.

Individual differences

We all have different abilities. Some of us are good at maths, others at languages, and some are good at doing things with their hands. During our lives most of us discover those things that we are good at and those things that we do not do so well. In the same way that we develop different practical and academic abilities during our lives, some of us learn to use particular senses more effectively than other senses. For example, there are people who are very good at detecting things that smell, and other people who have acute hearing and can hear the slightest sound. Some people are really observant and readily notice small details which other people miss. When I, David, learnt to be a scuba diver, the fellow who taught me was extremely observant and would frequently see things that I missed. He would see the heavily camouflaged and dangerous stonefish lurking among the rocks where I was probing, whereas I would fail to see it until it was pointed out to me.

Using different ways to think

Not only do people experience the world differently, but they also think in different ways. Some people think predominantly by using visual imagery (the seeing mode), others think in the hearing mode by talking to themselves mentally, and others think in terms of their feelings and bodily sensations (feeling or kinaesthetic mode). There may be people who are equally versatile and can think easily in all or any of the three modes, but most people seem to rely more strongly on one mode than the others. What mode do you think in? Are you predominantly visual, auditory, or feeling (kinaesthetic)?

If you listen to someone talking, and listen carefully to the words being used, you are likely to get some clues as to which mode they generally use when they are thinking. Let us consider a few examples. Some people use expressions like: 'I hear what you say', 'It sounds as though you are saying', 'It sounds as though', 'Tell me what happened', or 'That rings bells for me'. People who use that sort of language are using the hearing mode of thinking. There are other people of course who will say things like: 'I see what you mean', 'I've got a clearer picture of the situation', or 'It looks good'. People who talk like that are using the seeing mode to think. The third category of people are people who predominantly think and experience the world by using feeling methods. They say things like: 'It feels good', 'You touched a raw nerve there' or 'I sense your discomfort'.

Matching the client

Previously we've considered the value of matching the way in which the client behaves. We've talked about how it's helpful to sit in a similar way to the client, to talk at the same pace and with the same tone of voice as the client, and to match the client's breathing. Doing these things gives the client a feeling of connection with the counsellor, so that the client feels comfortable, safe and able to share openly. Another way in which a counsellor can join with a client is by using similar language to the client's. If a client is using predominantly 'seeing' language, then it is preferable for the counsellor to use 'seeing' language too, if they are to properly connect with the client. Similarly, if a client is using 'hearing' language, in order to join with that client properly, the counsellor will need to use hearing language, and of course the same is true when it comes to 'kinaesthetic' or 'feeling' language. It's really quite fun to try to learn the skill of matching the client's mode. When you are listening to people in general conversation, listen carefully to find out their preferred mode, and respond in the same mode. If you do this you may improve your rapport with them.

Learning to match the client's preferred mode

There is an enjoyable way of learning to recognise the type of language being used. If you wish you can use a practice session to play a game of 'spot the mode'. The game goes like this: one student, or player, talks about a problem, but continually changes the type of language that they are using, flipping from 'hearing' to 'seeing' and to 'feeling' language in random sequence. While this is happening, other students hold up one of three cards on each of which is written 'hearing' or 'seeing' or 'feeling'. If the listening students are correctly following the one who is talking, then they will all hold up a 'seeing' card whenever the speaker is using 'seeing' language, and similarly they will hold up a 'hearing' or a 'feeling' card at appropriate times, in order to match the language being used. For your practice now, here is a paragraph in which the mode continually changes. See if you can spot when the language changes from one mode to another.

Practice example of mode changes

Example 1A

'I remember the scene as I sat on the sand, which was cold and wet. As I sat there, I heard some seagulls squawking as they flew overhead casting shadows on the sand, and I could hear the waves crashing. On the horizon, I noticed a ship steaming along, and at the same time a young man's foot-steps thumped past me as he ran along the beach. I thought about what was going to happen later in the day and could picture the beautiful house that we were going to visit for tea. I imagined myself walking through the garden of the house and admiring the beautiful flowers that grew there. My body tingled with excitement in anticipation, and I told myself to be patient.'

We wonder how many changes of mode you found in the above paragraph. According to our count there were nine. You may wish to go to the end of this chapter to find out how we arrived at this figure.

Practice examples of counsellor responses

The following are some examples of client statements and counsellor responses. In each case, notice that the response is in the correct mode, that is, either the hearing, feeling or seeing mode. Once again it is suggested that you cover up the given response and invent a response yourself. You can then compare your response with the one provided.

Example 2

Client Statement: *I went back there once more, but as before, the place gave me bad vibes. I had to leave because my stomach was churning and my hands were sweating.*

Counsellor Response: You felt so uncomfortable that you left. (Feeling mode.)

Example 3

Client Statement: *In the past, my mother has frequently criticised my wife, and I have always listened to what she has said. Recently though, I've started to question what she's told me and I'm inclined to say that some of her statements about Monica may be wrong.*

Counsellor Response: It sounds as though you've got doubts about the accuracy of what your mother tells you. (Hearing mode.)

Example 4

Client Statement: *She gave me a bunch of flowers and I was really touched by that. In fact, I feel quite different about our relationship now because the coldness we experienced before has been replaced by warmth.*

Counsellor Response: Your feelings towards her have changed, and are now very pleasant. (Feeling mode.)

Example 5

Client Statement: *It seems to me that the writing's on the wall, there's nothing that I can do to save the situation, and I can see nothing but disaster from now on.*

Counsellor Response: The outlook's a really bad one. (Seeing mode.)

Example 6

Client Statement: *It's as though there is a brick wall around him. It has no door, and no way in or out. When I look over the wall I see a very strange person.*

Counsellor Response: You picture him as a strange man surrounded by a brick wall. (Seeing mode.)

Example 7

Client Statement: *When she spoke it was as though a bell was ringing in my head warning me not to prejudge what she was saying. Consequently I heard what she told me, responded sensibly, and then said to myself, 'Well done, you've avoided another terrible argument'.*

Counsellor Response: You listened to your own internal warning system and the outcome sounds good. (Hearing mode.)

Matching the client's metaphors

Many of us use metaphores in our daily lives without realising that we are doing this.

Rather than directly describing some specific aspects, situations or processes within our lives, we use a metaphor to provide an alternative description. The alternative picture and its contents are used to represent the real-life picture symbolically. For example, we might say, 'I'm trapped in the maze. Every time I turn a new corner it leads to a dead end' in order to describe feelings of frustration and the inability to find resolution to a problem. The maze is then a metaphor for the real-life situation.

Have you noticed how many people make use of metaphors in their everyday speech? In counselling sessions clients often make metaphorical statements. Here are some examples of the use of metaphor:

Example 8

'I can see myself being swept away by a river. I can't control my direction and I'm afraid that I'm going to drown.'

Example 9

'It's like being in a rock concert with the music turned up so loud that I can't think. The tune I want to hear is being drowned out by other people's music.'

Example 10

'I can't breathe. I'm being suffocated; the stale air is poisoning me.'

When a client uses metaphors such as these, it can be helpful if the counsellor responds by making use of the same metaphor and the same mode of speech.

In example 8 above, the client uses the seeing mode to describe a metaphor of a river. In this case, it could be helpful for the counsellor to respond by using the same mode and metaphor. The counsellor might respond by using reflection to say, 'You see the river as more powerful than yourself'.

In example 9, the client uses the hearing mode, and the metaphor is about music. The counsellor might respond by saying, 'The music is overwhelmingly loud'. This would match both the client's mode and metaphor.

In example 10, the client uses the feeling mode and a breathing metaphor. The counsellor could match the client by using reflection to say, 'You don't have the fresh air you need to breathe'.

Clearly, by using the same mode and metaphor, the counsellor joins more fully with the client.

Modelling appropriate behaviour

In this chapter we have focused on the usefulness of matching the client's mode of thinking and use of metaphor. In Chapter 4 we also considered the advantages of matching the client's non-verbal and verbal behaviour. However, there are times when it may not be sensible, appropriate or useful for a counsellor to match a client's non-verbal and/or verbal behaviour. For example, it is unlikely that it would be helpful for a counsellor to match angry or aggressive behaviour. In such situations it is generally more useful for a counsellor to remain calm and detached. By not getting caught up in the client's angry emotional experience, the counsellor may be able to model appropriate ways of dealing with aggressive encounters. This detached stance is not judgmental, but reflects the counsellor's willingness and ability to contain and accept the client's current emotional state.

When a client uses expletives that are not acceptable to some, we have a more complicated issue. The counsellor's own values are almost certain to become involved. Some counsellors believe that expletives can be used appropriately at times, and that in such cases matching the client's language may be helpful in the joining process and may enable the client to continue to talk freely. Other counsellors are uncomfortable with this, either because they do not use such language themselves and need to be congruent, or because they think that it is inappropriate to use such language in a counselling situation. Clearly, you will need to make a personal decision for yourself in this regard.

Building on skills already learnt

In your practice sessions, we suggest that you might wish to continue to practise those skills you have already learnt and to practise matching the client's language by using the same mode and/or metaphors. If you do this, then the words you use will be more meaningful for the client. Note that the ideas expressed in this chapter have their origins in neuro-linguistic programming. If these ideas strongly appeal to you then you may wish to learn more about neuro-linguistic programming once you have mastered basic counselling skills (see the suggestions below for further reading).

Modes used in practice example

Example 1B

I remember the scene as I sat on the sand,	Seeing
which was cold and wet. As I sat there,	Feeling (first change)
I heard some seagulls squawking as they	Hearing (second change)
flew overhead casting shadows on the sand,	Seeing (third change)
and I could hear the waves crashing.	Hearing (fourth change)
On the horizon, I noticed a ship	
steaming along,	Seeing (fifth change)
and at the same time a young man's	
footsteps	Hearing (sixth change)
thumped past me as he ran along the beach.	
I thought about what was going to	
happen later	Seeing (seventh change)
in the day and could picture the beautiful	
house which we were going to visit for tea.	
I imagined myself walking through the garden	
of the house and admiring the beautiful	
flowers that grew there. My body	
tingled with excitement in anticipation,	Feeling (eighth change)
and I told myself to be patient.	Hearing (ninth change)

Learning summary

- Three important modes of experiencing the world are the seeing, feeling and hearing modes.
- An individual may predominantly use one of the three modes.
- Matching a client's predominant mode and any metaphor used can help in the joining process between client and counsellor.

Further reading

Bandler, R. 1993, *Time for a Change*, Meta, Cupertino.
Bandler, R. & Grinder, J. 1990, *The Structure of Magic: A Book about Language and Therapy*, Science and Behavior Books, Palo Alto.
Bandler, R., Grinder, J. & Andreas, C. 1989, *Reframing: Neurolinguistic Programming and the Transformation of Meaning*, Real People Press, Moab.

Examples of client statements for use by trainers in teaching matching language

1. *'I really do need to complete the project in a hurry. I can hear the clock ticking by and know that if I delay any more the other members of the team will start to earbash me.'*

2. *'I feel as though I'm flying by the seat of my pants and that gives me the shivers right down my spine. I'm not secure.'*

3. *'I can visualise him now, doing nothing. All he does is to lie around getting in my way. I've half a mind to pick up his belongings and throw them out of the door. It would be interesting for me to watch his reaction.'*

4. *'I can picture the scene. Me lying dead in a pool of blood and then Frank rushing home to protect me. It will be too late then. He will have missed the bus.'*

5. *'I can sense when he's in a bad mood. He's like a time-bomb ready to go off. The atmosphere's tense and I'm scared in case I accidentally set off the detonator.'*

6. *'I need to listen to my own ideas and not Mum's. What she says always sounds good but I always get taken to the cleaners. I'm going to tell myself to be careful from now on.'*

chapter 15

Reframing

Have you ever noticed how two people who observe the same event, such as a game of football, will give different descriptions of what happened? We all have individual perspectives, and the way in which each of us sees things may well be different from the way in which you see things. Quite often clients have a very negative view of the world. They interpret events as they see them, but often viewed from a position of depression or of low self-esteem. The counsellor needs to listen very carefully to the client's description of the events or situation, and then try to look from the client's viewpoint and picture what the client has described. The client's picture, painted from the client's own perspective, will have a frame that is appropriate for them because it fits with their own partic-ular mood and viewpoint.

The process of reframing

Sometimes a skilful counsellor can change the way a client perceives events or situations by 'reframing' the picture the client has described. The counsellor, metaphorically speaking, puts a new frame around the picture so that the picture looks different. The idea behind reframing is not to deny the way the client sees the world, but to present the client with

an expanded view of the world. Thus, if the client wishes, they may choose to see things in a new way.

It would be quite useless to say to a client, 'Things are not really as bad as you think; cheer up!', if the client really sees the world in a very negative way. However, it may be possible to describe what the client sees in such a way that the client has a broader vision of what has occurred and thus is able to be less negative.

Examples of reframing

Example 1

The client has explained that she seems to be unable to relax, because as soon as she turns her back her young son misbehaves and she has to chase after him and punish him. The counsellor has reflected back her feelings about this and now the client is calmer. At this point the counsellor decides to offer the client a reframe concerning the behaviour of her son.

Counsellor Reframe: I get the impression that you are really important to your son and that he wants lots of attention from you.

By making this statement, the counsellor has reframed the son's behaviour in a positive way, so that the mother may, if she accepts the reframe, feel important and needed. Maybe she will start to believe that her son is really crying out for more attention and will see his behaviour not as designed to annoy her, but as designed to attract her attention so that he can get more of her time. By reframing the child's behaviour in this way, there is a possibility that the mother may feel more positive towards her son and that this change in relationship could bring about a change in behaviour.

Example 2

The client has explained that he is continually getting angry with his daughter who will not study and attend to her school work but instead prefers to play around with what he describes as 'yobbos'. He explains how he can hardly cope with his anger and is getting uptight and feeling very miserable.

Counsellor Reframe: It seems as though you care so much about your daughter, you care so much about her turning out to be the sort of person that you want her to be, that you are prepared to completely sacrifice your own needs for a relaxed and enjoyable life, and are willing to make your own life a misery by putting a great deal of energy into trying to correct her behaviour.

This reframe allows the father to feel positive about himself instead of feeling negative and angry. He may now be able to see himself as caring about his daughter, and also may be able to see that he is putting his daughter's needs ahead of his own. He is reminded of his need to be relaxed and enjoy his own life. The reframe might take some of the tension out of the situation by removing the focus from the daughter, and putting it onto the client himself.

Example 3

The client has separated from her husband against her will. Her husband is now pushing her away and hurting her badly by refusing to even talk to her or to see her at all. The client has shared her pain and suffering and the counsellor has reflected her feelings and allowed her to explore them fully. However the counsellor now reframes the husband's behaviour.

Counsellor Reframe: You've described the way you see your husband pushing you away and not being prepared to talk to you, and that hurts you terribly. I'm wondering whether it is possible that what he is doing is really a result of his own inadequacy. Maybe your husband can't cope with the emotional pressure of talking to you, feels guilty when he sees you, and it's easier for him to avoid seeing you altogether, rather than to face his own emotional pain. Do you think that's possible?

By tentatively putting up this alternative the client may see that there could be other reasons for her husband refusing to have anything to do with her, and that it may be that her husband is also hurting and can't face the experience of seeing her. The counsellor's goal is to try to make it easier for the client to accept her husband's rejection.

Example 4

A senior executive has described to the counsellor how terrified he is of having to stand up and address a large meeting of professionals the following week even though he wants to have the opportunity to tell them about the work he has done. The counsellor has reflected his feelings and allowed him, to some extent, to work through them. The counsellor then offers the following reframe.

Counsellor Reframe: It seems to me that you have mixed feelings about giving the talk. At times I almost get the impression that you are looking forward to it, and yet you say that you are very anxious about it. I am wondering if it would be possible for you to think of your anxiety as blocked excitement. Sometimes anxiety is due to our stopping ourselves from being excited, and if we let go and allow ourselves to be enthusiastic and excited, then the excitement can overshadow the anxiety.

The counsellor here is using a useful reframe from Gestalt therapy by reframing 'anxiety' as 'blocked excitement'. Very often, holding our emotional selves in and putting restraints on ourselves prevents us from enjoying the exciting parts of our lives as we negatively reframe exciting events as anxious moments. A good example of this is the way a bride may prepare for her wedding. One way of thinking about going through the wedding ceremony and the reception is to say, 'Wow, that's a really anxiety-producing situation'. Another way of looking at it, a reframe, is to say, 'Wow, this is going to be a really exciting day and it's going to be fun'.

Example 5

The client explains how he is frequently being hurt by the boss who ignores him. The boss doesn't even look at him and she doesn't say 'Hello' when she meets him in the morning. She walks straight past him.

Counsellor Reframe: You've explained to me how your boss walks straight past you without noticing you, and I'm wondering if there is an alternative explanation for what's happening. Sure, it may be that she really does intend to snub you. On the other hand, is it possible that she gets terribly preoccupied and really isn't on this planet half the time?

In this reframe, the counsellor is presenting an alternative that may be partly true. It's quite likely that the boss is sometimes preoccupied, and that may be a partial explanation. By putting this possible explanation up as an alternative, some of the sting is taken out of the boss ignoring the client, and the client may then feel less uptight in his relationship with her.

Example 6

The client explained to the counsellor his feelings of inadequacy and failure. He knew that he was intellectually bright and that made him feel worse because he never completed any project he started. He would start enthusiastically and soon lose interest. He was deeply depressed by a long string of past 'failures', things that he had started and then left half-finished.

Counsellor Reframe: You seem to be a very intelligent person who is quite capable of completing any of the projects you have started. My guess is that you are excited by new projects because they present a challenge, and that you lose interest only when you believe that the challenge is easy for you to meet. Because you are highly intelligent you very quickly get bored and look for new stimulation.

This reframe enables the client to feel good about himself instead of perceiving himself as a failure. He is then left with the possibility that he can decide to do the boring thing and complete a project if he wishes, or can choose to continue looking for excitement and stimulation without feeling so guilty.

As you can see, reframing needs to be done carefully, sensitively and tentatively. If it is done in this way, it is likely to be accepted by the client but may be rejected if it does not fit. Sometimes though, the client may not think that your reframe fits. However, by being offered an alternative way of viewing things the client may be able to broaden their perspective with a resulting reduction in hurt and pain.

Before reading the next chapter, you may wish to practise reframing by using the following examples of client statements. If you are in a training group, it might be useful to discuss and compare your reframes with those of other group members. Some suggested reframes for these examples are provided at the end of this chapter.

Practice examples for reframing

Example 7A

Client Statement: *I can't believe something so terrible should happen. My husband has been granted custody of my children and I'm only allowed to see them on alternate weekends. He claims that I can't cope with them, and I feel like a total failure because in some ways he's right. They used to drive me crazy. But I love them and want to have a good relationship with them. Now I'll have so little contact with them, they'll hardly know me.*

Example 8A

Client Statement: *I crave a long-term relationship with someone, and all I get is short relationship after short relationship. I just don't seem to be able to hold on to my lady friends. They always criticise me for being so restless and for never relaxing, and none of them want to stay with me.*

Example 9A

Client Statement: *My father hates me, I'm sure. He picks on me for everything I do. All the time he follows me around and complains about my behaviour. He wants me to behave like a toffy-nosed snob instead of a normal human being. Not only that but he's always nagging me to study more!*

Example 10A

Client Statement: *I've got so much that I have to do in a day and I get so angry with myself because I keep making mistakes. Sure, I get lots done, but I keep forgetting things and mixing arrangements up. I'm hopeless. When will I learn?*

Example 11A

Client Statement: *I'm furious with my mother. She lets my sister, Annette, manipulate her with suicide threats and her refusal to eat properly. Mum rushes around attending to her every need. It's just not fair on Mum and I wish she'd stop doing it.*

Example 12A

Client Statement: *My son's unemployed again, and I resent having to support him financially. Why should I spend my money on a person who's mean and nasty to me? It would serve him right if I let him starve. What annoys me is that he knows that he can treat me badly and then twist me around his little finger and I will support him. I'm angry at myself for being so stupid as to be manipulated so easily.*

Suggested reframes for practice examples

Example 7B

This reframe would be used only after fully reflecting and working through the client's distress in the usual way.

I'm wondering whether when the children are not with you, you will be able to do things for yourself to enable you to recharge, and regain your energy. Then when you do see the children you will feel good and be able to have some quality time in which to create a good relationship with them.

Example 8B

You must be attractive to the opposite sex to be able to start so many new relationships. By the sound of it, you have plenty of energy, and I wonder whether the woman friends you've had would have been able to satisfy you for very long.

Example 9B

Do you think it's possible that your father doesn't hate you but just worries excessively about you? Maybe he desperately wants you to be a success and worries in case you fail in life.

Example 10B

People who do nothing never make mistakes. Making mistakes could be a sign that you are, to use your words, 'getting lots done'. You could feel good about that.

Example 11B

Your mother must care a great deal about Annette to choose to do what she does.

Example 12B

You must be a very caring person to choose to support your son, especially as you don't like his behaviour much.

Learning summary

- Reframing provides clients with an expanded picture of their world which may enable them to perceive their situation differently and more constructively.
- Reframing needs to be done sensitively and carefully.
- Reframes should be offered in such a way that clients can feel comfortable in either choosing to accept them or in choosing to reject them.

Further reading

Bandler, R., Grinder, J. & Andreas, C. 1989, *Reframing: Neurolinguistic Programming and the Transformation of Meaning*, Real People Press, Moab.

Examples for use by trainers in teaching reframing—client statements

1. *My teenage daughter is a great disappointment to me. I thought that when she reached this age that she and I would be good friends and would spend lots of time together. All she wants now is to do her own thing. I'm just irrelevant as far as she's concerned.*

2. *My husband interferes in everything I do. I just need to start doing something and he's there, taking over. I'm starting to think that I must be an incompetent idiot who isn't capable of doing anything for myself.*

3. *'Don't sniff, stand up straight, don't be late, be polite', that's all I hear from Mum. She says she loves me but I don't think that she even likes me any more.*

4. *I don't know why the manager picks on me all the time. Whenever there is a difficult job to do or a difficult customer to deal with she always gives the work to me. She's obviously trying to make my life as difficult as possible.*

5. *I'm totally exhausted and realise I've been very stupid. In just a few months, I've completely redecorated my house, written several journal articles for publication while working full time in a very demanding job, driven 200 kilometres and back to see my dying brother most weekends, and organised a group project for the local community. I seem to be unable to stop working compulsively. I feel really depressed by my inability to relax and enjoy life.*

chapter **16**

Confrontation

What do you feel emotionally when you decide to confront someone? Many people feel apprehensive and worry about the outcome of confrontation.

What is it like for you when someone confronts you? Is it sometimes threatening? It may be.

Generally when we use the word 'confrontation' we think in terms of opposing parties and of people disagreeing as they confront each other. In such a situation the person being confronted is likely to feel threatened and may become defensive, while the person doing the confronting is likely to feel anxiety.

Confrontation in counselling

Confrontation as a counselling skill is different from the generally perceived view of confrontation. The micro-skill of confrontation involves raising the awareness of clients by presenting to them information that in some way they are overlooking or failing to identify. Correct use of this skill involves bringing into a client's awareness, in an acceptable way, information that the client may consider to be unpalatable and which is either being avoided or is just not being noticed.

How do you help a child to swallow medicine which doesn't taste nice? You can either force it down the child's throat, or use a more gentle persuasive approach. The problem with trying to force the medicine down is that the child may well vomit it up and your relationship with the young person will not be improved. Respecting the child's feelings is likely to have a more positive outcome than ignoring them. Similarly clients deserve a high degree of respect, and they usually don't like being told painful truths. Metaphorically speaking, the art of good confrontation is to help the client to swallow 'bad medicine' voluntarily, so that they can incorporate it into their bodily system and digest it.

Confrontation is clearly a difficult skill to master and should not be attempted until the skills previously described in this book have become a natural part of your counselling style. The skills you have learnt already are often sufficient in themselves, making confrontation unnecessary. Additionally, it is important to avoid using confrontation until a trusting relationship has been established with the client, as otherwise the client is likely to feel threatened and may withdraw from the counselling process without receiving the help they need.

Self-examination before confrontation

Before using confrontation look within yourself to examine your feelings, motives and goals. Ask yourself, 'Do I want to confront because I am impatient and not prepared to allow the client to move at their own pace; do I want to confront because I enjoy confrontation; am I wanting to use confrontation to put my own values onto the client; or am I feeling angry with the client and wanting to express my anger through confrontation?' If the answer to any of these questions is 'Yes', then confrontation is inappropriate. Satisfying the counsellor's own needs is no justification for confrontation. Confrontation is most appropriately used after the use of other micro-skills has failed to sufficiently increase the client's awareness.

When to confront

There are a number of situations in which confrontation is appropriate. For example, confrontation is appropriate where:

1. the client is avoiding a basic issue that appears to be troubling them;
2. the client is failing to recognise their own self-destructive or self-defeating behaviour;
3. the client is failing to recognise possible serious consequences of their behaviour;
4. the client is making self-contradictory statements;
5. the client is excessively and inappropriately locked into talking about the past or the future and is unable to focus on the present;
6. the client is going around in circles by repeating the same story over and over;

7. the client's non-verbal behaviour does not match their verbal behaviour; or

8. attention needs to be given to what is going on in the relationship between the client and counsellor, for example, where dependency is occurring, or where a client withdraws or shows anger or some other emotion towards the counsellor.

In situations such as these, the counsellor may decide to confront the client by sharing with the client what they feel, notice or observe. Good confrontation usually includes elements of some or all of the following:

1. a reflection or brief summary of what the client has said, so that the client feels heard and understood;

2. a statement of the counsellor's present feelings; or

3. a concrete statement of what the counsellor has noticed or observed, given without interpretation.

In addition to the above, good confrontation is presented in such a way that the client can feel OK rather than attacked or put down. These points are best explained by means of examples.

Examples to illustrate the use of confrontation

Example 1

The client had been referring obliquely to her concerns about her sexuality. She mentioned the sexual problem briefly several times and then immediately deflected away from it by talking about seemingly irrelevant trivia.

Counsellor Confrontation: I'm puzzled because I've noticed that several times you've briefly mentioned your sexual problem, and then have started talking about something quite different.

Notice how the counsellor first expressed her feelings by saying, 'I'm puzzled', and then gave a concrete statement of what she had noticed occurring. This response is minimally threatening as it merely feeds back to the client what the counsellor has observed, without judgment.

Example 2

An angry separated husband who had been denied custody of his children was threatening to burn down the matrimonial home when his wife and children were out. Even though he had been asked about possible consequences he failed to recognise the serious consequences of his threat. The counsellor had reflected back the client's anger and attitude towards his wife. This had reduced the client's anger level but he still felt excessively vindictive and admitted to this.

Counsellor Confrontation: You are so furious with your wife that you want to hurt her by destroying the family home. I'm very concerned when I hear you threatening to do this because you would hurt your wife, your children and yourself. Clearly, if you were to burn down the house your children would lose their home and possessions, and you might end up in jail.

Notice how the counsellor first reflected back the feelings and content of the client's message, followed this by a statement of his own feelings, and completed the confrontation by giving a factual statement of likely consequences. This latter statement was not a statement of the counsellor's opinion, but was an accurate statement of the likely consequences.

There is also an ethical issue here. Where people or property could be injured or damaged the counsellor has a clear responsibility to take action to prevent this from occurring (see Chapter 34). You may wish to discuss the issue of confidentiality in a situation such as this with your training group or supervisor.

Example 3

The client had come to the counsellor as a result of a crisis in her current relationship with a longstanding close friend. The counsellor helped her to explore past events at length, as she chose to do that. It seemed to the counsellor that nothing further would be achieved by continuing to focus on the past. However, although the client said that she wanted to talk about her present crisis, she continually recounted past events.

Counsellor Confrontation: I am puzzled. My impression is that you want to resolve your present crisis and yet you continually talk about past events. Unfortunately, the past can't be changed but what you can change is what is happening in the present.

The response started with a statement of the counsellor's feelings—'I'm puzzled'—followed by a reflection of the client's desire to talk about her present crisis, and then a concrete statement of what the counsellor had observed: 'You continually talk about past events.' In this example the counsellor adds another factual statement which might be useful for the client: 'Unfortunately the past can't be changed, but what you can change is what is happening in the present.'

Remember that it is appropriate for clients to deal with past events in a constructive way where those events are significantly influencing present thoughts and feelings. However, the suggested confrontation would be appropriate where a client was inappropriately and excessively using past history to avoid facing present problems.

Example 4

Here is an example of a counsellor response that addresses repetitive behaviour by a client, who kept repeating herself by going over and over the same ground.

Counsellor Confrontation: I've noticed that we seem to be going round in circles, so I'll summarise what we've talked about . . . (the end of this statement is a summary).

This example demonstrates how the client was confronted with her repetitive behaviour. The counsellor first told the client what she had noticed happening, and then gave a summary. By confronting in this way, a counsellor can increase the client's awareness of what is happening. With increased awareness the client may be able to move out of the rut in which she is stuck. However sometimes, even after confrontation, the client will persist in going around the track again and repeating the same details. It is here that stronger confrontation is needed and the counsellor might say, 'I'm starting to feel frustrated, because once again we are going around the same track'.

Example 5

The client said, 'I feel really happy in my marriage', using a very depressed tone of voice and slumping down in her chair as she spoke.

Counsellor Confrontation: I noticed that your voice sounded very flat and you slumped down in your chair when you said that you felt really happy in your marriage.

Here the counsellor confronted by reflecting back what he observed without putting an interpretation on his observation. The client was then free to make her own interpretation of the feedback given.

In summary, confrontation increases the client's awareness by providing the client with information which the client may have been unaware of. Confrontation is best done caringly, sparingly and skilfully!

Learning summary

- Confrontation involves bringing into the client's awareness information which:
  - may be unpalatable to the client; or
  - may have been ignored or missed and needs to be considered by the client if the counselling is to be optimally helpful.
- Good confrontation often includes a summary, followed by a statement of the counsellor's feelings and a concrete statement given without interpretation.
- Good confrontation leaves the client feeling OK and not attacked.

Examples for use by trainers in teaching confrontation

Write suitable counsellor statements of confrontation for the following examples.

1. The client tells the counsellor that he is very keen to receive counselling help but repeatedly arrives for appointments up to three-quarters of an hour late.

2. The client has made it clear on several occasions that she is coming to counselling to address the post-traumatic effects of abuse during her childhood. However, each time she arrives for counselling she deflects away from talking about the abuse by introducing a range of other unrelated issues.

3. The client admits to pushing and slapping his wife but minimises this behaviour and blames her for his behaviour, saying that she is provocative. He doesn't see that he needs to take responsibility for what he does.

4. When the counsellor reflects back what she sees as angry non-verbal behaviour the client denies being angry but continues to look and sound angry and to make statements which suggest that she is angry.

5. Although the client does not appear to be under any threat he is responding to others from a disempowered, victim, 'poor me', position instead of being assertive in letting others know about his needs.

chapter  17

Challenging self-destructive beliefs

We are all entitled to have our own attitudes, beliefs and thoughts. They are ours and no-one has the right to tell us that we should change them. Our attitudes are intrinsically ours, and we have the right to choose what we will believe and think and what we won't. Consequently, counsellors need to respect their clients' right to do this. However, an important role for counsellors is to help clients to change so that they will feel better. As discussed in Chapter 12, the most effective long-term change is achieved if emotions, thoughts and behaviours are all addressed. In order for this to happen, exploration of the client's attitudes, beliefs and thoughts needs to occur. Although any changes to attitudes, beliefs and thoughts need to be made by clients as a result of their own choice, counsellors have a legitimate responsibility to help clients recognise when attitudes, beliefs and thoughts may be self-destructive.

Counsellors may confront clients, as discussed in Chapter 16, if their attitudes, beliefs and thoughts are incongruent or may have socially undesirable consequences (see Chapter 36 regarding ethical issues). Although as we have said, as counsellors we do not have the right to impose our values on our clients, it is most certainly a legitimate part of our role, and a responsibility, for us to raise our clients' awareness of their choices. As a consequence of helping clients to bring into focus the choices that are available for them, they can be enabled to make new choices, if these fit for them and are appropriate, so that positive change may occur in their feelings, thoughts and behaviours.

Many clients do not seem to be aware of the possibility that they may if they wish change the way they are thinking, or the beliefs they have, in order to help them lead more satisfying lives. Many clients hold onto beliefs which are unhelpful for them, and indeed may be self-destructive. Albert Ellis, the originator of rational emotive behaviour therapy (see 'Further reading'), referred to self-destructive beliefs as 'irrational beliefs'. However, some self-destructive beliefs are not in our view irrational, and if we tell clients that they are irrational it is possible our clients may argue that they are not. It is clearly not helpful for counsellors to get into arguments with clients. We ourselves therefore prefer to refer to two categories of self-destructive beliefs, or SDBs for short. These are:

1. 'should', 'must', 'ought' and 'have to' beliefs
2. irrational beliefs.

'Should', 'must', 'ought' and 'have to' beliefs

Clients often make statements using the words 'I should', 'I must', 'I ought', or 'I have to'. Sometimes the words are spoken with enthusiasm, firmness and meaning, and it is clear that the client feels good about doing whatever it is that they 'should do', 'must do', 'ought to do', or think they 'have to do' and that's OK. At other times the words are spoken in an unconvincing way, as though some other person is saying to the client 'you should' or 'you must', 'you ought' or 'you have to', and the client is reluctantly, uncomfortably and maybe resentfully accepting that message. When this occurs, the client is likely to feel confused and emotionally disturbed. If the client conforms with the 'should' message, they may feel like a small child reluctantly and miserably doing as they are told by others. They will not feel as though they are fully in control of their life, and will not recognise their behaviour as being of their own choosing. If, on the other hand, they disregard the 'should' message, they may feel guilty, with consequent negative results. The goal of counselling in such instances is to help the person to feel more comfortable with their decisions, so that when they make a choice they do it willingly, and without feelings of either resentment or guilt. Provided underlying issues are correctly and fully addressed this goal is usually achievable.

Where do 'should', 'must', 'ought' and 'have to' beliefs come from?

As children we grow up in a world in which we have no experience. We do not know the difference between right and wrong, and we cannot distinguish good behaviour from bad behaviour. However, we learn, initially from our parents and close family, and then from others such as teachers, friends, and social and/or religious leaders. We learn from the people who care for us, from what they tell us verbally, and by watching and copying their behaviour. Gradually we absorb a system of values, attitudes and beliefs. It is right and proper that we do so.

As we grow through childhood and adolescence there comes a time when we start to challenge and rebel against some of the beliefs we have absorbed from others. Interestingly though, many people, by the time they are young adults, hold on to most of the beliefs and values of their parents while having rejected some. As children it is clearly appropriate that we learn and absorb the beliefs of our parents and significant others. There is no other way for us to learn, because as children our experience is too limited for us to make mature judgments for ourselves. As adults, we do have that experience and it is appropriate for each of us to determine for ourselves which beliefs fit and make sense for us as individuals and which beliefs do not fit. We can then keep what fits and reject that which does not. We can replace what doesn't fit by something new that does.

Beliefs that don't fit

Sometimes when a client uses the words 'should', 'must' or 'ought', they are stating a belief that has its origins in their childhood, and which they are holding on to, but which does not fit for them now. If they really accepted the belief as their own they would be more likely to say 'I've decided', or 'I want to', or 'I choose to', rather than 'I should', or 'I must', or 'I ought', or 'I have to'. Of course we are describing the general case and this is not always true. What is important is to encourage the client to own their choices as being morally right and fitting for them, rather than for them to attribute their decisions to an external moral code imposed on them by others or through childhood conditioning.

The problem with 'shoulds', 'musts', 'oughts', and 'have tos', is that often the words spoken are believed at a head or thinking level, but do not sit comfortably at a gut or feeling level. Where there is a mismatch between what is happening at a head level and what is being experienced at a gut level, the person will be confused and emotionally distressed. Human beings are holistic beings, so we cannot separate our emotional feelings, our bodily sensations, our thoughts and our spiritual experiences into discrete compartments. They all interrelate and must be in harmony with each other if we are to feel integrated and comfortable.

Challenging beliefs

Sometimes a client will use an 'I should' statement and then express reluctance to do what they have said they 'should' do. In such a case it can be useful to raise the client's awareness of what is happening internally so that they become more fully aware of their options. We like to explain to the client where many 'I should' messages come from, and to ask them where they think this particular 'I should' message has come from. We then encourage the client to check out whether the message sits comfortably with them. If it does, that is great. If it doesn't they can, if they choose, challenge the 'I should' message and maybe can replace it with something which fits more comfortably for them. Alternatively, they may decide that the message fits for them and accept it more willingly. A similar approach can be used when helping clients to challenge 'ought', 'must', and 'have to' statements.

Irrational beliefs

As well as 'should', 'must', 'ought', and 'have to' beliefs, SDBs include beliefs that are irrational. These irrational beliefs are also often absorbed from others during childhood. Irrational beliefs often, but not always, include the words 'should', 'must', or 'ought' or 'I have to', but additionally they are intrinsically irrational. For example, to have the expectation that life will be fair and just is unrealistic. Life experience clearly demonstrates that life is often unfair and unjust. It is therefore irrational to assume that it will be fair and just. A more rational belief might be: 'Unfortunately life is not always fair and just. If I can accept that, then I may be able to make sensible decisions to deal with those things which are unjust and unfair.'

Having unrealistic expectations of others

Another version of 'should', 'ought' and 'must' beliefs involves expectations regarding other people's behaviours. For example we frequently hear people say things like, 'she should . . .', 'people should . . .' and 'they ought to . . .'.

By saying such things the speaker is assuming that other people will have the same values as they do and is putting their own expectations onto other people. To do this is unrealistic and consequently irrational. Counsellors frequently encounter clients who are distressed as a result of others failing to live up to their expectations. When such clients recognise that their expectations are unrealistic, they often experience a sense of loss and need to be allowed to grieve. For example, a person might say, 'I expected my brother to care about me but he doesn't'. Having recognised this, the person experiences a loss of expectations and is likely to be saddened by the loss.

Table 17.1 gives some examples of common irrational beliefs and rational alternatives. Notice how the irrational belief is certain to make the client feel bad whereas the rational alternative helps them to feel better. For other examples of irrational beliefs see Chapter 25.

Table 17.1 *Comparison between rational and irrational beliefs*

Irrational belief	Rational alternative
I must never make mistakes.	The only way not to make mistakes is to do nothing. I'm active, and all active people make mistakes.
Other people should not make mistakes.	No-one's perfect. I can accept that other people will make mistakes.
Other people make me angry.	I make myself angry when I don't accept that other people don't live up to my expectations.
Other people should live up to my expectations.	Other people don't need to live up to my expectations.
My happiness depends on other people's behaviour and attitudes.	My happiness comes from within me and does not depend on others.
I must live up to other people's expectations.	I don't need to live up to other people's expectations to be OK.
I must win.	According to the law of averages most people only win 50 per cent of the time. I don't need to win to feel OK.

continued ...

Table 17.1 *continued*

Irrational belief	Rational alternative
Life should be fair and just.	Life is not fair and just.
Other people are bad if they do not have the same beliefs, attitudes and values as me.	All good people do not think the same or necessarily have the same beliefs, attitudes and values.
I must get my own way.	I do not need to get my own way to feel OK, and I can sometimes get satisfaction out of letting other people have their own way.
I need other people's approval to feel OK.	It's nice to get other people's approval, but I do not need their approval to feel OK.
I must always please other people.	It's unrealistic to expect that I can always please other people.
I must never get angry.	It's OK to be angry sometimes.
I should always be happy.	There is a time to be happy and a time to be sad.
I must not cry.	It's OK to cry.
I can't be happy if people misjudge me.	People sometimes will misjudge me. That's inevitable. But I know that I'm OK and that's what matters.

Challenging irrational beliefs

If a client verbalises an irrational belief, it can be useful to encourage them to question the belief by asking a question such as, 'Is it realistic to expect that life will be fair and just?' By doing this the client is very likely to challenge their own SDB, that life should be fair and just. If they do, you may invite them to suggest a rational alternative.

You may wish to explain the difference between rational and irrational beliefs to your client and to point out that irrational beliefs are not only irrational but also inevitably make people feel bad. You can then encourage your client to write down a list of their irrational beliefs and replace them by rational alternatives. Remember that a client has the right to retain their irrational beliefs if they wish. It is their choice, so do not attempt to persuade them to change, just raise their awareness of the consequences of irrational beliefs.

Care is needed

As when confronting, skill and care are needed when challenging SDBs. Ideally the challenge will come from the client rather than the counsellor. However, it can be helpful for a counsellor to explain the nature, origin and effects of SDBs, so that the client is able to recognise and challenge them.

Rational emotive behaviour therapy

The ideas expressed in this chapter have their origins in rational emotive behaviour therapy although, in contrast to the approach described here, rational emotive behaviour therapists are usually direct in their efforts to challenge and persuade their clients. If such an approach appeals to you then you may wish to learn more about rational emotive behaviour therapy once you have mastered basic counselling skills (see 'Further reading').

Learning summary

- Self-destructive beliefs include 'shoulds', 'musts' and 'oughts', and irrational beliefs.
- Most self-destructive beliefs come from messages absorbed during childhood.
- Self-destructive beliefs need to be challenged so that they can be replaced by constructive beliefs.

Further reading

Dryden, W. 1995, *Brief Rational Emotive Behaviour Therapy*, Wiley, London.
Ellis, A. 1995, *Better, Deeper, and More Enduring Brief Therapy: The Rational Emotive Behavior Therapy Approach*, Bruner/Mazel, New York.
Ellis, A. & Lange, A.J. 1995, *How to Keep People from Pushing Your Buttons*, Carol, New York.

Walen, S. R., DiGiuseppe, R. & Dryden, W. 1992, *A Practitioner's Guide to Rational Emotive Therapy*, 2nd edn, Oxford University Press, Oxford.

Examples of SDBs for use by trainers in teaching
Replace the SDBs below by rational beliefs.

1. Other people should always agree with me.

2. I should be able to expect that people will be reliable and trustworthy.

3. Other people should always respect me.

4. I should never be seen to make mistakes.

5. I need to be in control all the time or I will feel threatened.

6. Other people should care about my needs.

7. I need other people's approval to feel OK.

8. As a result of past trauma I can't enjoy life like other people.

9. I should do what other people want me to do.

10. People should never be impatient.

11. I will feel bad if other people reject me.

12. I must work hard all the time.

13. Things will sort themselves out if I just wait.

14. I must always help other people when they ask me to.

15. I must never refuse invitations.

16. Other people should appreciate what I do.

chapter **18**

Normalising

Some time ago a person came to me, David, in deep distress. 'I think I'm going crazy', she said. 'My head is buzzing with thoughts that flit in and out, I can't concentrate on anything for even a minute or two, and I'm getting nothing done in my daily life.'

I was concerned. Was this person really going crazy? Did she need medication or specialist psychiatric help?

I listened to her story using the basic skills and processes of counselling as described in this book. As the counselling session proceeded she sobbed as she got in touch with her sadness and I began to understand. Once again she asked me, 'Do you think I'm going crazy?' and this time I was able to say, 'No, I don't think you are going crazy. If I had suffered the trauma you've just described I think that I would also feel the way you do'. I continued: 'I think that what is happening to you is inevitable and normal for someone who has had your recent experiences.' I also said that maybe if she was finding the emotional pain too severe she could ask her doctor to consider prescribing medication. However she chose not to do so, and I was pleased to notice that when she came back to see me a week later she was slowly and naturally moving into a more comfortable emotional space.

The above is an example of the use of the skill called 'normalising'. I told the client that in my judgment what was happening to her was inevitable and normal. I noticed that she looked relieved and less tense as soon as I was able to tell her that I did not think that she was going crazy but saw her emotional distress as normal for the situation.

The skill of 'normalising' is a particularly useful and powerful one if used correctly. Often a person's anxiety can be considerably reduced if they can recognise that their emotional state is normal and appropriate for the situation.

The example given above involved normalising a person's emotional response to trauma. However, the skill can also be used to normalise behaviour and relationship changes which occur as part of life's normal developmental crises.

The need for care

Clearly we need to be careful in using the skill of 'normalising' because it would be irresponsible, unethical and possibly dangerous to tell someone who was experiencing severe problems of a psychiatric nature that they were OK and did not need specialist treatment. A counsellor who is in doubt about a person's psychological condition, should consult with their supervisor and refer the client to a professional who is competent to make a proper assessment.

Uses of normalising

Normalising can be used:
1. to normalise emotional states; and
2. to normalise changes in behaviours, roles and relationships due to developmental crises.

Normalising emotional states

The goal in normalising a client's emotional state is to help the client to reduce anxiety by letting them know that their emotional response is a normal one. Time and again clients become frightened by their intense emotions in times of crisis. Fear of their highly charged emotional experiences leads them to wonder whether they are going to fall apart completely and end up in a psychiatric ward. As we know, the reality is that this could happen to any one of us. A high percentage of the general population require psychiatric help at some point in their lives so it is not realistic to deny a client's fear of what could happen. Instead, recognition of the fear with a response such as, 'You're frightened that you're going crazy' is sensible. However if, as a counsellor, you think that the client's emotional response is appropriate for the situation, then it will probably be helpful if you tell the client that. If you are unsure about the need for more specialist help, it is sensible to give your client the option of seeking further assistance. You might say: 'The emotional state you are experiencing and describing seems to me to be a normal response to your situation but if you are unsure about your ability to cope then you may want to look for more specialist help. What are your options in that regard?' It might then be possible for you to make suggestions with regard to referral for assessment or treatment. If in doubt the appropriate thing to do is to consult your supervisor.

Normalising changes in behaviours, roles and relationships due to developmental crises

We all go through normal developmental stages in our lives. An example of a developmental stage is when a child takes its first few steps. Previously the child had been unable to walk and then their lifestyle changes as they learn to walk. The time when those first few steps are taken involves anxious moments, so in some sense it is a crisis time. However, it is inevitable and normal for a child to learn to walk and for there to be associated anxiety.

There are many developmental stages in our lives. Some of these are listed in Chapter 31, entitled 'Crisis intervention'. These stages are generally inevitable and normal but usually involve anxiety. Unfortunately most people do not recognise the normal developmental processes and tend to respond to them inappropriately with panic and sometimes despair.

Consider some examples of common developmental changes. Happily married couples frequently run into trouble when a second or third child comes on the scene. With the first child things are usually fine, because both partners are delighted and proud as new parents and lavish time and affection on the new member of the family. However, things naturally and inevitably change with subsequent children. Often, although not always in our contemporary society, it's the mother who has most responsibility for parenting young children and much of her energy is taken up in doing this. Consequently she does not have so much time or energy for her husband when the second or third child appears. She may feel resentful if she has interrupted her career by temporarily giving up her job with its associated social life. Her husband may feel resentful because his wife, due to the demands placed on her by the children, is no longer able to give him the attention and affection he previously enjoyed. Both partners may therefore be unhappy and may come to the conclusion that there is something terribly wrong with their relationship. However, this is a normal developmental crisis due to the changing nature of the family. It is to be expected and is almost inevitable. It can be a great relief to the partners in such a situation if the nature of the developmental crisis is explained. A counsellor might say, 'What is happening to you could almost have been predicted because you have reached this developmental stage in your family life'.

Often, as counsellors, we find that it is useful to use the word *inevitable* when we are 'normalising' a client's situation even though using this word may result in an overstatement. For example, we might say to the couple we have been discussing, 'It's *inevitable* that you would feel this way'. By saying this, the couple are likely to feel relieved because if they believe that what is happening to them is inevitable, they are likely to lose their feelings of failure. Thus, they may be able to recognise where they have succeeded rather than focus on their disappointments. They may realise that there is nothing fundamentally wrong with their marital relationship, but that there is a need for both of them to look for new ways to deal with this developmental crisis. Without blaming themselves or each other, they can then take action to make changes so that they are both more comfortable.

Another common time for distress due to a developmental crisis is when children grow to an age where they require very little parenting as they become more independent. This is a time when parents can feel a sense of worthlessness as one of their central life roles, that of 'parent', is diminished. Some people find considerable satisfaction in life through parenting and when this role diminishes they feel empty and lost unless they can find satisfaction in other ways. Additionally, they may feel rejected by their children who, in their search for individuation and independence, may naturally and appropriately distance themselves physically and emotionally from their parents.

Once again, 'normalising' the situation, by explaining to the client that what is happening is part of an inevitable and normal developmental stage in life, can help the client to feel better and to look for constructive ways in which to gain an increased sense of satisfaction.

If you stop to think, you will probably be able to identify a number of examples of times in your own life when feelings, behaviours, roles or relationships have changed due to normal developmental processes. It is often easier to recognise these for what they are when they happen to other people rather than to ourselves. This is why the skill of 'normalising' is so useful because it brings emotional relief as it raises awareness of the inevitable and normal characteristics of a situation.

Warning!

Normalising does not and must not involve minimising or devaluing the client's problem and pain. Normalising does not involve saying to the client, 'This situation is normal and inevitable, it's really no big deal, everybody has to go through the same process!' To do that would fail to address the client's genuine pain. What normalising does do is to give the client a better understanding of their situation by putting it in its developmental context. By doing this, they may see their situation differently, understand why they are experiencing emotional distress, but also recognise that they are going through a normal process. This recognition may enable them to deal more effectively with their pain and to move forward rather than to think that they are a failure and should somehow have been able to avoid the crisis. It is much better for them to be able to say, 'I couldn't have avoided this crisis, it is a normal and inevitable crisis that couldn't be avoided. Now I can look for ways to respond to this crisis constructively'.

Learning summary

- Normalising involves:
  - letting a client know that their emotional feelings are a normal response to their crisis; or
  - explaining to a client that they are experiencing an inevitable and normal developmental crisis that could not be avoided.
- Normalising needs to be carried out appropriately with attention to the possible need for onward referral if the client is at risk psychologically.
- Appropriate normalising does not minimise the client's problem or devalue their pain.
- Appropriate normalising may help the client to feel better and to respond more constructively to their situation.

Examples for use by trainers when teaching the skill of normalising

For each of the case descriptions below devise suitable counsellor normalising statements and explain how you would use that statement to help the client.

1. An elderly lady who had a successful career has recently retired. She is now bored with life, has no interests, and sees herself as a failure.

2. A man in his twenties who has previously enjoyed a single life has recently moved into a close live-in relationship with a friend. He is confused because he says that he loves his friend and wants to continue the relationship. However, he feels claustrophobic and unable to do the things which he would like to do for himself.

3. The father of a young child says that he and his partner (the child's mother) are having difficulty managing the child's behaviour and are arguing with each other about how to parent the child. It has emerged in the counselling process that the father's own family of origin was very easy going and that physical punishment was never used. However, his partner's family of origin believed in the use of strict rules with physical punishment for disobedience.

4. A middle-aged woman is unable to work or sleep and cannot understand 'what is the matter with her'. In counselling it transpires that there have been three deaths of near relatives in recent weeks. She herself worries about whether she has bowel cancer and is avoiding seeking medical advice.

5. In a time of very high unemployment a 50-year-old, who was retrenched as a senior executive nine months ago, says that he has been unable to find employment. He feels deeply depressed, has lost his motivation and feels a failure.

chapter **19**

Exploring polarities

We are stating the obvious when we say that the human personality is incredibly complex, because it certainly is. Even though it is complex, it can be useful to describe the human personality in terms of easily understandable models in order to help us conceptualise aspects of human behaviour. Any model we use is certain to be an over-simplification, but even so a model can be useful in helping us to understand more fully what happens in ourselves and in our clients. In this chapter we will consider two models which are of particular value with regard to our understanding of the existence of different parts of self in the human personality, and the way in which clients' awareness of opposites within themselves can be raised through counselling. These models can also be very useful if we explain them to our clients and use them in a way which enables them to change and feel more comfortable. The models are:

1. the iceberg model
2. the polarities model.

The iceberg model

A good metaphor to illustrate opposites in the human personality is the iceberg as illustrated in Figure 19.1. An iceberg floats so that most of it is below the waterline and cannot be seen. Human beings are a bit like that. As you get to know a person, you will see parts of their personality. You will see those parts that are, metaphorically speaking, above the waterline. There are other parts of that person's personality too, but you do not see these as they are submerged below the waterline. Even the person concerned is unlikely to be fully aware of all those parts which are below the waterline. Icebergs have a tendency to roll over from time to time and as they roll over some parts of the iceberg that had previously been submerged come into sight. From time to time, hidden parts of a person's personality come unexpectedly into view, rather like those parts of the iceberg that show when it rolls over. Sometimes it is other people who are surprised by what they see when this happens, and sometimes it is the person concerned who gets a surprise.

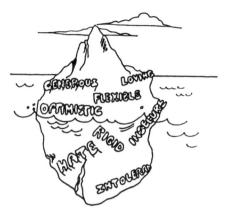

Figure 19.1 *The iceberg model of human personality*

The most commonly talked about opposites in human feelings are 'love' and 'hate'. How often have you heard someone talk about a love/hate relationship? You may be aware from your own experience that a love/hate relationship can exist. If we have a strong capacity for loving, then it is likely that we also have the potential to hate. We may of course deny our capacity to hate. Just imagine the iceberg with the word 'love' sitting on the top, out in the open for everyone to see, and the word 'hate' right down below the sea, and hidden from view. The danger exists that one day the iceberg will roll over and the 'hate' side will be all that will be seen for a while. Time and time again we see a relationship where a couple fall in love, and then the relationship breaks up, and the love that was there is replaced, not by something neutral, but by hate.

Hostility and friendship are on opposites sides of the iceberg. Sometimes if we are feeling very angry with somebody, our hostility prevents us from forgiving them and being friendly towards them. Forgiveness and acceptance are on the opposite side of the iceberg to anger and hostility. If the iceberg rolls around so that anger is uppermost, then forgiveness is buried beneath the sea.

Denial of 'negative' emotions

Many of us are taught from childhood to deny what our parents, teachers and other significant persons regard as negative emotions. Parents often put angry feelings into this category and tell their children not to be angry but to calm down. Similarly, some parents tell their children not to cry and teach them to disown feelings of pain and hurt. Stereotypically, such parental behaviour is often directed towards boys who may be told that, 'Boys don't cry'. As a result, many children learn to think that angry feelings and feelings of pain and hurt are negative emotions and start to disown them, saying things such as, 'No, I'm not angry', when they are really very angry indeed, or, 'No it doesn't hurt', when it certainly does.

A common example of client distress caused by suppressing a part of self is the depression caused by repressed anger. We have found that many clients who are depressed are unable to express their anger. Often, when we suggest to them that maybe they feel angry with a person who has wronged them, we will be met with a denial. 'No I'm not angry, I'm just sad', they will say. Gradually, however, as the counselling relationship builds, they will begin to express themselves more fully. After a while, as anger starts to emerge the depression will start to lift. At first the anger will be barely expressed and will be described in very mild terms using words such as frustration, but gradually it will gain in momentum. The more this happens, the more the depression recedes.

Similarly, repressed anger may block the ability of a person to forgive. Sometimes, a client with high moral values will be concerned because they wish to forgive someone but find themselves unable to do so. However, once they are able to get in touch with their anger towards the person they wish to forgive, and fully experience that anger, they are often able to allow the iceberg to roll over and experience forgiveness.

It is somewhat paradoxical that if we fully accept and own our anger, then we are more likely to be able to deal with it constructively rather than by expressing it destructively. By owning our anger, it will often disappear or reduce in intensity spontaneously, and in its place we are likely to experience a more comfortable emotion. It is important, however, to recognise that we have a potential to be angry, and to own that potential rather than to pretend it isn't there. Then, once it is owned, we have choice as to how we can deal with it.

Usefulness of the iceberg model in counselling

Sometimes it may be helpful for a client if a counsellor describes the iceberg model and explains that it is normal for human beings to have within them the capacity to experience a range of emotions and behaviours, some of which are opposite to others. In this way it may be possible to help the client to expand their self-awareness, and to get in touch with repressed emotions.

The polarities model

The polarities model, taken from Gestalt therapy, is in some ways similar to the iceberg model but with an important difference. As in the iceberg, Gestalt therapy recognises the existence of opposites in feelings, attitudes, beliefs and behaviours in each human being. This is seen as a normal human condition. In the Gestalt polarities model these opposites are viewed as separated polarities that cause inner conflict and confusion to the client unless they are fully accepted and integrated. Whereas in the iceberg model it is assumed that one polarity or the other will be submerged at any one time, the Gestalt model places emphasis on integrating the polarities so that both polarities are fully owned in the 'here and now' and can be accessed freely as a person chooses.

Usefulness of the polarities model

The polarities model can be useful for helping clients to feel OK about accepting and owning what they initially believe are undesirable or negative qualities or emotions. As counsellors, we can tell clients that for every so-called positive or desirable emotion, attitude, belief, behaviour or quality, normal human beings may also have an opposite emotion, attitude, belief or quality. This is normal and therefore OK. Such thinking frees clients to deal with all their emotions, personal qualities, traits and attributes.

Using a Gestalt therapy counselling approach the process involves integrating the polarities so that any two opposite polarities are seen as ends of a continuum rather than as discrete and separate from each other. Opposite polarities can then be accepted as co-existing parts of self. This allows the client to recognise and own any two opposite polarities and to feel free to move to a more comfortable position on the continuum between these. Thus, the client is empowered by the recognition that they can if they wish choose to be at either polarity or at any intermediate point on the continuum. Through this recognition they may be enabled to strengthen those parts of themselves that they would like to strengthen, and can grow as people accordingly. For example, someone who has previously seen themselves as timid may recognise an inner ability to be assertive. Having recognised this, they then have the choice to move along the continuum—timid to assertive—to a position that suits them at any particular time and in any particular situation.

Acceptance of polarities within self

It's important for all of us to recognise and own that opposites exist within us as human beings. If we want to strengthen a particular quality, then we need to accept and deal with its opposite. To be honest with ourselves we need to be able to say: 'I'm capable of loving and hating', 'I'm capable of being angry and I'm capable of being forgiving', 'I'm capable of being tolerant and capable of being intolerant', 'I'm capable of being generous and miserly', 'I'm capable of being optimistic and of being pessimistic', 'of being fun-loving and of being a kill-joy', 'of being light-hearted and of being serious', 'of being religious and of having doubts about my religious values and beliefs'. In order to feel integrated and comfortable within ourselves, we need to accept all the parts of ourselves, and not just those parts that are socially acceptable and consistent with being 'nice' people.

Clients often come to counselling because they are unable to accept parts of themselves. It seems as if parts of themselves have become submerged beneath the sea, never to be seen, and never to be owned. The submerged parts are continually wanting to surface, and there is an inner struggle to prevent the iceberg from rolling over. Naturally clients feel great discomfort when they try to keep parts of themselves submerged and try to deny parts of themselves that really want to be expressed.

Helping clients integrate polarities

There is more than one way in which to help clients to integrate polarities within themselves. We can do this by using the iceberg model with them, and helping them to recognise and own opposites within self. Alternatively, we can make use of an active experiential method which involves role-play and has its origins in Gestalt therapy and psychodrama.

New counsellors are often lacking in the confidence required to enable them to use active methods where the client is encouraged to take part in role-plays. This is understandable, and it is sensible for them to stay with the skills which are comfortable for them until such time as they can use these confidently and wish to extend and enhance their repertoire of skills. Our experience is that when active methods involving client role-play are used, outcomes for clients are usually greatly enhanced. We do need to point out that in our opinion it is generally not appropriate to use active experiential methods until a sound, trusting, counselling relationship has been established. Additionally, some clients are too self-conscious and unsure of themselves to be able to make use of these methods. When inviting clients to take part in an experiential exercise, we always make it clear to them that they have choice about whether they take part in the exercise, and that they may stop the exercise at any time.

We keep a pile of coloured cushions of various shapes, sizes, colours, designs and textures in a corner of our counselling room. When exploring polarities, we invite the client to go to the pile of cushions and choose a cushion to represent each polarity. For example, let us consider a case where a client is extremely submissive, and is afraid to use the powerful part of self. In this case we might ask the client to choose a cushion to represent the submissive part of self, and to choose another cushion to represent the powerful part of self. Having done this, we invite the client to place the cushions one or two metres apart on the floor. The client is next invited to stand beside either one of the cushions. Imagine that the client chose to stand beside the cushion representing the submissive part of self. We then invite the client to say what it is like being submissive. Next we invite the client to move and stand beside the other cushion that represents the opposite part of self. Once again the client is invited to talk about what it is like to be in this position; in the example given, in the powerful position. Additionally, the client might be invited to dialogue between the two polarities, so that the submissive part of self might talk to the powerful part of self and vice versa. As the submissive part of self, when standing beside the 'submissive' cushion, the client might say to the powerful part of self represented by the other cushion, 'people won't like you if you behave like that' and, 'nice people are like me, submissive'. When standing beside the powerful cushion, the client might say to the other cushion, 'people will walk all over you like walking on a door mat'.

In this experiential counselling method, the counsellor needs to invite the client to move from cushion to cushion so that the dialogue continues. While the client is engaged in the dialogue, or is moving from one cushion to the other, it can be very useful for the counsellor to feedback to the client any non-verbal behaviour which is observed. For example the counsellor might notice that the client hesitates in moving, moves reluctantly, or looks much happier when going to the opposite polarity. Rather than the counsellor interpreting non-verbal behaviour, it is more appropriate and useful for the counsellor to give direct feedback of what is noticed by making a statement such as 'you're smiling'. The counsellor might also wish to inquire, 'What are you experiencing inside right now?' As a consequence of the dialogue and feedback from the counsellor regarding non-verbal behaviour, the client is likely to recognise times when it is useful to be in one position or the other.

Finally, the counsellor might invite the client to walk slowly backwards and forwards between the two cushions, stopping in various positions. By encouraging the client to do this, the client is likely to recognise that they can move to any position they choose at any particular time and in any particular situation. Consequently, they are empowered to use both parts of self. Additionally, they may recognise that it is possible to be in an intermediate position where they are not totally powerful or totally submissive, but are somewhere in between.

As we indicated earlier, experiential methods are extremely powerful and very helpful for the client provided that the client is comfortable with such an approach. New counsellors who would like to explore the use of such experiential approaches would be sensible to undertake some practical training in either Gestalt therapy or psychodrama. Because the approaches are experiential, they are most effectively learnt through experience in a training course rather than just through reading a description in a textbook such as this.

Learning summary

- Human beings have polarities or opposites in their personalities.
- Generally we try to show the more acceptable polarities but sometimes the opposite polarities emerge.
- If we can accept the hidden parts of ourselves, then we will be better able to deal with them and to strengthen their opposites, if that is what we want.
- Experiential role-play methods can be useful in enabling clients to accept and integrate polarities so that they feel better.

Further reading

Clarkson, P. 2000, *Gestalt Counselling in Action*, 2nd edn, Sage, London.
Luft, J. 1969, *Of Human Interaction*, Mayfield, California.
O'Leary, E. 1992, *Gestalt Therapy, Theory, Practice and Research*, Chapman & Hall, London.

chapter **20**

Using the 'here and now' experience

We all know people who are in the habit of continually complaining about their life situations, and who like to talk at length about the injustices of the world. They talk about things 'out there', which are apparently out of their control and are the responsibility of others. Rather than saying, 'What can I do to change this situation?', they use statements with words in them like 'They should . . .', and 'They ought to . . .', and 'It's disgraceful that they don't . . .'. Such people often go over the same ground again and again. It is almost inevitable that they will fail to move ahead, because no one can change a situation that is not within their own sphere of control.

Do you ever behave like the people we've just described? Do you ever grumble, moan and complain about 'out there' things, things that are apparently other people's responsibility rather than yours? We both have to admit that at times, we do.

Taking personal responsibility

Notice how we started talking about other 'people who complain' in this chapter and are now looking at ourselves. My guess is that you were more comfortable when the discussion was about others than you were when owning your own ability to grumble and complain. It's usually easier for us to distance ourselves from our own dysfunctional behaviour and to blame others for our problems. Unfortunately if we complain about things that other people are doing or not doing, or about external events or situations, then we are likely to get stuck in a rut of complaining, and to feel frustrated because we are powerless to bring about change. Conversely, if we focus on what we ourselves are doing, and on what is happening inside us, then we can, if we choose, take action to change what we are doing, or we can change our thinking so that we are better able to accept what is happening.

Focusing on the 'here and now'

Similar logic to that just discussed applies to the present when compared with the past and future. We have no control over past events; they have already happened and we can't change them. Similarly, we have limited control over future events; they have not happened yet and we cannot be sure what the future will bring. Inappropriately focusing on the past or future is likely to lead us into unending philosophising, complaining and worrying, whereas focusing on the present allows us to make sensible choices for our own satisfaction.

The preceding discussion is not meant to imply that it is inappropriate and of no value for the client to talk about what other people are doing, to talk about situations beyond their control, or to talk about past or future events. It does imply that there is little point in the client doing these things unless they also focus on what is happening inside them at the present time, when they think about these situations or events. The focus in counselling needs to be on what is happening within the client at the moment in question, in the *here and now*, if the intervention is to be optimally therapeutic. The need to focus on the here and now is one of the central concepts of Gestalt therapy (O'Leary 1992).

Imagine a situation where a client is angry about the way his father treated him when he was a young child. He could talk about this past relationship time and again and make little progress. However, if the counsellor brings the focus onto what is happening within the client at the time when he talks about the past, then progress is more likely to be made. The counsellor might then tap into anger, resentment and bitterness that is present right now. As the counsellor listens to descriptions of past experiences, it is appropriate for the counsellor to ask the client how he feels as he talks about them. The counsellor might say, 'Tell me how you feel emotionally *right now*, as you talk about those past events.' By doing this, the counsellor brings the focus into the present, and brings current emotional feelings that are associated with the past experiences of trauma into the client's awareness. The client is then able to experience fully those feelings and deal with them appropriately. It is only by experiencing these emotional feelings fully that the client will be able either to reduce them or get rid of them, or to discover ways of dealing with them constructively.

Helping the client to focus on the present

One way of bringing a client's focus into the present is to watch their non-verbal behaviour and to tell them what you notice. Alternatively, you might ask a question about what they are experiencing emotionally. For example, the client's eyes may become watery as they recount some past event. Sensitively interrupting with the words, 'I notice the tears starting to form in your eyes', or 'Tell me what you are experiencing emotionally right now', is very likely to bring the client more fully in touch with their present internal experiences.

It can be useful to give a client permission to take time, to stay with their feelings and to experience them. In that way they are allowed to cry if hurting, are allowed to express anger if angry, and are allowed to own whatever other emotions are being experienced, so that they can move forward into a more comfortable space. If this is done, gradually the client will learn to allow themselves to experience their feelings rather than to deny them. This learning in the counselling situation will hopefully extend into the client's daily life and enable them to be more responsive to their feelings generally. Thus, they will be enabled to deal with their feelings as they arise rather than letting them build up to an intolerable level.

'Negative feelings'

As discussed in the previous chapter, a common cause of client distress is an inability to properly and appropriately express 'negative' feelings towards others. For example, for many people the expression of anger is repressed from childhood. Whenever small children get angry their parents tend to say, 'Don't behave in that angry way. Don't throw a tantrum.' As a result the child learns, incorrectly, that it isn't appropriate to express anger towards others even when an angry reaction is justified. Unfortunately blocked anger often leads to depression, anxiety or stress. What is worse, if we don't let other people know how we feel towards them, or how we feel about their behaviour, then we prevent ourselves from having fully functioning, open and genuine relationships. Bringing issues out into the open and discussing them enables emotional feelings to be expressed, rather than suppressed with the pretence that they don't exist. The immediacy of the counselling relationship can be used to demonstrate how feelings can be shared in a constructive way that enhances rather than damages a relationship.

Modelling

In the immediacy of the counselling situation there is a real-life relationship between the client and counsellor. A skilled counsellor will naturally model adaptive and constructive ways of relating, and will also help the client to explore feelings that are generated by the counselling relationship. By learning to explore these feelings and bring them into the open, the client learns appropriate ways in which to deal with the feelings generated by relationships with others, and hence is likely to improve the quality of their relationships generally.

Imagine that by carefully observing the non-verbal behaviour of a client, a counsellor suspects that the client is angry with them. The counsellor may have noticed, for example, an angry look flash across the client's face. However, because it is easy to misinterpret non-verbal behaviour it is important for the counsellor to check out whether in fact it was an angry look. The counsellor might say, 'I've got the impression that you looked angry then', and as a result the client may become aware of anger and may be willing to explore it, or may get more fully in touch with whatever it was they did experience. In this way the client's feelings are brought into the open and the counsellor can respond appropriately and genuinely so that the relationship with the client is more authentic.

Feedback

If counsellors are to be genuine in their relationships with clients, they need to stay in touch with their own feelings rather than suppress them so that they are not owned. Additionally, a counsellor's emotional feelings may provide important information about the counselling process. Consequently, by recognising, owning and responding appropriately to their own feelings in the immediacy of the counselling relationship, counsellors may be able to respond more effectively to the counselling process to the benefit of the client. However, counsellors do need to be careful in sharing their own emotional feelings, particularly if these are not positive, as it is not appropriate for a counsellor to unload their own feelings onto the client.

It does need to be recognised and admitted that some clients engage in annoying behaviours. Consequently, sometimes a counsellor may recognise that they are starting to be annoyed by a client as a consequence of a particular behaviour. When this happens the counsellor firstly needs to recognise and own their own feelings, and make a decision about how to deal with these. If the counsellor is not able to deal with these feelings in a way which ensures that they will not adversely affect the counselling process or intrude on the counselling relationship, then the counsellor needs to explore these feelings in supervision with an experienced counsellor. Having dealt with their own feelings, a counsellor may recognise that a client engages in a behaviour which interferes with the counselling process and may also be annoying to others. In this case it may be useful to give the client feedback in a way which is acceptable to the client. This may enable the client to learn how the behaviour is perceived. Then the client can, if they choose, change. Such change might significantly affect the client's life in a positive way, because it could be that the way in which the client behaves in counselling is similar to the way in which they behave when interacting with other people in the wider environment. Unfortunately, most people are too polite to give useful feedback to friends, even when their friends exhibit quite destructive and maladaptive behaviours. However, sometimes it is possible for a counsellor to give useful and appropriate feedback in a respectful way.

How to give feedback

Imagine that a counsellor was unable to complete appropriate responses because the client was continually interrupting. Initially, the counsellor would need to allow the interruptions to occur and to observe the process. However after a while, it might be appropriate for the counsellor to give the client some feedback. The feedback would need to be given in a way that enabled the client to feel respected rather than attacked. In giving feedback, a counsellor might say to a client, 'I feel concerned because I don't seem to be able to finish what I am saying.' Thus, the client may discover that their tendency to interrupt is interfering with the communication process, and they can, if they wish, change that behaviour. Obviously, such feedback needs to be given in such a way, and at such a time, that it is non-threatening and acceptable to the client.

When giving feedback, it is sensible to avoid starting a feedback sentence with the word 'you' because this might be seen as attacking and lead to a defensive response. Instead it is preferable to start by using an 'I' statement. A typical feedback statement has the following structure: 'I feel . . . when . . .' By starting with the words 'I feel' the counsellor is owning and sharing their own feelings and this makes it easier for the client to hear what is being said. It also makes it less likely that the client will feel attacked and become defensive. Other feedback statements start with the words 'I notice that . . .'. Once again, the statements begin with 'I'.

Consider the example previously given: 'I feel concerned because I don't seem to be able to finish what I am saying.' The statement after the word 'because' is a concrete statement of fact describing exactly what the counsellor noticed. It is not an interpretation. An example of inappropriate feedback in this situation would be to say, 'I feel irritated when you interrupt me because you don't want to listen to what I'm saying'. This statement would be likely to result in the client feeling criticised and attacked because the word 'irritated' implies blame. The statement also involves an interpretation of the client's behaviour which might be quite incorrect. As counsellors, we need to be careful not to include interpretation in feedback statements.

The following are some examples of appropriate and inappropriate feedback statements. See if you can decide which are appropriate and which are not, and then check your decision by reading the comments at the end of this chapter.

Examples of appropriate and inappropriate feedback statements

Example 1A

You keep coming late to appointments because you don't think it's worth coming for counselling.

Example 2A

I am puzzled when I notice that you continually come late for appointments.

Example 3A

You have put a barrier between us because you dislike me.

Example 4A

You are treating me like a father and I'm not your father.

Example 5A

I am uncomfortable because to me it feels as though you are relating to me like a son relates to his father.

Example 6A

Right now I have a shut-out feeling, as though there is a closed door between us.

From these examples and the comments provided at the end of the chapter you will have noticed that appropriate feedback involves the counsellor owning their own feelings in the relationship and sharing these together with a concrete statement of fact. Inappropriate feedback accuses, blames or interprets the client's behaviour and often starts with the word 'you'.

Note that it is sometimes useful to teach clients how to use 'I' statements instead of 'you' statements. We teach them using the 'I feel . . . when . . .' structure, as this is easy to understand. We also stress the importance of making concrete factual statements and of not making interpretations.

Appropriately given feedback will leave a client feeling cared for and valued. Remember that a counsellor does not need to like a client's behaviour to be accepting of the client. It is not inconsistent to say, 'I don't like it when you do that' and also to say, 'I care about you and accept you the way you are'. As human beings, we don't need to like everything a person does in order to care about them and/or like them.

Transference and counter-transference

The immediacy of the counselling relationship often raises questions regarding what psychoanalysts call *transference* and *counter-transference*. Transference occurs when a client behaves towards a counsellor as though the counsellor were a significant person from the client's past, usually the client's mother or father. Naturally, it is quite possible for the counsellor to inadvertently fall into playing the role in which the client sees them. That is, if the client relates to the counsellor as though the counsellor were his father, the counsellor might start feeling and behaving like a father. Such behaviour, on the part of the counsellor, is called counter-transference.

It is inevitable that transference and counter-transference will occur at times in the counselling relationship but, provided that this is recognised, brought into the open and discussed, it is not a problem. It would, however, be a problem if it were not brought out into the open, as it is not useful for the client to treat the counsellor as though they were someone from the past.

It may be that in some ways the counsellor is like the client's parent, but in other ways they are not, and it is important for the counsellor to make the distinction clear. This enables a genuine relationship between client and counsellor to be maintained instead of the relationship being inappropriately coloured by the client's past experiences with a significant other. When a male counsellor realises that transference may be occurring, the counsellor might say, 'I have an impression that you are relating to me rather like a son relates to his father.'

Where counter-transference is occurring, the relevant counsellor statement, for a female counsellor, might be: 'Right now I feel rather like a mother to you.' The counsellor needs to point out caringly that she is not the client's mother or any other significant person from the client's past, and that she is herself—unique and different. As a consequence of bringing the feelings into the open they may be discussed and dealt with directly, so that an inappropriate relationship does not persist. In situations where the counsellor does not feel as though it is appropriate to bring the transference or counter-transference issue directly into the open, the counsellor needs to address the issue in supervision.

Sometimes a counsellor will not recognise when transference or counter-transference is occurring. It is here that supervision can play an important role in helping a counsellor to recognise what is happening and to explore appropriate ways of dealing with the issue.

Projection

Through the immediacy of the counselling relationship the client may learn something about their tendency to project characteristics of significant others from the past onto people in their current life. Thus, they may be able to recognise when inappropriate projection onto others is damaging relationships.

Usually when a counsellor notices what is happening in the relationship between themselves and their client, it is sensible to bring this into the open.

If as a counsellor you sense that something unusual, different or important is happening in the relationship, it will usually be useful to tell the client what you are observing so that it can be fully discussed and explored. By exploring such material the client is able to learn more about themself, to realise what they do in relationships, and to become more in touch with their emotional experiences and thoughts. As a result, they may be able to move forward and to develop more fully as a person.

Resistance

New counsellors are troubled at times by a client's apparent lack of cooperation with the therapeutic process. This is called 'resistance'. A good example of resistance is provided by clients who come late for appointments or who miss appointments repeatedly. Of course, there may be good reasons for a client doing such things. It is well to be aware, though, that often the explanations given may be more in the nature of rationalisations or excuses than the real reason why the behaviour is occurring. For example, a client may be finding counselling very threatening and worrying, and may, for subconscious reasons, be postponing attending. It is important for the client to realise what is happening so that the real issue is addressed, and the client's fear is addressed. Once again, what the counsellor needs to do is to verbalise what is noticed, rather than interpreting this.

Resistance may often involve the client deflecting away from talking about important issues when these are painful. Once again, the most useful strategy is for the counsellor to give feedback of what is noticed by saying something like, 'I noticed that you change the subject whenever you start to talk about . . .'

An example of resistance

As a trainer of counsellors, David noticed that often trainee counsellors came to supervision sessions and said to him, 'Unfortunately I haven't been able to make a videotape of a counselling session as promised.' He was then given a very convincing reason why it was quite impossible for them to make the videotape: 'Oh, I couldn't find a blank cassette', or 'The machine jammed when I put the cassette in', or 'I put the cassette in and unfortunately I pushed the wrong button and it didn't record', or 'Unfortunately somebody else borrowed the video before I did, as I had forgotten to book it'. Of course, all of those 'excuses' were valid. They were all genuine. The trainee counsellor was at no time lying but was being genuine and honest.

However, resistance was usually discovered when David said something like, 'I notice that for three weeks you have been unable to make a videotape, and have had perfectly good reasons. However, I am puzzled by this because you are a very capable person. I am wondering what happens emotionally inside you when you think about making a video.' Giving direct feedback often enabled a trainee to explore more fully what was happening, and as a result it was often recognised that it was threatening for the trainee to produce a video, and yes, if they had made a little more effort, it would have been possible to have produced the recording. David never needed to say, 'You must produce a video next week'. Rather, just drawing attention to what he had observed was sufficient to overcome the trainee's resistance.

Dealing with resistance

In the counselling process with clients, if a client is repeatedly late, or has missed several appointments in a row, it can be useful to draw the client's attention to what has happened. It may be necessary to say, 'Yes, I have heard your reasons and I understand and believe them, but I am still left wondering whether at some other level something else is happening. I am puzzled that you should be late so often.'

Resistance can, of course, take many forms. Sometimes resistance blocks a client from exploring a particularly painful area in their life, and as a counsellor you may feel frustrated by such avoidance. However, in our opinion, it is important to explore the resistance rather than try to burst through it. There are differences of opinion here, however, as some counsellors believe that directly breaking through the resistance is preferable. We prefer the opposite approach, probably because we have an interest in Gestalt therapy. We explore the resistance by drawing the client's attention to what is happening. We might say to a client, 'I notice that whenever you mention (a particular subject) you quickly change the subject. My guess is that it is too painful to talk about . . . (the subject in question)'. The client is then able to experience the avoidance fully and usually something important will emerge spontaneously. If it doesn't, then we might ask the client what they are currently experiencing emotionally. As a result the client would probably be brought in touch with what it felt like to avoid exploring a painful area of their life and consequently might decide how to deal with their avoidance. Alternatively they might say, 'I'm not prepared to explore that really painful area of my life. To do so would be like opening up Pandora's box. It's far too scary for me.' We need to remember that the client has a right to make that choice and to leave Pandora's box closed. If that is what they choose we respect their wishes.

Uses of the 'here and now' experience

In this chapter we have dealt with the ways in which the immediacy of the counselling relationship can be used to:

1. help the client to focus on their own behaviour, inner feelings and thoughts, in the present, rather than focusing on past behaviours or on the behaviour of others over which the client has no control;
2. help the client to learn to own and deal with their emotional feelings as they arise; this includes owning and dealing with so-called 'negative' feelings towards others;
3. give the client constructive feedback, in an acceptable way, with regard to inappropriate behaviours that cause annoyance to the counsellor and may annoy others;
4. help the client to recognise and deal with the human tendency to project the characteristics of significant persons from their past onto others; and
5. help the client to deal with their own resistance.

An effective counsellor will verbalise their observations of what is occurring in the immediacy of the counselling relationship so that client growth is promoted. Hopefully, what is learnt from the counselling experience will be carried into the client's everyday life.

Comments on examples of appropriate and inappropriate feedback statements

Example 1B

Inppropriate Feedback: The statement is threatening as it starts with the word 'you'. The words 'because you don't think it's worth coming for counselling' are an unverified interpretation of the client's behaviour.

Example 2B

Appropriate Feedback: The counsellor starts with an 'I' statement which describes how they feel: 'I am puzzled.' A concrete statement of what has been observed is then given: 'You continually come late for appointments.' The counsellor does not attempt to interpret the client's behaviour, but merely states what has been observed.

Example 3B

Inappropriate Feedback: The statement is inappropriate because it consists of a 'you' statement which could make the client feel attacked. Moreover, the counsellor is interpreting the client's behaviour. The statement, 'You dislike me' is guesswork and could be wrong.

Example 4B

Inappropriate Feedback: An inappropriate statement starting with 'you' which could be received by the client as a put-down.

Example 5B

Appropriate Feedback: This statement starts appropriately with an 'I' statement of the counsellor's feelings: 'I am uncomfortable.' Instead of accusing the client by using a 'you' statement, information about how the relationship feels for the counsellor is given. Compare this statement with example 4. It is very different.

Example 6B

Appropriate Feedback: Notice how in this statement the counsellor's own feelings are described rather than blaming the client for putting up a barrier. Compare this statement with example 3.

Learning summary

- Talking about the past and future, and about other people, is not constructive unless the client also focuses on the 'here and now' experience.
- Staying in the 'here and now', and focusing on current experiences, emotional feelings and thoughts is therapeutically useful.

- The immediacy of the counselling relationship can be a useful learning experience for the client.
- A counsellor can model adaptive behaviour and relationship skills and give feedback to the client.
- Appropriate feedback can start with 'I feel . . .', followed by a concrete non-interpretive statement.
- 'Transference' is when the client treats the counsellor as a parent (or significant other).
- 'Counter-transference' is when the counsellor responds to the client's transference as a parent (or significant other).
- Transference and counter-transference usually need to be brought into the open when they occur.
- 'Resistance' may involve a client's apparent lack of cooperation with the therapeutic process or direct avoidance of painful issues.
- A good way to deal with resistance is to the raise the client's awareness of what is being observed.

Further reading

Clarkson, P. 2000, *Gestalt Counselling in Action*, 2nd edn, Sage, London.
Kennedy, E. & Charles, S. C. 1990, *On Becoming a Counsellor: A Basic Guide for Non-Professional Counsellors*, 2nd edn, Gill & Macmillan, Dublin.
O'Leary, E. 1992, *Gestalt Therapy, Theory, Practice and Research*, Chapman & Hall, London.

Exploring options

When a client comes to see a counsellor it is often because they feel hopelessly stuck in an intolerable situation in which they do not know what to do to ease their pain, and believe that there is no apparent solution to their problems. This hopeless feeling may lock a client into depression, anxiety and tension. Use of the reflective and other skills described previously enables the client to explore their issues and to clarify them. This process alone may be helpful in reducing their distress, and they may spontaneously move towards exploring options and finding solutions for their problems. Sometimes however, the client does not move forward in this way and appears to reach an impasse, without properly exploring possible options. An appropriate way for the counsellor to deal with this situation is to reflect the feeling of being 'stuck' and then to ask the client whether they can see any options.

Finding options

An open question such as, 'You are obviously in a very uncomfortable situation. What do you see as your options?' can be useful in helping the client to identify options. By asking this question, rather than suggesting options, the counsellor encourages the client to take responsibility for solving their own problems. The client is then able to think about and hopefully suggest options for consideration. Some of these options might be discarded immediately as being impossible or unacceptable. However, be careful to remember all the options the client suggests, because an option that the client has ruled out initially may turn out to be the one that will eventually be chosen.

New counsellors often feel pressured into trying to find options for their clients. Our experience is that generally it is not necessary to do this, and that it is far better if clients are able to come up with their own options. Of course there are times when for some reason a client fails to see an option that is obvious to the counsellor, and in such a case the counsellor may choose to tell the client about that option. However, when a counsellor does put forward an idea of their own, it's preferable that it should be put forward in a tentative way, so that the client sees it as nothing more than a possible suggestion and does not take it as advice which needs to be followed.

Exploring options

When helping a client to explore options, we let the client talk in a general way about the various alternatives and then summarise them clearly. We then encourage the client to explore each idea individually and to talk about the positive and negative aspects of each option. There are some advantages in dealing with the most unlikely or least preferred options first. Thus, the client gets these out of the way, and this leaves a smaller range of options, which makes it easier for the client to move towards a decision.

It is sensible to encourage the client not only to look carefully at the consequences, both negative and positive, of each option, but also to take into account their own gut feelings about the various alternatives that are available. Quite often a person's logical thinking will be pulling in one direction whereas their gut feelings will be pulling in a different direction. It is, for example, quite common to hear a client say: 'That is what I really ought to do, that is what I should do, but I don't want to do that, it doesn't feel right for me.' Obviously the client needs to feel very comfortable with the decision they make, or they are unlikely to stay with it. Logical thinking alone does

not provide sufficient grounds on which to choose an option. In fact, we believe that it's more important for the client to feel comfortable at a gut level with an option than to think that the option is the most sensible one. However, any option chosen obviously has to be the client's choice and may not be the choice the counsellor believes to be the most desirable, sensible or appropriate.

Making a choice

Imagine that your client is in a dilemma and is unable to make a choice between two options, option A and option B. In order for the client to resolve the dilemma, we suggest that you might wish to help the client to fully explore what it would feel like to have chosen option A, and to explore what the consequences of this choice would be. After this is completed encourage the client to do a similar exploration for option B. This enables a clear comparison between the two options to be established.

One of the problems in making a choice between two alternatives is that whenever we make a choice, almost invariably there is a loss or cost involved. Let us give you an example. We are both working on revising the manuscript of this book on a Saturday and don't have to work today unless we choose to. It's a warm sunny day and we are only five minutes walk from a beautiful sandy beach. We have two options. One option is to continue writing and the other option is to stop work and to go down to the beach for a swim, so we have a dilemma. In situations like this we might ask ourselves the question, 'What should we do?' However, remembering Chapter 17 on self-destructive beliefs, it would be better for us to replace the 'should' question by the question, 'What do we *want* to do?' By asking this question we can make a choice which is genuinely ours, is not excessively influenced by injunctions from the past, and fits with our current experience. We enjoy writing and quite enjoy what we are doing now, but it would also be enjoyable to go for a swim and maybe lie on the beach afterwards. Now this is not a heavy choice, but whichever choice we make will involve a loss. If we decide to keep on writing then we lose out on the exercise, the fresh air and the relaxed feeling of being down at the beach; but if we go down to the beach we'll have a different loss. We'll lose the satisfaction of continuing to do something creative—our writing—and we may feel frustrated by not having made more progress with our writing when tomorrow comes. So, whether we continue to write or whether we go to the beach, we have to accept that there is a loss either way. If we choose one alternative we lose the other.

The loss or cost involved in making a choice

One of the main blocks to making decisions occurs when people don't properly look at the loss or cost component involved. Frequently we discover that accepting the loss or cost associated with a decision is more difficult than choosing between the positive aspects of the alternative choices.

It can be very helpful to tell clients about the loss or cost component in decision-making, and to explain this as applied to their particular dilemma. We might say to a client, 'If you choose option A, what are your losses going to be?' and 'If you choose option B, what are your losses going to be?' And then ask them whether they would be able to accept those losses. The choice is not just a choice between two positives, but also a choice that involves choosing between two losses and deciding which loss is acceptable, if either. By focusing on the loss or cost component as well as the positive component of options, clients are more readily able to make decisions and resolve their dilemmas.

The effect of polarities

Resolution of dilemmas is difficult for most people. Part of that difficulty is due to the polarities that exist within us. Let me, Kathryn, go back to the previous example where David and I looked at the dilemma of continuing to write or going to the beach. Right now it is as though there are two parts of me. One part of me wants to go for a swim, and the other part of me wants to stay here and continue writing this book. I have found that it is very helpful for clients if I describe their dilemmas in terms of parts of themselves. Sometimes I say to a client, 'Part of you wants to make choice A and another part of you wants to make choice B. These are both valid parts of you. They both exist in you at the same time.' I ask the client to tell me about the part that wants option A and to explore that part fully, and then to tell me about the part that wants option B and to explore that fully. By doing this, I allow the client to integrate and own two opposite parts of self and not to feel confused, but rather to accept that both are valid parts of self (see Chapter 19 which dealt with parts of self). The client is then empowered to accept that choosing one of the options means letting go of the other option, and that involves a cost or the acceptance of a loss, the loss of the option that is not chosen.

The myth of the 'right' choice

Many people have been taught as children that there is always a correct choice, and that in dilemmas the choice of one option is correct and the choice of the other is wrong. Confusion often arises from the unrealistic expectation that choice involves a decision between black and white, or between right and wrong. In reality, most human decisions involve deciding between shades of grey where both options have advantages or positive qualities and both have costs or disadvantages.

Remember, if I choose option A, I lose option B, and that loss is part of the cost of choosing option A. To resolve a dilemma, and choose one option, I have to let go of the other. The letting go is the hard part. If you let your client know that, they may find it easier to reach a decision.

Creative solutions

At times dilemmas can be resolved by doing some creative thinking and introducing a new option so that the extent of any loss is reduced. If we use the example regarding whether David and I should continue writing or go to the beach, there is a third option. We could decide to continue writing for a while and then stop and go to the beach. This new option might provide a win–win solution! In fact, having talked about our choice with each other, this is what we have both decided to do. We have decided to continue writing for another hour and then go to the beach. This is convenient because we both like working and relaxing together.

Giving the client permission to stay stuck

Sometimes a client will stay stuck and will be unable to resolve a dilemma even though the issues are clearly understood. As a new counsellor, I often worried when a client was stuck and would sometimes prolong a counselling session unnecessarily in an effort to try to unstick the client and lead the client to a satisfying solution. I now realise that such counsellor behaviour is very inadvisable. It is much more helpful to reflect back to the client their 'stuckness', and to say, 'Look, it seems as though we've come to an impasse. There doesn't seem to be an easy solution, and today you seem to be stuck and don't know which way to go. Let's leave it there. Come back another time and we will talk together again.' By saying this, the counsellor gives the client permission to remain stuck, reduces the pressure to make a quick decision, and lets the client know that they are welcome to come back again to continue working on the issue. Sometimes the client will come back the next time saying, 'I've made a decision', because they were given permission to stay stuck and effectively given time to think through what was discussed in the previous session without pressure. At other times a client will remain stuck. Then the counsellor's goal is to assist the client to come to terms with the consequences of being stuck in what may be a painful or uncomfortable situation. The counsellor does this by assisting the client to verbalise emotional feelings about being stuck, and then encouraging them to talk about how they will cope with being stuck.

In the next chapter we will try to develop a deeper understanding of the process required to help clients deal with blocks to decision-making. However, remember that it is OK to allow a client to remain 'stuck'. Often experiencing being stuck for a while is necessary before progress can be made.

Learning summary

- It is preferable for counsellors to ask their clients to suggest their own options before suggesting additional ones.
- New options may be tentatively suggested if important alternatives have been missed (are there any 'win–win' options?).
- All the options need to be summarised clearly before discussing each in turn.
- Dealing with the least desirable options first may be helpful as it may exclude them.
- It can be useful for the client to examine the positive and negative aspects of each option, carefully considering likely consequences.
- There is a loss or cost involved in making any choice and often accepting the inevitable loss is the hardest part of making a decision.
- Many, if not most, decisions are not choices between black and white but rather choices between shades of grey.

chapter **22**

Facilitating action

By using the micro-skills described in the previous chapters an effective counsellor will most probably enable the client to move out of confusion and anxiety, and into a more comfortable emotional space. If that is achieved, then the client has clearly been helped by the counselling process in the short term, and for some clients that is sufficient. However, for many clients, their emotional distress is a consequence of entrenched life situations, and unless action is taken to change those life situations then emotional distress may well recur.

Some clients exhibit the 'cracked record' syndrome. They go to see a counsellor again and again, with the same unresolved problem. The experienced counsellor needs to have the necessary skills to assist such clients to move forward by making specific and observable changes to their life situations.

Have you ever experienced resistance from a person when you have tried to persuade them to make useful life changes? We human beings are rather like the proverbial donkey. The more someone pushes or pulls us, the more we tend to resist! If we are to enable clients to take action to change then we must resist the temptation to push for change and use a different strategy. The strategy needed was admirably described in Gestalt therapy theory by Zinker (1978) and more recently by O'Leary (1992). A modified version of the *Gestalt awareness circle* is shown in Figure 22.1. An understanding of this circle enables counsellors to help clients to take action, and consequently to feel better, after they have progressed through the necessary preliminary steps.

The Gestalt awareness circle

We will now look at the awareness circle (Figure 22.1) in some detail starting at the point of *arousal*.

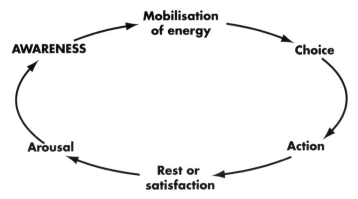

Figure 22.1 *Gestalt awareness circle*

Clients generally come for counselling when they are emotionally distressed—when they are at the *arousal* point on the *awareness circle*, with their emotions unpleasantly aroused. The counsellor's task is to enable the client to move around the circle towards *satisfaction* or *rest*. This is achieved by raising the client's *awareness*.

The arousal stage

In the *arousal* phase, the emotionally disturbed client is unable to focus clearly, and sees a confused picture of their world. It is as though they were looking at an overgrown forest, choked by too many trees and much undergrowth. They are unable to clearly see any one tree, but instead are overwhelmed by a blurred and confusing picture. In this state, the client's energy is depleted. They will be unable to see their options, and will therefore have little hope of taking any action to change their situation.

Raising awareness to mobilise energy

If the client is to feel better, they need to *mobilise their energy* so that they can work constructively to resolve their issues. The counsellor can facilitate this mobilisation of energy by raising the client's awareness of their inner experiences. As a trainee counsellor, if you have mastered the skills described in the previous chapters, then you have the tools required to do this. By using these micro-skills you will inevitably raise the client's awareness, and consequently will *mobilise their energy*.

Moving round the awareness circle

Sometimes, once awareness is raised, the client will move with ease around the awareness circle. To use the previous analogy, the overgrown forest of trees will become a background against which the clear outline of one tree will emerge. The client's confusion will disappear and they will move naturally around the circle into making a *choice*, taking *action*, and coming into a state of *satisfaction* or *rest*.

In life, we do not stay in a state of rest, and if we did we would probably achieve nothing. What we do is to move around the awareness circle again and again.

Blocks to progress around the circle

Unfortunately, most people don't move naturally and easily around the awareness circle but instead run into blocks as discussed in the previous chapter. Blocks often occur, as shown on the circle in Figure 22.2, before *choice* or *action*. If a client is blocked in either of these places, then it is tempting for the counsellor to focus on encouraging the client to make a choice or to take action. Such counsellor behaviour is usually very unhelpful, creating greater difficulties for the client. Instead of achieving the counsellor's goal of helping the client to make a choice or to take action, pushing for choice or action usually returns the client to an even higher state of arousal (see the arrows in Figure 22.2).

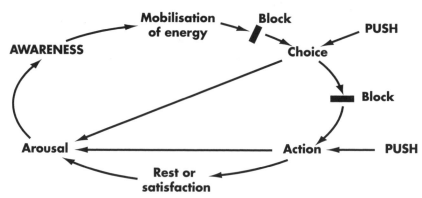

Figure 22.2 *The effect of pushing for choice or action*

If you want to help your client to make a choice or to take action, then a prerequisite is to enable the client to work through any block which might be impeding progress around the circle. The most common blocks which inhibit choice and action are identified in the simple dilemma model in Figure 22.3.

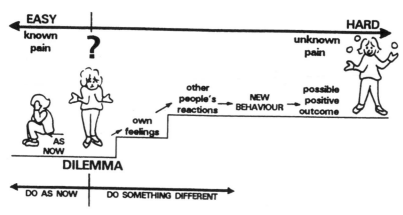

Figure 22.3 *Dilemma model*

A client who makes decisions and takes action to change their life has to cope firstly with their own feelings, and then with other people's reactions. This is often difficult, particularly if the decisions or actions displease others. Also, if a client does something new, then they take a risk; there may be unknown consequences, and these could be painful. It may be easier to go on living as now, with no changes and with known pain, rather than to take a risk and do something new and different with its unknown pain. Thus, it is easy to understand how client choices and actions are often blocked by internal fears and anxieties including the following:
- inability to deal with own feelings;
- inability to cope with the reactions of others;
- fear of consequences;
- fear of a repetition of past bad experiences;
- the intrusion of inappropriate 'shoulds', 'musts' and 'oughts';
- fear that something comfortable or rewarding will be lost; and
- lack of skills to carry out the desired action.

Dealing with blocks

Whenever a client is blocked and unable to make a choice or take action, resist the temptation to push the client into doing so, and instead return to the awareness point on the circle. Raise the client's awareness of their block and encourage them to explore how it feels to be blocked and unable to move forward. Encourage them to become aware of what they are experiencing internally. Ask them what messages they are getting from their body, from their emotional feelings, and from their thoughts, when they experience their inability to decide or act. This may enable the client to explore and to deal with the block, and thus free them to move around the circle to a more comfortable position. It is also possible that, by dealing with the block, the client may discover that they have another more important issue which needs confronting.

Remember, the more you push a client to make a choice or to take action, the more blocked they are likely to become. If you want to help a client to move on then you need to raise their awareness of the block.

Suitable questions to help clients explore blocks are as follows:

'Tell me what you are experiencing emotionally as you think about making this decision (or taking this action)?'
'What are you aware of happening inside you when you think about making this choice (or taking this action)?'

For most clients, if you, the counsellor, use the micro-skills you have learnt to raise *awareness* and to work through blocks, then the client is likely to move spontaneously around the awareness circle, to make *choices* and to take the necessary *action* to achieve goals. However, for some clients this approach alone is not sufficient.

Clients who need additional help to take action

Some clients repeatedly use the counselling process to enable them to continue to exist in unsatisfactory life situations without change. Sometimes in the counselling process it appears as though they are replaying the same tape over and over again. When they do this they may well sink further into despair and hopelessness. Such clients need specific help in facilitating action, if they are to bring about meaningful changes to their lives. Also, there are some clients who, after deciding what they want to do, find themselves unable to move forward into action, not because of psychological blocks, but rather because they do not have the necessary skills or confidence to carry out the action they wish to take. These clients need additional help. The rest of this chapter deals with ways of helping clients who do not have the necessary confidence or personal resources to make and implement action plans on their own.

Clearly, it is not helpful for a counsellor to do the client's work. By doing that, the counsellor would reinforce the client's sense of helplessness, and lead the client to believe that they needed assistance each time new goals were to be targeted. What is helpful is for the client to learn how to organise, plan and execute decisions so that in the future they are able to do these things for themself. A good way of helping a client to learn is to walk alongside them, and to work with them as they struggle with the issues involved in achieving one important goal. You can then, if you wish, explore with them the processes used in achieving their goal. Thus they may identify those processes which were most useful to them so that they can use them in achieving future goals.

Although every situation is different, there are some basic steps that are useful in enabling clients to take action to achieve goals. These steps are listed in the action plan below.

ACTION PLAN

1. Make psychological preparation.
2. Identify the goal.
3. Identify the first step towards goal achievement.
4. Concretise the first step towards goal achievement.
5. Decide how to carry out the first step.
6. Acquire the skills to carry out the first step.
7. Decide when to carry out the first step.
8. Carry out the first step.
9. Reward self for carrying out the first step.
10. Reassess the overall goal.

We will now look in detail at these steps in the order presented above. In order to make the exercise more meaningful consider the specific example of a father who has a dysfunctional relationship with his teenage son.

Psychological preparation

This has been dealt with earlier in this chapter. The counsellor raises client awareness, to enable the client to work through blocks and to come to a decision.

Identifying the goal

Imagine that the father in our example had come to the decision that he wanted to work on improving his relationship with his son. For many clients, identifying such a goal would be sufficient to facilitate action, and the counsellor's work would be over. For other clients, further help would be needed.

Identifying the first step towards goal achievement

For some clients, the goal of trying to improve a relationship with a son would be too broad and non-specific. It might not be clear how the goal could be achieved and consequently positive action would be unlikely to occur. Such a client may need to identify the first step towards achieving the goal. This first step needs to be realistically achievable, so that the client is likely to be rewarded by success rather than discouraged by failure.

The counsellor might ask, 'How are you going to set about improving your relationship with your son?' Maybe the father would respond, 'Well, I'd like to start by having a talk with him, but that's scary, because we haven't said anything pleasant to each other for some months'.

Clearly at this point the counsellor would move the focus away from the contemplated action and return to raising awareness of the client's fear of talking with his son. If this were not done then the client might be blocked from action.

Concretising the first step in goal achievement

Once the first step in goal achievement has been identified, it needs to be concretised, so that it is clear and specific rather than vague. For example, the statement 'I'd like to have a talk with my son' is very general. The value of such a talk is likely to depend on what the purpose of the talk is, and on what the content of the conversation is likely to be. Questions by the counsellor, such as, 'What do you want to say to your son?' and 'What do you hope to achieve as a result of this talk?', might yield more specific information such as, 'I want to tell him why I am so angry with him, so that I can get that garbage out of the way and can start relating to him in a positive way'.

Deciding how to carry out the first step

This decision needs to take into account the likely consequences of the proposed action. For example, the statement in the paragraph above, 'I want to tell him why I am so angry with him . . .' suggests that the client intends to confront his son in a way likely to lead to further alienation rather than reconciliation. At this point the counsellor could usefully carry out some role-plays to allow the client to experience what it would be like to be the recipient of the intended message.

Acquiring the skills to carry out the first step

The client may need to acquire new skills to be able to competently carry out the first step. In our current example the counsellor might coach the client in the use of 'I' statements, and carry out further role-plays to determine the likely impact of client statements.

Deciding when to carry out the first step

Sometimes when people have to carry out unpleasant tasks they will delay doing what they have decided to do by using the excuse that the time is not right. Do you do that? We think that most people do, and delayed action often results in no action. We find that for us it is usually easier to carry out what we plan if we have made a clear decision about the proposed timing. We think that it's the same for many clients, and it's therefore useful to explore the issue of timing with them. This may result in more awareness raising—back to the awareness circle again!

Carrying out the first step

Whether or not the client carries out the first step is unimportant. If they do, then they can feel good about that, and if they don't then there will be some learning from the process. The client can once again get in touch with their inner experiences to discover what stopped them from carrying out the first step, and from that awareness a new decision can be made.

Rewarding self for carrying out the first step

Do you ever minimise your achievements? We sometimes do, but we are getting better at taking pride in what we do well. Many clients fail to give themselves positive messages when they succeed in performing difficult tasks. As a counsellor, help your clients to feel good about themselves by maximising their achievements. A client who is properly rewarded for carrying out the first step is more likely to continue making positive decisions and carrying them out.

Reassessing the overall goal

Often when the client has gone some way in one direction, they will realise that the goal originally targeted is one which is no longer desired. That is clearly OK, but the client will consequently need to reassess their overall goal.

In conclusion

In this chapter we have discussed the skills involved in facilitating action. Generally, if you use the previously learnt micro-skills and remember what you have discovered here about the *awareness circle*, you will be successful in helping clients to take appropriate action to bring about meaningful changes in their lives. Additionally, the action plan described above can be used when it is clear that the client is unable to move forward without more specific help.

Learning summary

- Pushing directly for choice or action is likely to fail and increase emotional distress.
- To maximise the possibility of choice or action, raise awareness of blocks.
- A major client dilemma concerns the choice 'to do as now' or 'to do something different'.
- Doing as now involves known pain.
- Doing something different involves unknown pain and outcomes. It's risky!
- Action plans are helpful for some clients.
- Action plans involve preparation for action, setting a specific goal, and having a reward for taking the first step.

Further reading

Clarkson, P. 2000, *Gestalt Counselling in Action*, 2nd edn, Sage, London.
O'Leary, E. 1992, *Gestalt Therapy, Theory, Practice and Research*, Chapman & Hall, London.
Zinker, J. 1978, *Creative Process in Gestalt Therapy*, Vintage, New York.

part **V**

Post-modern approaches

In the earlier chapters of this book we introduced you, the reader, to basic counselling skills and to additional skills that are helpful in promoting change. We have also discussed the ways in which counsellors can help their clients to change and have described the processes that are required for this to happen. In this part of the book, we will provide an introduction to what are known as the post-modern approaches. These contemporary methods are believed by some counsellors to be better than other approaches because they do not focus on the client's problems but instead focus on their strengths. Also the post-modern approaches tend to be brief and to produce quicker results than those obtained by using the more traditional skills described in previous chapters. For many community and government agencies, this is viewed as being a considerable advantage in these days when economic rationalism is fashionable.

We believe that there is considerable value in understanding the post-modern approaches. However, we suggest that it is preferable if these approaches are learnt after new counsellors have become competent in the use of traditional counselling skills. This may then enable them to integrate traditional skills with ideas from the post-modern approaches.

The post-modern approaches are based on some extremely useful and creative concepts, and are powerful when used by a skilled practitioner. However, they do have some limitations. As described in Chapter 12, which deals with the way in which change occurs when counselling clients, we believe that the most successful and enduring changes in clients occur when counselling methods directly target emotional feelings, as well as cognitions (thinking processes) and behaviours. The post-modern approaches use a process of inquiry by the counsellor who, through asking specific types of questions, helps the client to recognise future possibilities, and so to change their thinking and behaviours. A limitation is that these approaches do not directly target emotional feelings, and are heavily dependent on language. Because these methods do not directly target emotions they may be particularly useful for those clients who are not able or willing to get in touch with their emotional feelings. However, for other clients, there may be some disadvantages in using the post-modern approaches because the counsellor does not promote direct exploration of feelings. Another limitation is the heavy reliance of these methods on the use of language. This may make them less suitable for use with those clients who do not have an adequate level of language development, and those who do not have a high enough level of intellectual ability.

We wish to make it clear that because this book is an introductory text for new counsellors, that Chapters 23 and 24 provide only a brief introduction to solution-focused counselling and narrative therapy. We suggest that readers who find these approaches appealing might like to read some of the books recommended for further reading, and then to attend a training course in their preferred approach.

chapter 23

Solution-focused counselling

In this chapter, we will give a brief overview of the solution-focused approach. The solution-focused approach to counselling emphasises:

1. a respectful partnership between the client and counsellor
2. strengths and resources and an optimistic view about the future
3. counselling as a conversational process.

In solution-focused counselling the relationship is viewed as a respectful partnership between the client and counsellor where the client and counsellor work together to find solutions. A major difference between solution-focused counselling and traditional counselling methods is that many traditional counselling methods tend to spend a significant proportion of time exploring those parts of the client's story which are troubling, painful, problematic and dysfunctional. In direct contrast, solution-focused counselling places the emphasis on strengths and resources and an optimistic view about the future. Rather than spending a significant amount of time exploring what might be considered to be client's disabling emotions, negative experiences, failures, disappointments and general pathology, the solution-focused model puts energy into identifying strengths and resources and finding solutions. The attitude generated is one of optimism about the future rather than one of despair about the past.

A major difference between Rogerian counselling and solution-focused counselling is that in the former the counsellor is primarily a reflective listener throughout the counselling process, whereas in solution-focused counselling, counselling is seen as a conversational process where the counsellor is an equal partner in helping the client to find solutions.

Underlying assumptions of solution-focused counselling

In this book we have attempted to avoid the use of jargon. However, in this and the following chapter we will need to make use of some words which may not have clear meaning for members of the general population but do have meaning for the solution-focused counsellor and are essential for understanding and using solution-focused counselling.

It is assumed that to understand their lives people generally engage mentally in a building process to construct models (or *constructions*) that represent their world, or various parts of their world. When they stand back and look at the 'constructions' that they have built in their minds they can recognise that these constructions have been influenced by what they have learnt in life, mainly in a biological, physical and scientific sense. Also, their constructions are influenced by what other people say about them and their lives, and how other people behave towards them. The constructions are then used to help them make sense of themselves and their world. Sometimes a person's constructions become weak or develop problems that need fixing. Generally, people tend to use what they have learnt scientifically to try to fix their problem. They spend a lot of time focusing on what is wrong, in trying to fit the problem into the right pigeonhole so that it makes sense, and in discovering how the problem occurred. They sometimes consult an expert in the area believing that the expert will then be able to discover the solution to the problem. They may begin to see themselves as incompetent and deficient as they persevere in trying to fix their problem in a scientific way. Delving further into the problem often results in an individual becoming overwhelmed and pessimistic about change. The solution-focused approach contrasts radically with this as it emphasises and amplifies the client's strengths and resources when solving problems. The counselling process is then seen as a journey out of a problem-saturated world into a world of increased autonomy and personal success.

Many of the ideas in solution-focused counselling come from the innovative and pioneering work of Milton H. Erickson who was committed to utilising people's competencies in creating a context for change. Milton Erickson believed that viewing the world only through physical and biological understanding severely limited people's ability for problem solving because with this view, the individual focuses on the problem rather than on the solution (Erickson, Rossi & Rossi 1976). Additionally, solution-focused counsellors believe that the constructions that people build are strongly influenced and defined through day-to-day conversation and interactions with one another using language. In the view of the solution-focused counsellor the ways in which we perceive the world and ourselves are organised and maintained through the stories we tell ourselves as a result of our interaction with others. Consequently, solution-focused counselling emphasises the importance of a conversational process that intentionally uses language to, metaphorically speaking, open the door to new constructions. This process is often referred to by solution-focused counsellors as *solution talk*. Problems, rather than being seen as something to be fixed, are viewed as stories which can change and develop different meanings through a conversational collaborative process.

Solution-focused counselling generally follows a specific sequence that includes:

- engaging the client
- constructing pathways for change
- generating creative solutions and tasks.

Engaging the client

The solution-focused counsellor engages the client by listening and, while listening, respects the client's description of the problem. Emotions are not directly targeted but respect for the client's description of the problem does include validating the client's emotional experience. Even though the amount of time spent directly exploring feelings in solution-focused counselling is less than in many other styles of counselling, it is recognised that expressing powerful feelings can be a catalyst for change (O'Connell 1998). However, solution-focused counsellors argue that helping a client to change the *'meaning of their experience'*, that is their understanding of the world they experience, will automatically bring about a change in emotional feelings connected with the problem.

The counsellor's task is to channel the flow of the conversation, identifying the client's goals and identifying exceptions to the current difficulty, rather than focusing on the problem. The counsellor focuses on approaching the client with a curious, open and inquisitive mind, and with an optimistic view to the future.

Listening and responding to the client's description of the problem

Clients generally come to counselling with a negative view and often see their problems as intractable. In responding to the client's description of their problem, the solution-focused counsellor uses language in a way that enables the client to have a more optimistic view about the possibility of change. This does not mean that the counsellor is not interested in hearing about the client's difficulties, but while listening, the counsellor gives responses which open up the possibility that solutions will be found.

Clients will inevitably talk about their past experiences as contributing to their current issues. In solution-focused counselling the belief that current problems are caused by negative past experiences is viewed differently. Negative experiences in the past are viewed as experiences that have brought about something positive. For example a client may blame their current situation on the actions of a punitive father. The counsellor's task is to maintain a position of curiosity about how the client was able to cope and survive despite receiving punishment. The client might then be able to view the possibility that the father's excessive discipline is not related to the problem, but rather may explain how the client now has some useful resources in being able to cope with difficult and/or unpleasant situations.

Normalising the client's difficulties by indicating that others have had similar experiences can also be helpful in this initial stage (see Chapter 18). While normalising, the solution-focused counsellor also uses a method that is similar in some ways to reframing (see Chapter 15). Many clients describe their situation by using labels that are unhelpful for them. For example a client might describe themselves by using the label 'depressed'. In response, the counsellor might refer to the client as 'feeling down a lot of the time'. This statement normalises the client's situation, as most people feel down at times. It also describes the client's condition in a way that suggests that the client doesn't feel down all the time, and therefore there is a possibility that the times when the client doesn't feel down can become longer and/or more frequent.

Sometimes, a solution-focused counsellor will describe the client's current predicament as a stage, or speak about the problem concerned as a stage; something that the client might grow out of, or will get over. Once again this opens up the possibility that change will occur. For example, a client might say, 'My mother died two years ago and I still feel depressed'. In response, the counsellor might say, 'Losing your mother was a major event. Before they can move on, all people need time to grieve when they suffer a major loss. They need to give themselves permission to fully experience it rather than fighting it or trying to avoid it'. This statement is designed to help the client recognise that they are in a stage where it is appropriate to grieve, and that the stage will pass.

Identifying the client's goals and resourcefulness

During the engagement process the counsellor helps the client to identify goals and encourages the client to recognise that they have the resources to determine the future path of their lives. The counsellor's goal is to lead the client to a view that the future they would prefer is possible. The counsellor pursues this goal by reflecting, summarising, clarifying, and by using words that convey an expectancy that the client's preferred future will come about. The counsellor raises the suggestion that at some time in the future the problem will end or things will be better. When a client talks about their problem, the counsellor reflects what the client has said in a way that re-states the client's concerns in terms of goals to be achieved rather than problems to be removed. For example, the client may say, 'My husband and I fight all the time', and the counsellor might respond by saying, 'It sounds like counselling will be successful when you are getting along better most of the time'. By responding in this way the focus has been removed from fighting and instead directed towards a positive goal.

Identifying exceptions to the current difficulty

Solution-focused counsellors use examples from the client's story to help the client to get in touch with their ability to be resourceful. The counsellor can use questions to help the client remember and identify past times when they were competent, skilful and hopeful. For example the client might say, 'I don't ever seem to be able to say what I mean. I get overwhelmed with other people's points of view'. The counsellor might respond to this by saying, 'Let's look at when you had to write assignments. Tell me how you went about putting your point of view forward then'. By saying this, the solution-focused counsellor assumes that helping the client to go into detail about things they have actually done and felt will be useful, even though these are not directly related to the issue at hand.

During the engagement process the solution-focused counsellor will spend time inquiring about the client's interests, pleasures and areas of competence, and will get details of these and highlight and expand them. Thus the focus is on helping clients to recognise that at times they are confident and feel at ease, and identifying situations where they are competent and effective, rather than focusing on times when they feel worthless. For example, the client might say, 'The teachers at school say I'm not good for anything'. In response, the counsellor might say, 'Your mother told me that you spend a lot of time skateboarding. How did you become good at that?' The young person might reply by saying, 'I repeat the same tricks over and over until I get expert at doing them. Each time I do a trick I notice the things that I do wrong so that I can correct them the next time.' By asking, 'How did you become good at that?', the counsellor will have enabled the young person to recognise the strategies they have used for learning particular skills. The counsellor might then be able to help the client to transfer these strategies and/or skills which the client has identified for use in the problem area.

Constructing pathways for change

This stage in the process is characterised by the counsellor asking questions with some specific purposes in mind. By asking these questions the counsellor aims to channel the conversation into:

1. helping the client to view the past positively
2. identifying current behaviours that the client is using to cope with their difficulties
3. looking at how change can occur in the future.

This lays the groundwork for generating solutions to the client's difficulties. We will now describe four types of question which are particularly useful at this stage of the counselling process.

Cheerleading

The use of cheerleading questions has been described by Walter and Peller (1992). Solution-focused counsellors engage in cheerleading when they show enthusiastic reactions of emotional support when clients tell them that they have used behaviours which are positive and different from behaviours which have led to undesirable outcomes. Typical cheerleading questions are:

> 'How did you do that?'
> 'How did you manage to make that decision?'
> 'Well done. That must have been really difficult to do; how did you do it?'

Additionally, there are some statements which have a similar effect such as:
'That sounds good!'
'That's amazing!'

Cheerleading questions are useful as they help the client to recognise and be encouraged by the knowledge that they have the ability within them to behave differently so that positive outcomes occur.

Questions which exaggerate consequences

These questions can be used to help a client recognise that they have coped extremely well under adverse situations. They are aimed at encouraging the client to view their behaviour in a positive light and discover unrecognised strengths. Such questions can be extremely useful for clients who are unsure about how well they are coping with life.

Examples of this kind of question are:
'How come things aren't worse?'
'What stopped total disaster from occurring?'
'How did you avoid falling apart?'

Scaling questions

Scaling questions help the client to be specific when identifying and discussing goals. Additionally, they help the client to place the current difficulties within a context, which suggests that it is possible to move towards something better. Often scaling questions lead into goal-oriented questions as they are related to goals.

Examples of scaling questions are:
'On a scale of one to ten, one being hopelessly incompetent and ten being really competent, where do you think you fit right now?'
'On a scale of one to ten, where would you like to be in the future?'
'On a scale of one to ten, where one represents terrible and ten represents wonderful, how would you rate your relationship with your partner?'

Questions which presuppose change

An example of a question which presupposes change is:
'What has been different or better, since you saw me last?'

This question presupposes that some change has occurred and may help the client identify things which have improved, so that they can feel good. Quite often, positive change goes unnoticed unless a deliberate question is asked in order to identify change. For example, although they may have had fewer arguments during the week, the client might not have recognised this. By using a question which presupposes change, the counsellor can bring the change which has occurred into focus and make small changes newsworthy so that there is a recognition that improvement has begun. Once improvement has been identified, there is an incentive to make further improvement so that significant change can occur.

Generating creative solutions and tasks

Up to now we have explained how the solution-focused counsellor initially concentrates on finding out all they can about the client. This includes finding out information about the client's resources, interests, likes and dislikes, and how the client has attempted to deal with their difficulties up to now. The solution-focused counsellor's task now is to use this information to create solutions.

At this point in the counselling process the counsellor makes use of the following:
1. viewing the client as the expert
2. highlighting exceptions
3. externalising the problem
4. goaling.

Viewing the client as the expert

Solution-focused counsellors let their clients know that they have heard and understood their problems and concerns, their experiences and points of view. They assume that the client is an active agent in directing their own life and consequently suggest that any successful achievement must be a result of the client's efforts. For example, a client might say, 'She walks all over me. She'll only do things if she knows there is a reward,' and the counsellor might respond by saying, 'It seems to me that *you* have been able to change her behaviour by using rewards as a useful strategy'. By saying this the counsellor clearly attributes positive change to the efforts of the client instead of focusing on the negative part of the client's statement.

Solution-focused counsellors explore in detail times when the client made a choice or a change which resulted in a positive outcome. They may share with their client what has worked for them in similar situations, or what has worked for other people with the same difficulty. For example, the counsellor might say, 'When I feel like that I know it's best for me to go for a long walk by myself'. Alternatively, the counsellor might say, 'Other people have told me that when they experience what you are describing, they find it is helpful to do something active'.

Highlighting exceptions

A powerful technique in solution-focused counselling is to highlight exceptions by using exception-oriented questions. Exception-oriented questions aim to promote change by drawing attention to times or situations where an undesirable behaviour does not occur. With almost every client there will have been past and present problem-free times. However it is quite possible that many clients may not have recognised these problem-free times. A task for the counsellor is therefore to help the client to identify those times or situations when the client's current difficulty didn't occur. Once these have been identified, the counsellor can inquire about them in detail. The counsellor can ask what, when, and with whom this exception to the difficulty occurred. For example, the client might say, 'I'm concerned because I'm drinking every night', and the counsellor might respond by saying, 'Are there any nights when you haven't had a drink?' The client might be able to identify some times when they haven't been drinking. In this case the counsellor might explore further by saying something like, 'Tell me about those times'. The counsellor then may use the client's views of facts, feelings and ideas associated with these times to help the client to pro-actively plan how to spend another night without drinking. It needs to be recognised that the client may be unable to identify any recent times when they have not been drinking. In this situation the counsellor will suggest that there must have been a time when the client didn't drink every night. The counsellor will then ask questions to help the client remember the skills they used in times when the problem didn't occur. This may include exploring thoughts, behaviours and emotional feelings which the client experienced in those times when the problem did not occur.

When looking for exceptions it can be useful to look for times when the client expected the problem to occur, but something happened differently or the client acted differently. For example a client might say, 'Last year on my birthday was the only time we didn't fight' and the counsellor might respond by saying 'What did you do differently?' or, 'What is your guess about why you didn't fight?' The focus is on what worked, helping the client to expand on the details of how it worked, and helping the client to retrieve how it felt to have things work.

Examples of exception-oriented questions are:

'When do you not get angry?'

'When do you not get into arguments with your father?'

'In what situations do you have control of your impatience?'

Exception-oriented questions aim to help the client discover that there are times and/or situations where they behave differently, and to recognise what it is that enables them to do this. Gaining understanding in this way helps the client recognise that they can take more control of their behaviour and/or their environment. By recognising this, they may be able to make choices to bring about positive change.

Externalising the problem

When externalising the problem the counsellor separates the problem from client. This enables the client to see the problem as something separate from themselves that they have the resources to deal with, rather than as something within themselves over which they have no control.

Solution-focused counsellors take the view that they don't work with problems: they work with people who believe they have problems. For example, a client may see themselves as alcoholic, a drug addict, as depressed, anxious or a failure. The counsellor might ask such clients where these perceptions came from and encourage them to expand on these perceptions. If this is done, usually a client will talk about the cause of the problem or how the problem influences or interferes with their behaviour. At this point the counsellor has an opportunity to separate, or *externalise*, the problem from the client by talking about 'depression', 'alcohol', 'failure' or 'anxiety', instead of talking about *the client* being depressed, being an alcoholic, being a failure or being anxious.

When externalising the problem it can be helpful to find out how 'the problem' has interfered with or influenced the client's life, and then to discover how the client has attempted to overcome the problem. Here are some questions which can be used to help clients discover how a problem has interfered with or influenced their life:

'When and how did the problem first gain a foothold in your life?'

'How has the problem restricted your life?'

'How does the problem manage to trick you into letting it control you?'

'What is the worst thing that the problem has done to your life?'

'When you try to get on top of the problem what does it do to hook you back in?'

'How is the problem stopping you from doing what you'd like to be doing?'

'How is the problem holding you back?'

'What is maintaining the problem now?'

These questions help the client to recognise that they can separate the problem from themselves and that because the problem has an entity of its own they can, if they wish, control or manage it.

The following questions can help the client to discover when and how they have been able to overcome the problem in the past:

'Can you recall some occasions when you have prevented the problem from influencing your life?'

'How did you restrict the problem's influence on these occasions?'

'What have you noticed about yourself that has made you think that you might be able to overcome the problem?'

'What retaliatory measures could the problem use to try to put you back where it wants you?'

'What would the problem do as a last desperate measure if you continue to become stronger and more independent?'

Goaling

'Goaling' is a word that has been coined by solution-focused counsellors. Goaling is a process that changes and broadens the client's perceptions with a view to finding solutions. While goaling the counsellor attempts to help the client to formulate clear, concrete goals. However, the goaling process does not always result in achieving a specific goal. When goaling, the following types of question are commonly used:

• scaling questions

- miracle questions
- goal-oriented questions.

Scaling questions have been described previously. Miracle questions are used to help the client begin to find hypothetical solutions to the problems they are experiencing. Typical miracle questions are:

'If a miracle happened and the problem was solved, what would you be doing differently?'

'If things changed miraculously, what would life be like?'

This type of question appeals to many clients because it lets them use their imagination to explore what would be different if their situation changed for the better. As a result of thinking about ways in which things might change, they are likely to explore new ideas that might be useful in helping them to make changes.

Goal-oriented questions are direct questions and are similar in some ways to exception-oriented questions because they invite exploration of ways in which things could be different. They help the client identify broad changes which they might like to make. In exploring how things could be different, goal-oriented questions invite the client to look ahead to the future. Examples of goal-oriented questions are:

'What do you think your life would be like if you didn't get angry?'

'How would you know that you had resolved this problem?'

'Can you tell me what your life would be like, and what sort of things you would be doing, if you were no longer feeling miserable?'

'If you had a particular goal that you wanted to achieve with regard to . . ., what would it be?'

'How would you like things to be?'

Sometimes formulating clear, concrete goals might involve the counsellor helping the client to modify goals which are impractical because they are too idealistic. To help the client identify achievable goals the counsellor may invite the client to think about discrete steps which need to be taken in order to achieve the desired goal. For example, imagine a client who says, 'I want to feel happy'. In this case the counsellor might ask the client to describe in detail what they would be doing if they were happy. In response the client might say, 'I would be having dinner with my partner on my own'. Having identified this the client may decide that a goal might be to ensure that they have times when they can have dinner with their partner on their own.

Some useful questions to ask the client to help formulate future life goals might be:

'What will the future look like without the problem?'

'If you were successful what would you be doing differently?'

'If the same situation arises during the coming weeks what do you think you will do?'

Goal-oriented questions can also identify perceived restraints which, in the client's mind, interfere with their ability to achieve particular goals. They help the client to identify ways to overcome these restraints. Examples are:

'What stops you from achieving your goal?'

'What would you need to do to achieve your goal?'

Learning summary

- The solution-focused approach to counselling emphasises:
  - a respectful partnership between the client and counsellor
  - strengths and resources of the client
  - an optimistic view about the future.
- Solution-focused counselling emphasises the importance of a conversational process that intentionally makes use of language.
- The counsellor's task is to channel the flow of the conversation, identifying the client's goals and identifying exceptions to the current difficulty, rather than focusing on the problem.
- Well-formed goals are:
  - concrete and action-oriented
  - achievable by the client
  - the client's choice and in the client's language
  - goals that make use of the client's resources.

Further reading

De Jong, P. & Berg, I. K. 1998, *Interviewing for Solutions*, Brooks/Cole, Pacific Grove.

de Shazer, S. 1988, *Clues: Investigating Solutions in Brief Therapy*, Norton, New York.

de Shazer, S. 1991, *Putting Difference to Work*, Norton, New York.
Erickson, M. 1976, *Hypnotic Realities: The Induction of Clinical Hypnosis and Forms of Indirect Suggestion*, Irvington, New York.
Hoyt, M. F. (ed.) 1988, *Constructive Therapies*, Guilford, New York.
O'Connell, B. 1998, *Solution Focused Therapy*, Sage, London.
Walter, J. & Peller, J. 1992, *Becoming Solution Focused in Brief Therapy*, Bruner/Mazel, New York.

chapter 24

Narrative therapy

In the last chapter we discussed solution-focused counselling. In this chapter we will give a brief overview of another post-modern approach: narrative therapy. As you read this chapter you will recognise that there are some similarities between solution-focused counselling and narrative therapy. Additionally, you may notice that there are some fundamental and important differences.

In this book we have attempted to avoid the use of jargon. However, narrative therapy does have a language of its own and involves the use of some words which are not commonly understood but have particular meaning for narrative therapists. We will define these words in the following discussion and italicise them when we first use them so that they are recognised as being specific to narrative therapy.

It is important to recognise that counsellors who use narrative therapy are working in a very specific way that is based on a particular and well-defined belief system. The narrative therapy style of counselling is quite different from the styles of counselling described in the earlier parts of this book. However, an eclectic counsellor may be able to introduce some narrative therapy ideas into more traditional counselling methods. Readers who are interested in the ideas on which narrative therapy is based may wish to learn more by consulting the books referred to at the end of this chapter. In order to learn to be an effective narrative therapist, counsellors need to attend a practical training course run by an experienced practitioner.

Narrative therapists assume that everyone has stories which describe themselves and their lives. They also believe that sometimes these stories are unhelpful and instead of enabling the person to live a satisfying life, the stories that they live out cause problems for them. The narrative therapist's approach is to help the person to replace problem stories with other more useful stories. To use narrative therapy language, the therapist helps a person to *deconstruct* problematic and unhelpful stories and then to *reconstruct* more useful stories about themselves and their lives. These more useful stories are referred to as *preferred stories.*

The narrative perspective suggests that human beings try to make sense of their lives by interpreting their experiences as they live their lives. Each experience is interpreted in the context of the person's stories. As the person interprets each life experience, their stories, which grew out of similar past experiences, will be reinforced and thus strengthened. Using narrative therapy language, new experiences *thicken* the person's stories. Consequently the interpretation of each experience will contribute to thickening the person's stories and these stories will determine how each new experience is interpreted.

The narrative perspective suggests that to use the narrative therapy approach we, as counsellors, must first acknowledge and accept that it is the stories that people have constructed about their lives that determine how they live their lives. Working from this assumption we are then in a position to help clients continue to build on stories that have been helpful for them or to help them alter the stories that have been problematic so that they can be more useful.

To use the narrative therapy approach to counselling we, as counsellors, need to understand how a person's life stories have been made. Stories are influenced by the culture the person lives in. For a moment consider the way in which people in Western culture make up stories about themselves and their lives. In Western culture there is a widely accepted story about what it means to be a person of worth. This story involves being individualistic and self-actualising. When we tell the story to others we tell it by describing behaviours that fit the story. What we do is to describe things that we have done that demonstrate that we are individualistic and self-actualising. For example, we might describe the way in which we take responsibility for ourselves, pursue activities that are in our best interests, own our own feelings, do not blame others for our mistakes, and set and achieve our goals. Additionally, the story will be influenced by our gender, family values, and socio-economic position.

We all have more than one story about our lives. For example, we have stories about ourselves like the one described above, and we also have stories about our desires, our relationships, our work, our achievements and our failures. The way we, and our clients, have developed these stories is determined by how we have linked certain experiences together and how we have interpreted them. The resulting stories about our lives influence the way in which we live out our lives. In narrative therapy language they are referred to as *dominant stories*.

Narrative therapists believe that people select out certain experiences as important because these experiences fit with their dominant story. This means that these experiences are *privileged* over others and are elevated in their significance over other experiences that do not fit the dominant story. As more and more experiences are selected and gathered into the dominant story the story gains richness and, in narrative therapy language, *thickens*. You will notice that this process applies to both stories that are positive and stories that are negative or problematic.

Narrative therapy is not seen as a process of discovering the true feelings of a person, the truth about who people are, or about fixing a particular deficit or problem. Rather, narrative therapy is seen as an exploration of how people construct meanings about themselves and their relationships. The task of the narrative counsellor is to help the client *deconstruct* old problematic and unhelpful stories and *reconstruct* preferred stories about themselves and their lives (Morgan 2000; Parry & Doan 1994; White & Epston 1990).

In narrative therapy it is helpful to follow a process, which generally progresses through the following stages:
- listening to and understanding the client's current story
- deconstructing problem stories
- re-storying
- sustaining change.

These stages will now be discussed.

Listening to and understanding the client's current story

When listening to the client's current story the counsellor must pay attention to the experiences that the client has chosen in order to develop their story. Clients will gather together many experiences from the past as well as the present to form their dominant story. The counsellor might also enquire about how culture has played a role in the formation of the problem by asking questions such as, 'Do you think the problem has influenced others in your family, or your friends, or only you?' The dominant story will usually contain within it a description of the problem which has brought the client to counselling. While listening to the client's current story, the counsellor will discover what the client sees as their preferred ways of living and interacting with others. The narrative therapist then uses this information to help the client to build what in narrative therapy language is referred to as a *preferred alternative story*.

For example a client who has a problem in forming lasting relationships might come to counselling. The client's dominant story might be as follows:

> *'I'm someone who is not able to get a partner. Other people see me as superficial. I am unattractive and not skilled at connecting with others. I believe that lasting relationships only happen if a person is consistently nice.'*

The narrative counsellor's role is to help the client to deconstruct this story and to reconstruct a new and preferred story. As a result of counselling the client might realise that there had been times when they had been able to develop a relationship for a while. The preferred story might be as follows:

> *'I'm a person who is particular about the type of person I want to spend time with and I believe that it is important for me to take time to get to know someone rather than to rush in.'*

Alternative stories

The client's problem story will usually be limited in focus so that other more useful alternative stories are blocked. The person's life experience is consequently repeatedly interpreted in terms of the dominant problematic story. As a consequence, the problem story usually disempowers clients by limiting their ability to see things in a different light.

Unique outcomes

In order to help the client to construct an alternative preferred story, the first thing the counsellor does is to try to discover any times when the client has not been influenced by the problem story. For example, imagine a client whose problem story involves a perceived inability to control angry outbursts which are damaging relationships. In this case the counsellor might ask, 'Have their been any times when you have felt angry but not had an angry outburst?' You may notice that this question is similar to a question which a solution-focused counsellor might use to discover exceptions (see Chapter 23). The counsellor might then ask, 'In that situation how did you manage not to have an angry outburst?' In response the client might say, 'Well, the children were around and I didn't think it was appropriate for them to see me explode.' In narrative therapy language, this exception to problematic behaviour occurring is referred to as *a unique outcome.*

The narrative therapist would then focus on the client's respect for children and would encourage the client to incorporate this quality (respect for children) into a story which would shift the client's perception of themselves as an angry person, to a perception of themselves as a respectful person. Thus, a new story would be created which would describe a preferred way of living and being.

As explained, it is the counsellor's task to seek out and identify experiences in the client's life that will help create stories that reflect contradictions or exceptions to the dominant story. These contradictions or exceptions which are referred to as unique outcomes may involve a plan, action, feeling, statement, quality, desire, dream, thought, belief, ability or commitment that the client may have had at the time when they would usually have been driven by their dominant story. In the example above the unique outcome was the absence of an angry outburst and this involved a belief that it is inappropriate to explode in front of children. Understanding what the unique outcome means to the client can help the alternative story to emerge. It is important to ask whether unique outcomes are preferred or not. The counsellor needs to work with the client to assemble as many unique outcomes as possible. In doing this there is less chance that the client can dismiss the unique outcomes as accidental. Alternative stories are created by linking unique outcomes into a coherent sequence over time.

Deconstructing problem stories

Prior to this stage the counsellor's intention has been to gain an understanding of the client's problem story by being curious. The process then moves into deconstructing problem stories by using what narrative therapists call *deconstructive questioning.* Deconstructive questioning involves a shift from that of understanding the client's story to that of deconstructing those stories.

Questions with a deconstructive intent invite the client to view their stories from a different perspective, to notice how they are constructed, to note how the story limits or constrains them, and to discover that there are other possible stories.

Externalising

Exploring alternative stories and unique outcomes, and using deconstructive questioning, begins the deconstruction process. Additionally, externalising conversations are particularly useful when the problem that the client experiences is all-encompassing and when other stories of self and relationships are not readily available. To accomplish this, inquiry is directed toward the beliefs, practices and feelings that support a particular story. Often externalising conversations involve tracing the influence of the problem in the person's life over time, and understanding the relationship between the client and the problem.

In narrative therapy the goal of externalising is to separate the problem which troubles the client from the client as a person. For example, a client might come to counselling with a story which describes them as an 'anxious person'. By using the strategy of externalising the counsellor describes the anxiety as having a separate and independent existence from the person. Thus, initially the person might say, 'I'm very anxious'. The counsellor might respond to this by asking, 'How does *anxiety* stop you from doing things you want to do?' By asking this question, the client's story changes from 'I am an *anxious person*' to '*anxiety* causes a problem for me'. The person is then in a position to be able to deal with the anxiety rather than seeing the anxiety as a part of self.

It can be seen that the concept of externalising is based on the premise that the problem is the problem, as opposed to the person being seen as the problem. It is important that during externalising conversations, the name of the problem fits the experience of the client, and that the client is actively involved in deciding how the problem is going to be referred to, or named. For example, externalising descriptions might include the following: 'anxiety', 'depression', 'failure', 'anger', 'procrastination', 'drugs' and 'victimisation'.

When externalising, the counsellor attempts to create a different atmosphere around the problem, one in which the client sees their problems as not being intrinsic to them, but as being something that is acting upon them from outside. Externalising conversations make it possible for the client to experience a part of themselves that is separate from the problem. This then opens up new possibilities for action. By externalising, the power is to some extent taken away from the problem and instead the client becomes empowered to control the problem.

Externalising requires a particular shift in the use of language. Rather than using sentences which begin with 'I am . . .' externalising conversations will use sentences beginning with 'The problem . . .'. For example, instead of saying, 'I am anxious' the language changes to 'anxiety gets in my way'. Helpful questions to use in externalising conversations can be found in Chapter 23 under the heading 'externalising the problem'.

Re-storying

The counsellor can help the alternative story to emerge by encouraging the client to describe stories of how they would prefer to be and how they would like to live. This is achieved mainly through asking questions. Narrative counsellors describe this process of questioning as the counsellor remaining in a position of 'not knowing' and the counsellor enquiring curiously about the client's story and the client's preferred story. When listening to the client's preferred story the counsellor will identify possible unique outcomes in the conversation and will invite the client to develop these into alternative stories. This can be done by asking questions such as, 'Did that surprise you?' or, 'Is this something that you want more of in your life?' Questions like these invite clients to consider whether a particular direction is preferred over the direction of the problem story. Sometimes clients will indicate that a particular unique outcome interests them. In such cases the counsellor can ask for more details about the client's activity in the situation as well as the meaning that the client attributes to the activity or behaviour in the situation.

Exploring unique outcomes more fully

Once the narrative counsellor has discovered that there were times when the problem did not occur, the counsellor asks questions to explore in detail what was happening at those times. For example, the counsellor might ask questions like:

'What were you doing at the time when you were able to beat the problem?'
'Can you describe your relationship with your partner at the time when the problem wasn't present?'

'What's your main experience when this problem is not around?'
'What strategies do you know that you have called upon in the
past and that you can also use now?'
'As you win more battles against the problem how will your life
look in the future?'
'Five years from now as you look back, what steps do you think
you will have taken to achieve (the preferred story) in your life
rather than the problem?'

Checking out the meaning of the client's preferred story

The narrative therapist also encourages the client to interpret the meaning
of unique outcomes in terms of a preferred story. For example, the counsellor may ask questions such as the following:

'As you see yourself succeeding more with regard to the
problem how are you thinking of yourself as a person? What do
these successes tell you about yourself?'
'Is this something you have known about yourself for a long
time?'
'If you were to describe your successes to others, how do you
think you might describe yourself?'

Questions asked may concern intentions, desires, preferences, values and
beliefs. Questions such as these frequently provide the most powerful means
of motivating clients to live out a preferred story.

Sustaining change

Once the client has been able to identify an alternative story to the dominant
story, the counsellor can help the client to connect past successes with
expected successes in the future. To do this, the counsellor might ask questions such as:

'Having developed these abilities, what new possibilities might
open up for you in the future?'
'What effect will these strategies have on your management of
the problem in the future?'

As we explained previously, narrative therapists believe that client stories
are influenced by family and culture. If a client's new preferred story is to
endure then the client will need to get support from others including the

family and people from their cultural background. To assist in this process the counsellor might ask questions such as:

'Now that you have made this commitment to yourself, who else would celebrate it with you?'

'If your partner could be here now, what might they say about your strengths in beating this problem?'

Asking these questions helps the client to feel supported by others and as a consequence the client may have more success in living out the preferred story.

As a new and preferred story emerges narrative therapists believe that it is important to assist the client to hold on to, to stay connected with and, in narrative therapy language, to *thicken* the new story. One way of thickening the alternative story involves finding other people, referred to by narrative therapists as *witnesses*, who will act as listeners to the new story and link their lives in some way to the new story. The witnesses may consist of people, present or absent from the counselling session, real or imaginary, or from the client's past or present. This process is referred to by narrative therapists as *re-membering*.

What witnesses do is to validate the client's experience of change. They do this by confirming that they have noticed particular changes and by drawing attention to instances of change that may not have been noticed by the client. They may also talk about times when they have had similar experiences to those of the client and may offer accounts of how they overcame similar difficulties in their lives. They focus on the client's preferred alternative story and are invited to ask questions or make comments about that story which in turn contribute to a richer description of the client's story.

Learning summary

- Narrative therapy has a language of its own.
- Narrative therapists help their clients to deconstruct problematic and unhelpful stories and then to reconstruct more useful stories about themselves and their lives.
- The narrative therapist listens to, and understands, the client's current story, deconstructs problem stories, uses re-storying and techniques for sustaining change.

- In helping the client to create alternative stories the counsellor looks for unique outcomes—these are times when the client was not influenced by the problem story.
- Narrative therapists use the process of externalising to separate the problem from the person.
- Change is sustained by involving witnesses to the preferred story.

Further reading

Morgan, A. 2000, *What is Narrative Therapy?*, Dulwich Centre Publications, Adelaide.

Parry, A. & Doan, R. E. 1994, *Story Re-visions: Narrative Therapy in the Postmodern World*, Guildford Press, New York.

White, M. 1995, *Re-authoring Lives: Interviews and Essays*, Dulwich Centre Publications, Adelaide.

White, M. & Epston, D. 1990, *Narrative Means to Therapeutic Ends*, Norton, New York.

part **VI**

Dealing with particular problems

This section of the book deals with angry, depressed, grieving and suicidal clients. It is inevitable that before long a new counsellor will find that some clients who come for help fall into these categories. It is important to know your own limitations as a counsellor and to refer such clients to experienced and skilled therapists, after consultation with your supervisor, whenever appropriate. However, the problems dealt with in this part of the book are so common that it is important for new counsellors to have an understanding of useful ways in which to work with such clients.

chapter **25**

Counselling the angry client

Counsellors frequently have to deal with angry clients. Bottled-up anger can be very destructive and also very dangerous because it may break out at some time or other and the client may do injury or damage to another person. Many counsellors, in the early stages of their counselling careers, become quite frightened when clients exhibit even moderate levels of anger. This chapter has been included to provide new counsellors with some practical ideas about how to deal with angry clients in cases where it is not considered necessary to refer them to more experienced counsellors.

Angry clients need to be able to dissipate their anger and then to change some of their thinking patterns and behaviours, if they are to feel better. We will discuss two different and complementary ways of helping clients to dissipate anger. One way is to encourage them to release their anger verbally in the safety of the counselling environment, and the other is to teach relaxation (see Chapter 29). We will also consider ways to help clients to think and behave differently, so that hopefully they can deal with anger more constructively in the future.

Helping clients recognise and express anger

Clients who are not dangerous or violent can be allowed to recognise and express anger verbally in the counselling room. However, if an inexperienced counsellor suspects that a client might have a potential for violence, the client should be referred to a suitably qualified and experienced therapist.

When a client starts to express anger use the normal reflective methods if you wish. However, if the level of anger starts to rise then it's sensible for you, the counsellor, to take control and to ensure that the anger is directed away from yourself. As a counsellor, do not allow the client's anger to rise significantly while they are talking directly to you, or you may end up feeling tense yourself. Instead, protect yourself by using a method borrowed from Gestalt therapy (if you want to learn more about Gestalt therapy read Clarkson (2000) or O'Leary (1992) and if you like what you read, enrol in a Gestalt therapy training course after you have completed your basic counsellor training). The method is as follows.

Use of the empty chair

Start by asking the client, 'Who are you most angry with?' Next, place an empty chair facing the client and a metre or two away from them. Tell the client to imagine that the person who is the target of the anger is sitting in the empty chair. Say to the client something like, 'I don't want to be the recipient of your anger, so I don't want you to tell me how angry you are; rather I'd like you to talk to the imaginary person who is sitting in that empty chair, about your angry feelings towards him or her.' Preferably you should now stand beside your client and join them in facing the empty chair. You can then 'coach' the client in their expression of anger towards the imagined person. For example, if the client starts saying, 'Well, actually I'm very angry with Fred, because Fred has consistently offended me with his behaviour', then, as counsellor, you can say yourself, '*I'm* very angry with you, Fred, because you've consistently behaved badly.' The client will then pick up the way in which they are expected to address the imagined person on the empty chair instead of talking to you, and they can then be encouraged to express the anger openly and fully. This method is useful for the client as it enables them to verbalise the anger, and avoids a situation where the counsellor becomes the recipient of the anger, because the counsellor is standing beside and joining with the client. If this method appeals to you, then after completion of your basic counsellor training, you may wish to train as a Gestalt therapist and learn other powerful techniques for enabling clients to release their anger.

Warning!

Remember that some clients have great difficulty in controlling inappropriately high levels of anger. Among these are people who perpetrate violence against spouses, others, children, and/or property. They must be referred to skilled psychotherapists and are not suitable clients for a new counsellor. Moreover, rather than getting in touch with and expressing their anger they need to learn ways to manage and to control it.

Helping the client to change thoughts and behaviours

Once counselling has been effective in enabling a client's high anger level to moderate, the next stage is to teach the client how to deal with anger in the future. You may find it useful to give your client a copy of the chart shown in Figure 25.1 and discuss it during a counselling session.

Although the chart is fairly self-explanatory, it can be useful to work through it step by step. The first step is for the client to learn to recognise physiological cues. When we start to get angry, things happen to our bodies. What happens in your body when you are starting to get angry? We are all different, some people will notice their heart rate increase, others will breathe more rapidly, they may start to sweat, their muscles might tighten up, or they might have an uncomfortable feeling in their stomach. Some people freeze on the spot and feel their hair standing on end. Because we are all different, each individual needs to identify for themselves what happens to them physiologically when they start to get angry. Once a client has learnt to recognise the physiological symptoms that occur as their anger starts to rise, they can use these as cues to indicate that action is required to take control of the anger. In fact, they have a choice, they can either let the anger take control of them and allow an angry outburst to occur, or they can decide to take control of the anger, stop and respond differently. At times it may be better to allow controlled angry outbursts to occur, rather than to bottle up the emotion. Clearly, uncontrolled angry outbursts are dangerous, but letting off steam by occasionally having small controlled outbursts does enable anger to be dissipated. Unfortunately, people who continually behave angrily are certain to damage their relationships with others.

Thought-stopping

The alternative to having an angry outburst is for the client to recognise the physiological cues that indicate a rise in anger and immediately to say 'STOP' sharply but silently to interrupt their thoughts. The method is called thought-stopping. Some counsellors demonstrate thought-stopping by getting their clients to shut their eyes and to take time to imagine a scene that would make

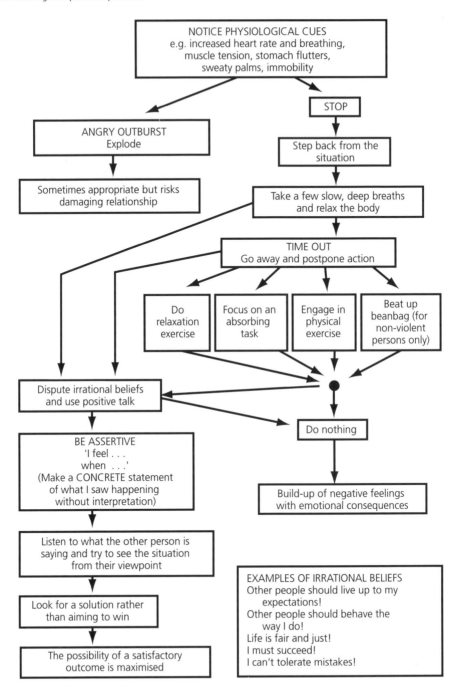

Figure 25.1 *Anger control flow chart*

them angry. When the client is concentrating on that scene, still with their eyes closed, the counsellor slams a book down on the desk and shouts 'STOP'. The sudden impact is almost certain to stop the client in their tracks. In fact, it would give the client such a fright that we do not use this method ourselves for fear of unpleasant consequences! However, providing the client does not suffer a heart attack or some other undesirable consequence, this method does demonstrate effectively to the client that their thoughts can be interrupted instantly, and that they can change the direction of their thoughts if they choose to do so.

An alternative to demonstrating thought-stopping, is to get the client to practice saying 'STOP' and interrupting their thoughts as soon as they recognise that angry thoughts are starting to preoccupy them. Once a client has interrupted the thoughts promoting anger, and thus stopped letting their thoughts hook them into an angry outburst, they can make the choice to step back from the situation, to move back in their imagination by 10 metres, so that they are, in effect, looking at themselves and their situation from a distant vantage point. They can then, if they choose, take a few slow, deep breaths and allow the muscles in their body to relax as they would when engaged in a relaxation exercise (see Chapter 29). As the client takes those few slow, deep breaths, each time they breathe out they can say silently, 'Relax', and allow their body to relax.

Clearly, part of the process of helping clients to learn new ways of dealing with anger involves teaching relaxation. Clients can then use the method described. By learning how to relax and how to recognise their patterns of behaviour, some clients are able to lower the intensity of their emotional feelings in future times of crisis and hence are able to deal with their anger more appropriately (see Chapter 35).

Taking time out

The next stage in the process of anger control involves several options as shown on the chart. The 'time out' block shown gives the client time to cool off and reduce their anger level before deciding what action, if any, to take. The client may literally walk away from the situation and distance themself physically from it. In order to do this, they may need to negotiate with some significant person in their life, so that the person concerned allows them space when they ask for it.

After time out has been used to allow emotions to cool down, the emotional level may be further reduced by doing a relaxation exercise, by becoming fully absorbed in carrying out a task (such as putting full concentration into cooking a meal), or by engaging in physical exercise (like going jogging).

For people who are not violent, and not likely to become violent, another alternative is for them to dissipate their anger by beating up a beanbag, mattress or punching bag. This method can be very helpful for people who do not usually experience high levels of anger, but are angry as a result of a short-term life crisis. However, a word of warning: physically releasing angry feelings in this way is not recommended for clients who are likely to become violent with either people or property. These clients need to learn how to control their anger in other ways and should be referred to specialist counsellors and counselling programs. Teaching them to vent their anger by acting it out physically may be potentially dangerous because it could reinforce violent tendencies.

Making a decision

From this point in the anger control process, the options are either to do nothing further, or to move into the action described in the left-hand column on the anger control chart. Sometimes doing nothing is satisfactory. It may be that as a result of 'time out' followed by one of the anger-dissipating activities, the client will realise that they were overreacting and will feel OK. However, there is a danger in doing nothing at this stage as emotions may still be bottled up with a consequent increased likelihood of a future outburst.

Challenging self-destructive beliefs

If 'action' is the preferred option, then the first step involves disputing irrational beliefs and using positive self-talk. We all at times, when angry, give ourselves messages that are destructive because they make us feel even more unhappy and angry. Such messages have been discussed in Chapter 17 and include statements such as: 'Other people should live up to my expectations', 'Other people should behave the way I do', 'Life is fair and just', 'I must win', 'I must succeed' and 'I can't tolerate mistakes'. Statements like this are absurd. Why should other people live up to my, David's, expectations? Who said that other people should behave the way I do? I wouldn't like other people to tell me how to behave and it is not rational for me to expect them to live up to my expectations. Life is patently not fair or just. Some people have lots of luck, and other people just don't. It isn't necessary or likely that

I will always win. If I win 50 per cent of the time that would be pretty fair, and even that might not happen. So I need to remember that it is not necessary for me to win, it is not necessary for me to succeed every time, and I can, if I wish, choose to tolerate other people's mistakes. I can, if I choose, allow other people to behave in ways that are different from the ways in which I would behave myself.

Once I have put aside my irrational beliefs, I can replace them by positive ideas which will help me to feel better. For example, when someone fails to live up to my expectations I could say to myself, 'He doesn't care enough about me to try to please me. I just don't matter to him.' That would be irrational. It is equally likely that the person concerned is just a bit careless. A more positive self-statement would be: 'Maybe that person is naturally careless. His behaviour may have nothing to do with the way he feels about me. For all I know he might think I'm a great guy. What's more, it's not important what he thinks about me, because I know that I'm OK.'

Table 25.1 gives some specific examples of irrational self-statements which are likely to make a person feel angry, together with alternative self-statements which are more likely to have a positive outcome.

Once I have translated the negative, irrational messages that I am giving myself into positive messages, then I am in a situation where I can make other positive choices. I can do nothing, at least for the time being. That is a valid choice and it may be a sensible one. Sometimes it is better to let things cool off before taking action. However, it is important to be sure not to allow negative feelings to build up as a result of inaction. If negative feelings start to build up, then they need to be dealt with and that probably means confronting the person with whom I am annoyed. Where confrontation is the choice, it needs to be done in a way likely to lead to a positive outcome with a minimal risk of damage to the relationship.

Being assertive

Constructive confrontation requires assertive rather than aggressive behaviour. An assertive person has the goal of wanting to be heard, but not the goal of definitely getting all they want. An aggressive person is determined to win at any cost and also is intent on hurting the other person. Assertion involves communicating as an equal. It involves respecting the rights of the other person, and demands that the other person's point of view must be respected. Consequently, two assertive people may well come to the

Table 25.1 *Comparison of anger-producing irrational self-statements with positive self-statements*

Irrational anger-producing self-statement	Equivalent positive self-statement
1. If I don't get him to give me what I want, I'll be humiliated and made to look like a loser.	It's not reasonable to expect that I can make anyone give me what I want. I can feel proud of my ability to ask for what I want and to accept that I may not get it.
2. People should not let me down. When they let me down, I know that they don't respect me enough to want to please me.	I am a worthwhile person. It's not realistic to expect other people to live up to my expectations. When they let me down, it says more about them than me.
3. I can't feel OK unless Bill agrees that I'm right.	I can't control the way Bill thinks. If he's illogical, that's his problem, and I'm not going to make it mine. I'm OK.
4. Mary's behaviour is ruining my life. Unless she starts to do things to please me, I'm going to get very angry.	If my happiness depends on other people's behaviour, I might never be happy. I can be happy if I accept other people, including Mary, the way they are and the way they behave.
5. I've been victimised and that just isn't fair. I've got to get even.	Life often isn't fair and it's unrealistic to expect that it always will be. I can get on with enjoying life, instead of harbouring disturbing thoughts of revenge.

Note: For other examples of irrational beliefs see Chapter 17.

conclusion that they have different opinions. They will, however, respect the right of each other to have a different opinion. It is sufficient for the assertive person to be heard rather than to win an argument by convincing the other person to change their mind. Sometimes I, David, will not be heard and it is not rational of me to expect that the other person will necessarily be capable of hearing me. I can accept being misunderstood if I choose to do so.

One of the best ways to make assertive statements is to use 'I feel . . . when . . .' statements as explained in Chapter 20. An example is, 'I feel frustrated when you interrupt me in the middle of a sentence'. By using the

'I feel' statement, the speaker is owning their feelings rather than blaming the other person, and consequently they are more likely to be heard. After the feeling statement follows a concrete statement about the behaviour that caused the feeling. As explained before, it needs to be an objective statement of behaviour, and not an interpretation of the facts. By contrast with an assertive statement, an aggressive statement would be one that began with the word 'you', and implied blame. For example, I could say, 'You are very rude because you deliberately try to annoy me by interrupting me'. Such a statement implies blame, makes an unjustified interpretation, and is likely to lead to an argument.

Another good way of making an assertive statement is to make a request which might lead to some common agreement. For example, I might say, 'Would you mind waiting until I've finished what I'm saying? If you do that, I'll feel heard and will be more receptive to what you have to say.'

The goal of making assertive statements is to get a positive outcome. After making an assertive statement, the speaker needs to listen carefully to what the other person says in reply, with the intention of hearing and understanding their point of view, rather than with the intention of disputing what they say.

The use of role-playing

A good way of helping a client to practise anger control is by role-playing in front of a video camera. By video recording and role-playing a real situation that recently made the client angry, the client is able to see how other people perceive them. The client can gain if they role-play both themself and the other person. They will need to continually change position and role to do this. A review of the video recording enables the client to see how tempers become inflamed. The counsellor can then coach the client in the anger control methods described, and in particular can teach ways to make assertive rather than aggressive statements.

Remember that very angry clients may be dangerous. As a new counsellor you need to be conscious of the need to consult your supervisor and refer clients to other more experienced and qualified counsellors when necessary.

Externalising anger

A completely different way to deal with anger control is to use the narrative therapy approach of externalising the anger as explained in Chapter 24. The process of externalising separates the anger from the client so that the client perceives the anger as something which they have the power to manage or control rather than the anger being seen as a part of themselves which they are unable to influence. In the narrative therapy approach to anger control it can be useful to explore how anger influences and constrains the client's life. Exceptions can also be explored to discover times when the client is in control so that the client is able to recognise that they can in fact control the anger when they wish. As we have repeatedly suggested, counsellors are all unique individuals, and some may prefer to use the approach described in this chapter whereas others will prefer a narrative therapy approach.

Learning summary

- Refer potentially violent clients to experienced professionals.
- Encourage clients to direct anger to an imagined appropriate target person on an empty chair.
- Encourage the client to verbalise their anger.
- Teach relaxation.
- Teach the client to use the process described by the 'anger control flow chart' (Figure 25.1) starting with the recognition of physiological cues.
- Teach the client how to replace irrational beliefs by positive self-talk, how to be assertive, listen to others, and to look for solutions rather than to try to win.

Further reading

Clarkson, P. 2000, *Gestalt Counselling in Action*, 2nd edn, Sage, London.
Feindler, E. L. & Ecton, R. B. 1986, *Adolescent Anger Control: Cognitive Behavioral Techniques*, Pergamon, New York.
Goldstein, A. P. & Keller, H. R. 1987, *Aggressive Behaviour: Assessment and Intervention*, Pergamon, New York.
O'Leary, E. 1992, *Gestalt Therapy, Theory, Practice and Research*, Chapman & Hall, London.

chapter 26

Counselling the
depressed client

When do you get depressed?
Why do you get depressed?

We all get depressed from time to time. Being depressed some of the time is a normal human condition and as counsellors we are sure to be working regularly with clients who are depressed. Depression only becomes a serious problem when it is either very deep or very prolonged. It is then dangerous and requires specialist treatment, so counsellors need to be aware of this and refer for appropriate professional help when necessary.

There can be many reasons for depression. Some people become depressed as a consequence of what they see as overwhelming pressure in their lives. Others are depressed as a direct result of sickness. People who are unable to meet their own expectations of themselves are usually depressed. Then there are those people whose depression is due to their inability to accept that other people do not live up to their expectations. There are people who are depressed because they are grieving as a consequence of loss, and my guess is that you can think of a range of other circumstances that are likely to produce depression.

It is also important to recognise that there may be organic reasons for depression. Problems with body chemistry, organic problems in the brain and other medical conditions can cause depression.

Use of the normal counselling processes

With many clients the normal counselling processes previously described will produce changes in emotional feelings and thought patterns so that depression lifts. Why then are we writing a special chapter on depression if the normal counselling processes are usually sufficient? We are doing this because for some people who suffer from prolonged depression, a heavy emphasis on the reflective counselling techniques described in the early chapters of this book will not be useful, and may even have a detrimental effect. This is particularly so in cases where the depression does not seem to be related to recent or specific causes.

Generally, when depression can be directly related to the client's personal life and can be attributed to specific life events, personal situations or identifiable crises, it is appropriate to use the counselling techniques previously described. While doing this, it is useful to remember that depression can often be understood in terms of 'blocked anger'.

Depression as blocked anger

When a person suppresses or is unable to recognise anger towards someone else, it is quite likely that they will become depressed.

Can you imagine yourself being very angry with someone but being unable to express that anger? You might be unable to give vent to your anger for a variety of reasons. Maybe you care so much about the person who is the target of your anger that you do not want to hurt them by expressing anger. Perhaps you recognise that really your anger is unjustified, although real. Possibly you have been taught not to blame others or not to express angry feelings. After all, how many times do parents say to children, 'Don't be angry'? Sometimes we parents do this at times when it is appropriate for our children to be angry, and by doing so we encourage our children to block or suppress their legitimate feelings with inevitable negative consequences for themselves.

How are you going to feel if you suppress angry feelings? Probably frustrated. If you are not able to deal with your frustration by letting that anger out, then you are likely to experience feelings of helplessness and depression.

Exploring the possibility of blocked anger

During the counselling process it is often sensible to confront a depressed client with the possibility of anger underpinning the depression. A variety of counsellor responses can be used for raising awareness of underlying anger. Below are some examples:

> 'When you think about what has happened to you, who are you most angry with?'
>
> 'If you weren't depressed, who would you be angry with?'
>
> 'If instead of feeling depressed you felt angry, what would that anger be about?'

Sometimes, the client's response to one of these questions will be to deny that they are angry with anyone or anything, and this may be true. However, it may be that they are unable to get in touch with their anger, if it exists, or that for some reason they don't want to own it. If a counsellor suspects that anger is blocked then it may be useful to give the client a message that implies that it is OK to be angry in the client's particular situation. A counsellor might say, 'If I had experienced what you have experienced I think that I would feel very angry'. This may enable the client to recognise and access anger. If it does, then the empty chair technique described in Chapter 25 can be used so that the client is allowed to express anger verbally in the safety of the counselling environment. Be careful, however, to help your client to recognise appropriate and inappropriate ways of expressing anger.

Sometimes people who have learnt to disown angry feelings will tell you that they are not angry, but instead are just frustrated. There is a thin dividing line between frustration and anger. If a client is frustrated, the approach used for the expression of anger may be equally appropriate in dealing with the frustration.

Often when a depressed client expresses anger, there will be a change in their demeanour with depressed lethargy being replaced by an energised state in which the person becomes more active and looks more in control.

People suffering from depression due to the loss of a relationship are often angry with the person who has walked out of their lives. Appropriate expression of that anger in the therapeutic environment may enable them to deal with it in a constructive way. However, remember that some people have the potential to be dangerous to others (see Chapter 25). These people need to learn to control their anger and should be referred for appropriate professional help for the protection of yourself and others.

Clients who need referral

Counsellors need to be able to identify those clients who need referral for specialist counselling and/or for medical or psychiatric assessment and treatment. Included in this group are people who:

- are so depressed that they are a danger to themselves or others;
- are unable to function satisfactorily in their daily lives due to depression;
- have been depressed for long periods; and
- have no clearly identifiable cause for their depression.

If you are in doubt regarding referral to a suitable professional then we suggest that you talk with your supervisor.

Regardless of the need for referral in cases such as those described above, counsellors working in crisis counselling agencies will frequently become involved in counselling chronically depressed clients. Many of these may be either unwilling to seek specialist treatment or are engaged in long-term psychiatric treatment with little positive effect. We believe that it is appropriate for such people to talk to counsellors from time to time, provided that any other professionals involved are comfortable with that. Certainly, counselling by a skilled counsellor will, at the very least, enable the client to feel that someone cares enough to listen, and there may be other beneficial effects.

Counselling people who suffer from chronic depression

When counsellors are working with clients experiencing long-term depression, the effect of continually reflecting back depressed feelings is likely to do little more than heighten the client's experience of feeling depressed. Unfortunately, this may confirm to the client a belief that they are hopelessly and chronically depressed and are beyond help. To do such a thing is clearly destructive! In dealing with such clients we therefore need to limit our use of reflection and to use a different emphasis in our counselling. This does not mean that we should discard our ideas about the counselling relationship or forget the basic micro-skills. We need all that has previously been learnt, but with a change in emphasis.

We suggest that you might like to refer to the 'Process of a counselling session' chart (Figure 13.1 on page 123). The difference in dealing with chronically depressed clients is that we need to move forward more quickly and decisively from the active listening stage into the facilitating attitude change, options and action stages (see the left-hand side of the chart). By doing this, the emphasis is taken off emotions and replaced by an emphasis on thoughts and behaviours (see the right-hand side of the chart). Thus, rather than accompanying the client on a journey down into depression by reflecting feelings, invite the client to join you on a journey of exploration where together you will explore the influence of thoughts and behaviours on the depression, with some limited but positive goals in mind. In this process the counsellor needs to be more active and confronting then might be the case with clients who are not chronically depressed.

We suggest that when counselling chronically depressed clients, the counsellor may wish to start by attending carefully to the client using active listening to allow the counselling relationship to develop. However, once the client's feelings of depression have been validated by reflection, then it is not wise to continue by reflecting feelings of depression because this will merely accentuate the depressed feelings. Instead, the counsellor may refer to the depression as something to be dealt with, rather like a piece of baggage that can be picked up or put to one side. In this case the counsellor is using a process similar to externalising in narrative therapy (see Chapter 24).

Counselling goals for people who suffer from chronic depression

When counselling someone who is chronically depressed, make a decision about what are realistic counselling goals and what are unrealistic goals. New counsellors sometimes believe that it should be possible, with skill, to help every person who is chronically depressed to feel better. Unfortunately this is unrealistic. However, if counsellors choose suitable goals many people who are chronically depressed can be helped to enjoy a better quality of life. You might like to try to think of some realistic goals yourself before reading our suggestions:

- To help the client to identify what makes them feel better and what makes them feel worse.
- To help the client to recognise that they have choice regarding their current behaviour at any time. For example, the client could choose to do what makes them feel better or what makes them feel worse. They could choose to sit around and do nothing, or they could choose to do something active.
- To encourage the client to focus their mind on what they are actively doing instead of focusing on being depressed.
- To enable the client to take action.

- To enable the client to make a decision to seek appropriate specialist or psychiatric help.
- To enable the client to come to a decision with regard to one of the practical problems in their life.
- To help the client to challenge a self-destructive belief which is making them feel worse.
- To help the client feel a sense of importance because you are listening. (Note that some depressed clients will deny that the counsellor cares because there is a limit to a counsellor's caring. However, as a counsellor you do care enough to listen and you can tell your client that. Be specific though. A statement such as 'I care about you' is likely to be challenged, whereas a statement such as 'I care about you enough to want to listen to you' can't be sensibly challenged.)
- To be able to give the client a positive message about themselves at the end of the counselling session. For example, 'I'm impressed by the way you were able to clearly identify what makes you feel better and what makes you feel worse.'

If you decide that the goals described above might be too difficult to achieve, you could set an easier goal such as:

- My goal will be to listen to this person so that for a time they are not alone but will have my company. (In this case, you are really offering company rather than counselling so you may end up chatting together rather than using counselling skills.)

Even if the previous goals listed are not attainable, this last goal is definitely achievable and therefore realistic. If you decide to try to achieve one of the earlier goals mentioned, we suggest that you may wish to set one goal only because it will be hard for someone who is deeply depressed to find the motivation required to make several choices and take action to carry them out. The nature of depression leads to loss of motivation and consequent inactivity. Unfortunately inactivity reinforces depression which makes it hard for the person concerned to make changes.

Using a different approach

If you are to achieve a selected goal, once you have secured a warm and trusting relationship with the client by using active listening and problem identification, you will need to break the rules you have previously learnt. You will need to take control of the direction of the counselling intervention rather than walking alongside the client. You may also need to temporarily change your counselling style so that you are more confronting, but in a friendly, caring and non-threatening way. As explained, people who are chronically depressed lose their motivation and consequently find it hard to change. They find it hard to identify ways to reduce their pain. However, by confronting with care you may enable a client to explore options and take some positive action.

Encouraging action

It can be useful for a client to be able to recognise any behaviours and situations that make them feel less depressed. If they can discover what they need to do or where they need to go in order to feel less depressed, they may be able to escape from the intensity of their depression for a time. A good approach is to ask the client, 'Was there ever a time when you weren't depressed?' Most people can identify some times in their lives when they enjoyed themselves. If you can find out when those times were for your client, then you may be able to help them discover some way of partially regaining some pleasant experiences.

Remember how difficult it will be for your client to think positively. When we are depressed we all tend to think negatively so don't be too optimistic yourself or you might set yourself up for failure. For example your client might say something like, 'I was only happy while Judith was alive. She's dead now and so my life is meaningless.' If this were to happen then you would need to use your ingenuity to try to discover what it was that Judith did, apart from being present, that helped your client to feel good. The question, 'What sort of things did you do when Judith was around?' might lead to the answer, 'We used to go for long walks in the bush'. You could then explore whether, at the present time, a long walk in the bush would be more or less depressing than not going for a walk.

The question, 'Would that be more or less depressing than doing what you are doing now?', is a smart way of avoiding a 'Yes but . . .', answer. Even so, you might get the answer, 'Yes, but I would still be depressed'. You can agree with your client: 'Yes, you would still be depressed but would you be more depressed or less depressed?' Smile to yourself if you get the answer, 'I'd be just the same, miserably depressed', and change to a less ambitious goal for the session, but do not give up. Remember that this person is in pain and deserves respect and help.

The use of activity

Research over many years has shown that generally people who suffer from depression tend to be less depressed when they are active. This is why occupational therapy is used in psychiatric settings to help the seriously depressed. Even a simple action such as going to have a shower or take a bath can be a useful activity which might temporarily ease the depressed feeling.

Setting time limits

There may be limited value in talking for lengthy periods with people who are chronically depressed. Short interventions tend to be more useful, particularly if they encourage the client to undertake some activity. To encourage activity, remember to reward clients with praise when they do engage in meaningful activity, and when they succeed, for a time, in feeling less depressed.

Because depressed people are often bored and preoccupied with negative thoughts, they may wish to talk at length without purpose and to travel the same road, in their thoughts, over and over again. Because of these tendencies counsellors may need to use good termination skills. A useful way to terminate a counselling session is for the counsellor to be directive in suggesting that the client go to perform a task. For example, the counsellor may say, 'I would like to finish our conversation now and suggest that you might like to go home and prepare a meal for yourself right away. Next time we meet I would like you to tell me whether you felt more or less depressed when you made and ate the meal.' Once again, the suggestion is action-oriented and includes the goal of identifying the usefulness of activity.

Debriefing

Counsellors who work with clients who are depressed, if they join empathically with their clients, will pick up negative and depressed feelings themselves. It is therefore important to debrief and to look after your own needs (see Chapter 38).

Learning summary

- Normal people suffer from depression.
- Sometimes depression results from 'blocked anger'.

- Depression calls for specialist treatment when it is either very deep or prolonged.
- For many depressed clients the normal counselling processes are recommended.
- For chronically depressed clients:
  - continual reflection of feelings can be counter-productive;
  - set goals for the session and take control of the counselling process;
  - be confronting;
  - encourage activity; and
  - keep counselling sessions short and energised.

Further reading

Braiker, H. B. 1998, *Getting Up When You're Feeling Down*, Pocket Books, New York.

Burns, D. 1999, *Feeling Good: The New Mood Therapy*, Avon, New York.

Conroy, D. L. 1991, *Out of the Nightmare: Recovery from Depression and Suicidal Pain*, Liberty, New York.

Craig, K. D. 1995, *Anxiety and Depression in Adults and Children*, Sage, Thousand Oaks.

Gilbert, P. 1992, *Counselling for Depression*, Sage, London.

chapter 27

Grief and loss counselling

We have noticed that a high proportion of client problems are concerned with relationships. Relationship problems fall into four major categories. These are:

1. dysfunctional relationships;
2. failure to form meaningful relationships;
3. lost relationships through death and separation; and
4. negotiating the normal and/or developmental challenges and changes in relationships.

Loss associated with relationships

In each of the categories listed above issues of loss and grief may arise. In dysfunctional relationships there is a loss of expectation that these relationships will be functional and harmonious. People who are unable to form meaningful relationships may have to cope with the loss of their expectations. When couple relationships break up both people need to adjust to the loss of a partner. In the case of married couples there is also the loss of marital status and the loss of the expectation that marriage is for life. If children are involved, then each parent has a loss of support from their spouse in the day-to-day rearing of the children, and usually one parent has a significant loss of contact with the children and so their parental role is greatly diminished.

When relationships are functioning normally new situations will arise from time to time and changes will naturally occur due to changes in roles and developmental stages of the relationship. There is therefore a need to confront the challenges incurred by change, and change often involves loss.

Other losses

Counsellors also hear about many other types of loss; for example the loss of a limb, loss of an internal part of the body, loss of mental functioning due to ageing or brain damage, loss of a job, loss of a home or loss of self-respect.

Helping a person who is grieving

In order to be effective in helping people who are grieving over a loss, counsellors need to understand the process of grieving. There are many books on loss and grief counselling. A selected list of these is provided at the end of this chapter for those who wish to do further reading on the subject.

When counselling somebody who has suffered a loss, or who is grieving, it is important to be able to reassure them that the feelings they are experiencing are normal for a person who is grieving, and that it is normal to take time to grieve. In this regard it may be useful to self-disclose if you yourself have in the past taken time to grieve over a similar loss.

Restricting counsellor self-disclosure

Although at times self-disclosure is appropriate, it should be used sparingly, and never solely to satisfy the counsellor's needs. Before self-disclosing, we suggest that you may wish to examine what is going on within yourself and to make a decision about whether your motive is to satisfy your own needs or is genuinely to help the client. Where self-disclosure is used more than occasionally, its impact is lost, and the counsellor is certainly putting their needs before those of the client.

Disclosure of information about other counsellors or other people is unethical and should never occur in the counselling process. Additionally, it can be most unhelpful for telephone counsellors to self-disclose to regular callers (see Chapter 30) who may gather and distort information about a counselling team to the detriment of both the counselling process and the agency concerned.

Counselling skills to use

When clients are grieving, all the micro-skills previously discussed can be used to allow them to verbalise thoughts and feelings, to experience rather than suppress pain, and to generally explore whatever is happening within themselves as they experience their loss. Additionally, it is useful for a counsellor who is helping a client who has suffered a loss to have an understanding of the process of grieving. This understanding will enable the counsellor to recognise and appreciate the client's experience more fully so that an empathic counselling relationship can be established and maintained.

The stages of grief

People tend to go through a number of stages in the grieving process. For some people these stages follow a particular sequence, but for other people the stages overlap or occur in a different order. Everyone is unique and grieves in a uniquely personal way, so it is inadvisable to try to fit a predetermined grieving pattern onto a client. However, if as a counsellor, you know what the commonly experienced stages in the grieving process are, then you will be better equipped to deal with the grieving person. You will be able to explain to your client that their experiences are not strange or unusual, but are normal for someone who is grieving.

The most important stages of grief in the usual sequence are:

- shock
- denial
- emotional, psychological and physical symptoms
- depression
- guilt
- anger
- idealisation
- realism
- acceptance
- readjustment
- personal growth.

If a person is unable to work through the stages of grief, then they are likely to be stuck in a trough of hopelessness and despair. They may become neurotically obsessed by their loss, and become deeply depressed and possibly suicidal. The following paragraphs explain the stages of grief in more detail.

Shock

Usually, the first stage of grief is shock. This may be particularly severe in cases of sudden loss, or where a person has not been prepared adequately for an expected loss. In this stage the person almost seems to stop functioning, is numb, in a daze and is incapable of doing anything constructive.

Denial

Along with shock, and following on from shock, comes denial. The grieving person can't believe that what has happened is really true.

The denial process can be prolonged for people who separate from a living partner. Very often a rejected partner will deny that the relationship is over, even though the other partner is clearly saying, 'It's finished and I'm not ever going to come back to you'. This is hard for a counsellor to deal with because the grieving person needs to have time to move through the denial stage. Perhaps the most useful approach is to reflect back the client's expectation that their partner may return, and to add to this concrete statements of fact that seem to indicate the opposite. The counsellor might say, for example, 'I get the strong impression from you that you believe that your partner will come back to you. I also notice that she said to you that she would not do that, and that she has rejected all your approaches to her since she left. Do you think that it's possible that she may not come back?' This tentative statement and question enables the client to stay in denial if they need to do that for a while longer, or to move forward. When the client is starting to accept the possibility that the loss may be permanent, it may then be useful to let them know that denial is a normal part of grieving. By doing this they can feel OK about their difficulty in not wanting to accept reality in its entirety.

People who are dying often grieve in anticipation of dying and such people sometimes have real problems with denial. When a person is told that they are dying, they may try to convince themself that what the medical practitioner is telling them is not true. They may look for and try unorthodox methods to find a cure, and may start to bargain with God in an effort to get an extension to life.

Emotional, psychological and physical symptoms

Grieving people experience feelings of depression, despair, hopelessness and worthlessness. Very often they will exhibit symptoms such as insomnia, inability to concentrate, loss of appetite and physical ill-health. This is normal. There is little that the client can do but accept that such symptoms will pass with time as the painfulness of grief diminishes. Naturally if such symptoms are severe or persist, the client should consult with a medical practitioner.

Guilt

Guilt often occurs in the grieving person. A counsellor will frequently hear a client say how guilty they feel because they didn't tell the deceased how much they loved them, didn't tell them how much they cared for them, didn't apologise for something they had done wrong, or didn't make peace over an issue where there had been a disagreement. If, as a counsellor, your clients describe such feelings, allow them to fully explore them.

Anger

Often after shock, denial, depression and guilt, anger follows. Remember though, that the stages often overlap, and sometimes a person will move forward from one stage and then go back to an earlier stage.

In the case of a person who is dying, anger may be directed at the medical practitioners involved. The client may feel that they haven't had satisfactory medical treatment. Maybe they will believe that their illness was diagnosed too late and consequently that it's the doctor's fault that death is inevitable. Similarly, a person who has lost a loved one through illness may blame the medical practitioners who treated the deceased before their death. Additionally, a bereaved person may well experience anger towards the person who has died. They may feel that the deceased person 'had no right to die' and has hurt them by leaving them alone to cope in the world. This may be especially so in cases where the deceased has committed suicide.

Often it is hard for a client to accept that they are capable of being angry towards somebody they loved who has died. This is especially so for children who have lost a parent through death, and not had adequate counselling. They invariably feel guilty and confused by their anger and resentment towards the deceased parent. Without counselling, these feelings may endure for years.

People whose partners have rejected them often become very angry and, while being angry, desperately want to get back into the relationship. They inevitably make it hard for themselves to do this and probably spoil their chances of reconciliation because while saying, 'I love you and I want to be back in a relationship with you', they may also be experiencing anger, and are likely to express it in some way. Thus they give mixed messages to their partner because they are simultaneously giving 'Please come back' messages and angry messages. The anger, of course, can easily be understood as part of the process of grieving.

Sometimes a person who has Christian beliefs and is grieving will feel angry with God, and will blame God for the loss that has occurred. For deeply religious people this may cause feelings of extreme guilt. When counselling such people a counsellor can explain that it is normal to experience anger in grief. The counsellor might also ask the client whether they think that God is quite capable of accepting, forgiving and loving someone who is angry with Him. When counselling clients who have faith in other religions similar issues may arise. Here it is important for the counsellor to gain sufficient understanding of the client's beliefs to be helpful (see Chapter 34 regarding cultural issues).

Idealisation

Idealisation often follows the angry stage of grieving. It is very common for people who have suffered loss through death or separation to idealise the lost partner. The grieving person temporarily forgets any faults or negative characteristics of the deceased and remembers only an ideal person. They remember everything positive that the deceased did and convince themself that they loved them without reservation, and never had any negative feelings towards them. This is idealisation, and once again it is normal. It takes time for a person to move through idealisation and the counsellor needs to be careful not to try to move the client forward too quickly, but rather to let the grieving process occur naturally. When it is appropriate, a counsellor may ask tentatively whether the lost person had any bad points, any faults, and whether they sometimes made mistakes. Slowly the realisation will dawn that yes, there were polarities in the deceased person. The deceased was a real person, a human being with both strengths and weaknesses.

Acceptance, readjustment and personal growth

The client will hopefully, in time, come to terms with their grief and start to accept the reality of their loss. They will start to be more realistic about the person they have lost, and to accept the loss as a permanent reality. They are then free to move forward and to create a new life as an individual. This may be scary for some clients, particularly for those who were heavily dependent on the relationship which is now lost. In this stage of the grieving process the client needs to be active rather than passive, to try new experiences and thus to experience personal growth. New experiences, by their very nature, involve some degree of risk, and so may understandably cause the client to be apprehensive. Taking risks can be frightening and can also be exciting. Reframing 'risk taking' as 'exciting' may be helpful.

Allowing the grieving process to occur

Finally, as a counsellor, do not try to calm or soothe the grieving person. Do not try to cheer them up or help them to contain their sadness and fears. Instead, help them to express emotions freely, to cry if they wish, and to grieve fully. It is only when grief endures for an excessively long period that it becomes maladaptive. In such cases, clearly professional help from an experienced counsellor, psychologist or psychiatrist is required. Once again, know the limits of your own competence, and refer clients to others more qualified and experienced than yourself when appropriate.

Learning summary

- People grieve for lost expectations, relationships, bodily functions, jobs and losses of all kinds.
- Normal stages of grief include shock, denial, psychological and somatic symptoms, depression, guilt, anger, idealisation, realism, acceptance, readjustment and personal growth.
- It's usually a mistake to try to calm or soothe a grieving person. Encouraging free expression of emotions is more therapeutic.

Further reading

al Qadhi, S. 1996, *Managing Death and Bereavement: A Framework for Caring Organisations*, Policy Press, Bristol.

Attig, T. 1996, *How We Grieve: Relearning the World*, Oxford University Press, Oxford.

Bright, R. 1996, *Grief and Powerlessness: Helping People Regain Control of Their Lives*, Jessica Kingsley, London.

Corr, C. A., Nabe, C. M. & Corr, D. M. 1997, *Death and Dying, Life and Living*, Brooks/Cole, Pacific Grove.

Humphrey, G. M. & Zimpfer, D. G. 1996, *Counselling for Grief and Bereavement*, Sage, London.

chapter 28

Counselling the suicidal client

David's initial training as a counsellor was with a crisis telephone counselling agency. As a new telephone counsellor, his greatest fear was that he might get a call from a suicidal person. Later, he continued to be anxious when counselling suicidal clients. We believe that for most, if not all, counsellors such counselling is stressful. However, hotline counselling services frequently get calls from people who are contemplating suicide and sometimes such callers have already overdosed on prescribed pills before ringing for help.

Ethical issues

There are ethical issues involved when dealing with suicidal people, and before choosing strategies that are acceptable for you, as a counsellor, you may need to clarify your own values with regard to suicide. As counsellors, it is desirable that, if possible, we do not impose our own values on our clients. However, we do need to be congruent and genuine, so each of us needs to do whatever is necessary to satisfy our own conscience. In addition, we need to be aware of any legal obligations and the legal implications of our actions. We must remember that we owe a duty of care to the client and that we need to respect the policies of the agency for which we work. If there are internal conflicts for us when dealing with suicidal clients, then we need to resolve these for both our own and the client's wellbeing.

Does a person have the right to take their own life if they choose to do so? Your answer to this question may differ from ours, and our answers may differ from the client's. We suggest that you discuss this question in depth with your training group if you are in one, or with your supervisor, so that you have a clear idea of your own attitudes and beliefs regarding suicide and of your supervisor's expectations. You will then be better equipped to deal with the suicidal client.

Some counsellors believe that a person has the right to kill themself if, after careful consideration, they choose to do so. Others strongly oppose this view and believe that firm intervention is justifiable and necessary to prevent suicide from occurring. Many counsellors believe that a person who is contemplating suicide may be temporarily emotionally disturbed and not capable of making a rational decision at that time. This belief is reinforced by experiences with clients who were suicidal and then later have thanked the counsellor, because they have found new meaning and satisfaction in their lives. Consequently, some counsellors see the need for firm intervention, involuntary hospitalisation and subsequent psychiatric treatment where other options fail. Clearly, there are duty of care issues involved when making the relevant decisions. Whatever your view, suicide involves a one-way journey and suicidal clients need to be taken seriously. Remember that people who repeatedly make suicide attempts often succeed in killing themselves eventually. Their cry for help needs to be heard before it is too late.

Reasons for contemplating suicide

People who are considering suicide broadly fall into four categories although three of these overlap to some extent.

The first category comprises people whose quality of life is terrible, and who see little or no possibility for improvement. Included in this category are people who are chronically ill, in chronic pain, are seriously disabled, or are in extreme poverty with little possibility of changing their situations. Such people are often severely depressed and are seriously at risk of killing themselves because they can see little reason for living. This is particularly so if they are alone and do not have adequate social support systems.

The second category includes people who have experienced a recent trauma. These people are very much at risk around their time of crisis. Included in this category are people who have suffered losses such as those described in Chapter 27.

The third category comprises people who use suicidal talk or suicidal behaviour as a last resort in an attempt to get others to hear or respond to their pain. Sometimes their goal is to manipulate the behaviour of others. They are still genuinely at risk, but their motivation is different. They often have considerable ambivalence towards dying and may not really want to die. Some people in this category are openly manipulative and, for example, might say to a spouse who has left them, 'Come back to me or I will kill myself'.

The fourth category includes people who are having a psychotic episode and may be hearing voices that tell them to kill themselves. Clearly, these people need urgent psychiatric help.

We have drawn up a list of possible reasons why a person might contemplate or talk about the possibility of suicide. As you read the list you may wish to think about whether there might be other reasons which have not been included in this list:

1. Because they despair of their situation and are unable to see an alternative solution to their problems which seem to them to be unsolvable, intolerable and inescapable.
2. Because they are emotionally disturbed, are afraid that they may commit suicide, and want to be stopped.
3. To make a statement.
4. As a way of hurting others: an ultimate expression of anger.
5. To make a last-ditch effort to draw attention to a seemingly impossible situation, when other methods have failed.
6. To manipulate someone else.
7. Because they have positively decided to commit suicide, want to do it, and want other people to understand the reasons for the proposed action.
8. To be in contact with another human being prior to, or while, dying.
9. To say 'Goodbye', as preparation for death.
10. Because the person is having a psychotic episode and is hearing voices telling them to kill themselves.

Assessment of risk of suicide

Any client who says that life is not worth living may be at some level of risk. However, many people who have no intention of killing themselves experience times when they despair and start to question the value of their lives. A difficulty for counsellors is to determine the level of risk for a particular client. It is here that experience can be helpful in estimating level of risk, in deciding whether action needs to be taken or not, and in choosing the action to take if action is needed. Consequently, new counsellors need to consult with their supervisors.

There are some factors that are commonly considered in the relevant literature to be useful in determining level of risk (see the further reading suggested at the end of this chapter). A number of risk factors will now be discussed.

Gender and ethnicity

Although women attempt suicide more often than men, males are associated with higher risk. This is because males are more often successful in completing suicide than females. In particular Aboriginal males are associated with high risk.

Age

Suicide is more likely to occur in the young and old, with the risk being higher in people up to the age of 18 years and above 45.

Intense and/or frequent thoughts of suicide

Whenever a person thinks of suicide it is wise to assume that there is some level of risk. However, if the thoughts are persistent and/or strong with little ambivalence, risk is increased.

Warning signals

People who commit suicide have often given out warning signals over a period of time. Unfortunately sometimes these are disregarded because they may have been given many times and been seen incorrectly as threats that will not be carried out.

Having a suicide plan

If a realistic plan for committing suicide has been developed, then clearly the person has moved beyond vague thoughts that life is not worth living and there is a risk that the plan may be carried out.

Choice of a lethal method

Some methods of committing suicide are more likely to reach completion than others because they are quick and/or provide little opportunity for withdrawal if the person concerned has a change of mind as death approaches. Examples are when a person uses a gun or jumps off a high building.

Availability of method

Risk is higher if the person already has the means to carry out the plan. For example if a person has a loaded gun, or enough pills to cause death, then the plan may be carried out.

Difficulty of rescue

Risk is increased in cases where it would be difficult for others to intervene and prevent the suicide attempt. Examples are where a person is in an isolated place or when the location is unknown or when someone has climbed a structure, making it difficult for others to follow.

Being alone and having lack of support

People who are alone, single or separated, and believe that no-one cares for them are vulnerable to depression and suicidal thoughts and action. It may also be easier for them to carry out a suicidal plan without interference.

Previous attempts

Previous attempts are an indication of increased risk. This is particularly so if the attempts have been frequent, are recent and have been serious.

A friend or family member has died or suicided

Risk of suicide is increased where a family member, close friend, colleague or peer suicided. Additionally there may be risk where a loved one or pet has died.

Listening to songs about death

Some people, particularly the younger members of society, tend to listen obsessively to songs about death, dying and suicide. This increases risk.

Depression

People who are depressed, feel hopeless, helpless or in despair are at risk. This is particularly so with severe depression where there may be symptoms such as loss of sleep, or an eating disturbance.

Psychiatric history

Psychiatric illness or history is another indication of increased risk.

Loss of rational thinking

Loss of rational thinking can occur for a variety of reasons. People who have been traumatised, are under the influence of alcohol or drugs, are suffering from dementia or have a psychiatric disorder may not be capable of thinking rationally. They therefore present increased risk and there are clear duties of care for the counsellor.

Unexplained improvement

Someone who has been exhibiting severely depressed feelings with suicidal thoughts and then suddenly changes to display a calmness and sense of satisfaction for no recognisable reason may be at very high risk. The person may have completed preparations for suicide and have a sense of relief at the thought of impending relief from ongoing pain. By misleading the counsellor into thinking that everything is now OK, they can effectively mislead the counsellor so that preventative action is not taken.

Giving away possessions and finalising affairs

Behaviours such as giving away personal possessions, making a new will or terminating a lease may be indication that the person is preparing for suicide and at high risk.

Medical problems

Medical problems which severely interfere with quality of life, are painful or are life-threatening increase the risk of suicide. Chronic illness with little perceived hope of a cure or respite may increase a person's desire to terminate life. Here, there are both values and duty of care issues, as some people firmly believe that euthanasia is morally justifiable while others strongly disagree.

Substance abuse

Excessive use of alcohol or drugs, both illegal and legally prescribed, raises the suicide risk. Certainly, alcohol or other substance abuse is associated with completed suicides.

Relationship problems

People who believe that they are locked in to highly dysfunctional relationships and cannot leave are at increased risk. Similarly, there may be risks for people whose relationships are breaking up, who are separating or separated, and for those who are going through the process of divorce. When relationships change through, for example, remarriage, moving into a new step-family, having a new child in the family or children leaving the family, there may be an increased risk. Additionally, some people worry excessively and start to despair when a family member is sick or not coping.

Trauma, loss or significant life changing events

Suicidal thoughts and tendencies may occur as a consequence of significant traumas. For example, if a person's home or business is destroyed by fire, the trauma may push that person into deep depression and lead to suicidal thoughts and behaviour.

Changes in lifestyle and/or routine

Many people find it difficult to adjust to changes in their lifestyle or routine, so times of change can precipitate suicidal thoughts and increased risk. Examples are when a person changes job, school or their place of residence. This may be particularly relevant when a person moves to a new locality and may lose access to long-term friends.

Financial problems

Issues involving poverty, unemployment and financial difficulties, where the person concerned is depressed and feeling helpless to change the situation, lead to an increased risk. Important examples are bankruptcy and cases where a person loses a business or home.

Trauma and abuse

Traumatic events and the experience of abuse or perceived abuse, both in the past and present, may contribute to suicide risk. This includes emotional, physical, sexual and social abuse.

Loss

All losses of importance contribute to suicide risk. Examples include loss of job, employment opportunities, business, home, possessions, self-esteem and loss of role. People who experience failure either at work or academically or believe that they have failed others are likely to suffer loss of self-esteem.

The risk factors which have been discussed are included in Table 28.1. This table may be photocopied for personal use and used as an aid in identifying risk factors when counselling clients with suicidal thoughts and/or

Table 28.1 *Assessment of suicide risk*

Risk factors—tick boxes where risk is indicated

☐ Gender
☐ Age
☐ Ethnic background

☐ Intense and/or frequent
thoughts of suicide
☐ Warning signals given out over a
period of time
☐ Has a suicide plan
☐ Choice of a lethal method
☐ Availability of method
☐ Difficulty of rescue
☐ Is isolated or alone
☐ Lack of support

☐ Previous suicide attempts
☐ A friend, peer, colleague or
family member has suicided
☐ Listening obsessively to songs
about death, dying or suicide
☐ Death of loved one, friend or pet

☐ Depression
☐ Psychiatric illness or history
☐ Loss of rational thinking

☐ Unexplained improvement
☐ Giving away possessions
☐ Finalising affairs

☐ Relationship highly dysfunctional
☐ Relationship break up,
separation or divorce
☐ Relationship changes—
remarriage, new step-family,
addition of new child, children
leaving family
☐ Relationship worries—fear of
losing a family member or partner or that someone is not coping

☐ Medical problems

☐ Alcohol and/or drug abuse

☐ Significant life-changing events
☐ Change in lifestyle and/or
routine
☐ Change in job, school or house
locality

☐ Financial problems
☐ Socio-economic situation

☐ Trauma
☐ Abuse or perceived abuse—
emotional, physical, sexual or
social abuse in the past or
present

☐ Loss of employment or
employment opportunities
☐ Loss of business, home or
possessions
☐ Loss of self-esteem—feeling a
failure at work or
academically—or belief that
others have been let down
☐ Loss of role

☐ Other factors not listed

_____

_____

_____

_____

_____

_____

tendencies. However, it must be remembered that there is no precise formula for assessing risk because we human beings are each unique possessing our own individual qualities. All talk of suicide needs to be taken seriously and appropriate help sought where necessary.

Counselling strategies

Perhaps the biggest problem for a new counsellor in dealing with suicidal clients is the counsellor's own anxiety. Sometimes new counsellors try to deflect clients away from suicidal talk rather than encouraging them to bring their self-destructive thoughts out into the open and deal with them appropriately. Unfortunately, such avoidance of the issue may increase the likelihood of a suicide attempt.

Bring suicidal thoughts into the open

Whenever counselling a depressed or anxious client, counsellors need to look for the smallest clues that might suggest that the client is contemplating suicide. Clients are often reluctant to say, 'I would like to kill myself'. They tend instead to be less specific and to make statements such as, 'I don't enjoy life any more', or 'I'm fed up with living'. When a client makes a statement such as this it is sensible for the counsellor to be direct, and ask the client, 'Are you thinking of killing yourself?' In this way, suicidal thoughts are brought out into the open and can be dealt with appropriately. We need to remember that a significant proportion of people are at some times in their lives ambivalent about wanting to live and that many consider the possibility of committing suicide before rejecting it.

Deal with your own feelings

You will be a very unusual person indeed if your hair doesn't stand on end the first time that a client tells you that they intend to kill themselves. As a counsellor, allow yourself to experience your feelings and then you will be able to decide what to do about them. One thing that you can do is to give yourself new messages, after discarding the irrational messages that may be contributing to your tension. Table 28.2 presents some typical irrational and alternative rational self-statements for the situation.

Challenge your irrational self-statements, and if your feelings of tension don't subside then share them with the client. For example, you might say: 'I feel really uptight because I know that you are thinking of killing yourself.

Table 28.2 *Comparison between irrational and rational self-statements for counsellors dealing with suicidal clients*

Irrational self-statement	Rational self-statement
I am personally responsible if this client suicides.	Sadly, in the long term, no-one can stop this client from killing themselves if they firmly decide to do that. Ultimately it will be their choice.
I should stay with the client until they no longer have suicidal thoughts.	It's impossible for me to watch over the client 24 hours a day. In the long term they have to be responsible for themselves. However, if I wish, and am able, I can take steps to arrange appropriate psychiatric supervision.
I have the power to change this person's mind if I am skilful enough. OR I must persuade this client not to suicide.	I don't have the power to change someone else's mind. The most I can do is to help them explore the issues involved, and then take any other action available to me.
I'm not as well qualified as other counsellors.	I am me, with my skills and limitations. If I am able to refer this client on to someone more qualified I will, and in the meantime I'll do my best.
If I am incompetent I will be to blame for this person's death.	It's unrealistic for me to expect to be a perfect counsellor in such a stressful situation. I cannot take responsibility for their decision. I can only do what I am capable of doing.
I must live up to the client's expectations.	I do not need to live up to the client's expectations.
I can't cope.	I can cope provided that I set realistic expectations for myself.

I guess it must be really scary for you too.' By bringing these feelings into the open, trust can be created. A genuine and open sharing is now possible, and it is likely that the counsellor's tension will diminish.

Counselling skills

The micro-skills that have previously been learnt, together with an appropriate counselling relationship, are the basic tools for dealing with a suicidal client. We suggest that initially it is important to concentrate on building a relationship with the client so that when trust has been established the question of responsibility can be addressed. The way this is done will depend on the client's personality and actual situation, and on the counsellor's own personal style and value system. We believe that it is important to acknowledge that in the last resort responsibility rests with the client. For example, the counsellor might say, 'It is very sad for me to know that you are thinking about killing yourself. In the long term, even though I might like to stop you, if you are seriously determined to kill yourself then I will be unable to prevent you from doing so, because I can't be beside you for 24 hours each day'. This is the reality, because even if the client is hospitalised for a while, they will eventually be discharged. The counsellor may continue by saying, 'I am concerned for your safety and wellbeing and it is important for me to understand fully how and why you feel the way you do'. By taking this approach the client will understand that they are responsible for their own life and are likely to feel as though the counsellor is joining with them rather than working against them.

Focus on the client's ambivalence

We recognise that each individual counsellor needs to make a decision for themselves about how to counsel a suicidal client. Some counsellors prefer a direct approach where they will try to convince the client that they should not kill themselves, and we will discuss this approach later. For some clients this may be the best approach. However, in our view this is not always the best approach because it puts the counsellor in opposition to the client. We think that usually it is more useful to focus on the client's ambivalence— 'Should I kill myself or not?'—than to try to convince the client that suicide is not the best option. Most, if not all, suicidal clients have some degree of ambivalence towards dying. After all, if a client was 100 per cent convinced that they wanted to kill themself, they probably wouldn't be talking to a counsellor, they would just go ahead with their suicide plan. We have found that exploring the ambivalence is usually the key to the successful counselling of people who are contemplating suicide.

Exploring the client's options

As explained in Chapter 21, when a person chooses between two alternatives they lose one of the options and may also have to pay a price for the chosen option. By choosing suicide, a person loses life, contact with others and the opportunity to communicate with others about their pain. In addition they lose hope, if they had any, for a better future. The cost of dying is likely to include fear of the unknown and for some religious people fear of being punished for killing themselves.

By joining with the client, the client is free to explore the 'I want to die' part of self with the counsellor walking alongside during the exploration, rather than trying to deflect the client away from fully exploring negative thoughts. Later, the client can be invited to move on to look at the opposite part of self that still wants to continue living, or at least has reservations about wanting to die.

We think that it is advantageous to make a client aware of their ambivalence, and to help them to look at the consequences, costs and pay-offs of dying and of living. In the first instance, we try to avoid directly pressuring the client to stay alive and instead help in the exploration of options. In this way the client is likely to feel understood and has the opportunity to work through their pain and feel sufficiently valued to reconsider their decision.

An alternative approach

An alternative approach, as mentioned previously, is to try to persuade the client that living is the best option. This approach is not usually our personal preference because it sets up a struggle between the client who is saying, 'I want to die' and the counsellor who is saying, 'I want you to live'. There is then heavy pressure on the counsellor to convince the client of the rightness of living, and this may be difficult as the counsellor and client are in opposition rather than joining together. Even so, this approach can be successful with some clients. There is no universal 'right way' to go. Every client is unique and so is every counsellor. Each counsellor needs to choose an approach that seems right for them and for their client. If counsellors concentrate on establishing and maintaining a good relationship with their clients then they optimise their chances of success.

Dealing with depression and anger

Suicidal clients are usually in deep depression, and depression, as explained in Chapter 26, is often due to repressed anger. Very often suicidal clients are turning anger, which could be appropriately directed at others, inward and towards themselves. It may be useful to ask the question, 'Who are you angry with?' If the client replies by saying, 'myself', you can agree that that is obvious and consistent with wanting to suicide. You might say, 'You are so angry with yourself that you want to punish yourself by killing yourself'. This reframe of suicide as self-punishment rather than escape may be useful in some cases in helping to produce change. You could also ask, 'After yourself, who are you most angry with?' Then, if you can help the client to verbalise their anger and direct it away from themselves and onto some other person or persons, their depression and suicidal thoughts may moderate.

Looking for the trigger

Another way of entering the client's world is to find out what triggered off the suicidal thoughts *today*. Very often a single event is the trigger and this trigger can sometimes give important clues about the client's intentions. For example, is the client's intention partly to punish someone who has angered or hurt them? If so, there may be better ways of achieving this.

Recognise your limitations

Don't forget that it is unrealistic, unfortunately, to expect that the client will necessarily decide to stay alive. Although you may be able, if you choose, to take measures to ensure that the client stays alive in the short term, in the long term, if they are determined to kill themselves, they are likely to succeed. However, as counselling progresses you will need to decide, in consultation with your supervisor, whether direct action to prevent suicide is warranted and necessary. This decision is a heavy one and is certain to be influenced by your own values and those of the agency that employs you. There are some cases where the decision to intervene is clear. It would, for example, be unethical and irresponsible to allow someone who was psychologically disturbed due to a temporary psychiatric condition or a sudden trauma, to kill themselves without determined and positive action being taken to stop them.

A suicidal client is likely to need ongoing psychotherapy from a skilled professional, so be prepared to refer appropriately. The eventual wellbeing of such a client depends on them being able to make significant changes to their thinking and way of living, and this is unlikely to be achieved in one counselling session.

Learning summary

- People who make repeated suicide attempts often succeed in killing themselves.
- Suicidal people include those who are locked into miserable lives, those who have recently experienced trauma, and those who are wanting to manipulate others.
- When counselling suicidal clients it is important to deal with your own feelings as a counsellor and challenge any irrational beliefs you may have.
- When counselling suicidal clients focus on the counselling relationship using normal micro-skills:
  - find out what triggered the suicidal thoughts;
  - bring the client's anger into focus;
  - hook into the client's ambivalence if that can be useful;
  - explore the client's options and particularly the costs of dying;
  - use a more direct confrontationalist approach if you think that it is more likely to be effective;
  - decide what direct action is warranted and necessary to prevent suicide; and
  - finally, refer to suitable professionals for ongoing help.

Further reading

Appleby, M. & Condonis, M. 1990, *Suicide Prevention: What to Look For, What to Do, Where to Go*, ROSE Education Training & Consultancy, Narellan, Australia.

Bongar, B. (ed.) 1992, *Suicide: Guidelines for Assessment, Management and Treatment*, Oxford University Press, Oxford.

Donnelly, J. (ed.) 1998, *Suicide: Right or Wrong?*, Prometheus, New York.

Fremouw, W. J., de Perczel, M. & Ellis, T. E. 1990, *Suicide Risk: Assessment and Response Guidelines*, Pergamon, New York.

Jenkins, R., Griffiths, S., Wylie, I., Hawton, K., Morgan, G. & Tylee, A. (eds) 1994, *The Prevention of Suicide. A Conference Organised by the Department of Health, Faculty of Public Health Medicine, Royal College of General Practitioners, and the Royal College of Psychiatrists*, HMSO, London.

Pritchard, C. 1995, *Suicide—the Ultimate Rejection? A Psycho-Social Study*, Open University Press, Buckingham.

chapter 29

Teaching clients to relax

Some clients who are very tense and anxious find that counselling alone is insufficient help. Sometimes it's advisable to refer such clients to a medical practitioner or psychiatrist for assessment so that appropriate medication can be prescribed if necessary. However, for many clients considerable benefit can be achieved through the use of relaxation techniques.

Most clients find it easy to learn relaxation, enjoy relaxing and can be encouraged to use it regularly. However, there are a minority of clients who find relaxation techniques quite threatening. Instead of becoming relaxed during a relaxation exercise, these people experience increased tension and anxiety. For some, this can be severe. Be careful therefore to give your clients permission to stop the relaxation exercise if they find it is stressful rather than relaxing. With such clients it may be useful to explore the stressful experience, if this is not too threatening, because it may well be related to other stressful experiences in their present or past lives.

Preferably, a room used for relaxation will be quiet and will have subdued rather than glaring lighting. It will be protected, as far as possible, from external noises such as phones ringing and also from the intrusion of others. It is not helpful to have someone open a door and walk in while a client is trying to relax!

There are many different ways of teaching relaxation. The following relaxation exercise is one that we use. If you wish to use it, read the following instructions to your client using a quiet, slow, monotonous tone of voice. Pause between each statement for a few seconds.

Relaxation exercise

Lie on the floor with your head on a cushion, your hands beside you, and your legs straight.

Move around until you feel comfortable.

Close your eyes.

You will probably enjoy this exercise and find it pleasurable, but if at any time you are feeling uncomfortable and want to stop you may either choose to lie quietly and ignore my voice, or you may speak up and tell me that you want to discontinue the exercise.

Notice where your body touches the floor.

Move yourself so that you are more comfortable.

Be aware of your whole body from head to toe and stretch any part of you that is uncomfortable.

Let your body press down on the floor.

Notice the floor pressing up on you.

It's a good feeling.

You are in contact with the ground and the ground is in contact with you.

Notice your breathing.

Allow yourself to breathe comfortably and naturally.

(*Longer pause.*)

We are going to go through a series of exercises during which you will relax various parts of your body starting from the tips of your toes and finishing at the top of your head.

For each set of muscles, I will suggest that you tighten those muscles while breathing in deeply, and then relax them as you breathe out.

Whenever you remember, say to yourself the word 'relax' as you breathe out.

In between relaxing each set of muscles, focus on your breathing again.

Breathe naturally and say 'relax' silently to yourself as you breathe out each time. By doing this you will gradually become more relaxed. If any intruding thoughts come into your mind, don't worry, just return to focusing on your breathing again.

Notice your breathing now.

Each time you breathe out say 'relax' silently to yourself.

(*NOTE TO COUNSELLOR: Observe the client's body, and notice their breathing. When they breathe out each time say the word 'relax' quietly. Do this a few times so that the client remembers to do it themselves.*)

Notice your body. If any parts of it are uncomfortable, stretch or move so that you are more comfortable.

Focus on your breathing.

When you are ready, I will ask you, as you breathe in, to take a slow, deep breath and as you do this to clench your toes tightly and tighten up the muscles in your feet.

(*Choose the time.*)

Breathe in deeply and tighten up the muscles in your feet.

Hold your breath and keep the muscles in your feet tight for a second or two.

Breathe out heavily and release the tension in your feet.

Continue breathing naturally and say 'relax' to yourself each time you breathe out.

(*Wait for a while as the client continues to breathe naturally.*)

Now tense your thigh and calf muscles as you breathe in deeply.

Hold your breath and keep your muscles tense.

Relax as you breathe out.

Breathe naturally and feel relaxed.

(*Pause a while.*)

Tense the muscles in your buttocks as you breathe in deeply.

Hold your breath and keep your muscles tensed.

Now breathe out and relax.

Breathe naturally and notice a feeling of relaxation flowing up your body from your feet to your buttocks.

(*Pause a while.*)

Tense the muscles in your stomach as you breathe in deeply.

Hold your breath.

Relax.

Notice your breathing.

(*Pause a while.*)

Clench your fists as you breathe in.

Hold.

Relax.

(*Pause a while.*)

Now tense the muscles in your arms and stretch your fingers out as you breathe in.

Hold.

Relax.

Notice a relaxed feeling flow up from your feet through your calves, thighs, stomach, hands, arms and chest.

Let your body sink into the floor and feel supported by the floor.

Breathe naturally.

(*Pause.*)

Tighten your shoulder and neck muscles as you breathe in.

Hold.

Relax.

(*Pause.*)

Clench your teeth, screw up your face, close your eyes tightly, and feel your scalp tighten as you breathe in.

Hold.

Relax.

(*Pause.*)

Breathe naturally and notice the relaxed feeling moving up and encompassing your whole body.

Be aware of your breathing. Each time you breathe out feel yourself becoming more relaxed.

(*Long pause.*)

Soon it will be time to start getting in touch with your surroundings again. When you do this, allow yourself to feel good, to be wide awake and alert.

(*Pause.*)

Notice the floor. Move your fingers and feel it.

Wriggle slightly and when you are ready open your eyes.

Lie where you are and look around. Allow yourself to take in what you see, to feel good, and to be awake and alert.

When you are ready, roll over sideways and support yourself with one arm in a half-sitting position.

Sit up when the time is right for you.

The above relaxation exercise can be taught to a client in a counselling session, and they can then be encouraged to practise it regularly in their own time. However, warn your client about the dangers of being too relaxed. It is not advisable, for example, to drive a car in a very relaxed state. A certain amount of tension is useful so that the client's reactions to danger are fast.

Therefore, do not go through the relaxation exercise with your client immediately before they are due to drive away!

Once a client has learnt to relax by muscle tensing and relaxing they will find it easier to relax when standing up and in a tense situation. Teach them to take a few deep breaths and each time they breath in to tighten up their muscles and then relax as they breathe out. With practice they will probably find that they are able to let themselves relax as they breathe out naturally.

Learning summary

- Use a quiet, slow, monotonous tone of voice when teaching relaxation.
- Relaxation exercises can be threatening for some people.
- Make sure that the client understands that the exercise can be discontinued whenever they like.
- Observe the client's body so that your instructions are correctly timed.
- Warn your client of the danger of being too relaxed when attention is required.

Further reading

Madders, J. 1993, *Stress and Relaxation: Self-Help Techniques for Everyone*, Optim, London.
Payne, R. 1995, *Relaxation Techniques: A Practical Handbook for Health Care Professionals*, Churchill Livingstone, Edinburgh, New York.
Wilson, P. 1995, *Instant Calm: Over 100 Successful Techniques for Relaxing Mind and Body*, Penguin Australia, Ringwood.

part **VII**

Telephone counselling and crisis intervention

chapter 30

Telephone counselling

Let us ask you, the reader, a question, 'Do you think that it would be harder to be a telephone counsellor or a face-to-face counsellor?'

We feel certain that you will have to think hard about this question because the two types of counselling are in some ways similar but in other ways very different. Before reading on, you may wish to think about what the major differences are.

One major difference is that the nature of the contact between the counsellor and client is obviously quite different in telephone counselling when compared with face-to-face counselling and this is sure to have an impact on the counselling process.

Advantages of having visual contact

A telephone counsellor has much less information about the client than a face-to-face counsellor. The telephone counsellor can't see the caller and is consequently denied a wealth of information.

By contrast a face-to-face counsellor can directly observe the client. From this visual contact they may be able to make tentative judgments about the client's emotional state, coping ability, age, social status, cultural background and temperament. They are also able to gauge more easily the client's willingness to share and their comfort with the counselling relationship. From visual observation the face-to-face counsellor has the benefit of many subtle clues that are not available to the telephone counsellor. Most importantly, the counsellor is able to give and to receive non-verbal messages. This is much more difficult to do by phone. Have you ever tried to smile down a telephone line? It's not the easiest thing to do, is it? Have you ever wondered whether the person talking to you by phone was crying or not? In the face-to-face situation those tell-tale tears would leave you in no doubt.

Time to build a relationship

Another significant difference between the two types of counselling concerns the counsellor's ability to build a relationship with the client. The face-to-face counsellor has more time in which to build a relationship by using both verbal and non-verbal cues. Rarely does a client walk out of a counselling session during the first minute or two. But for the telephone counsellor the situation is quite different. If some level of trust isn't established early on in the call, the caller might well hang up, thereby terminating the counselling process!

In many ways then, telephone counselling is more difficult than face-to-face counselling. The telephone counsellor, 'TC' for short, has to have good 'fishing' skills. They need to be able to engage their caller through a gradual process which is active but non-threatening, so that the caller feels safe enough in the relationship to begin and to continue talking.

Being prepared for a call

To be effective, a telephone counsellor needs to be ready to make the most of the first few moments of a call to engage the caller. The first minute or two of the call are often critical. A distressed caller in a highly emotional state will easily be frightened away, and is likely to hang up unless some immediate warmth and responsiveness comes through from the counsellor.

Influence of the counsellor's own problems

We counsellors are people with our own needs. If we are preoccupied by our own emotional problems and if our own unfinished business with other people is needing attention, then we are very unlikely to be ready to engage with a caller over the phone when it rings. It takes time to put aside our own stuff, and unless we have done that it will intrude.

Sometimes with face-to-face clients who are coming to a second or subsequent counselling session it's possible for a counsellor to let go of their own preoccupations by owning them openly and saying to the client something like: 'I have just had a difficult few minutes and haven't yet distanced myself from that experience. I'm letting you know this so that I can put that experience to one side and give you my full attention without being distracted by intruding thoughts.'

Sharing information like this can be useful in two ways. Firstly, it addresses the process occurring for the counsellor and will probably enable the counsellor to focus on the client without the problem of intruding thoughts. Secondly, there is good learning for the client as the counsellor models an appropriate way of displacing, or putting to one side, troubling thoughts. Unfortunately this technique can't be used in telephone counselling unless the caller is well known to the counsellor. The telephone counsellor–client relationship is usually too fragile for such a disclosure at the start of a call.

Preparing yourself for a call

As explained above, the telephone counsellor needs to be ready right from the start of the call to pay full attention to the caller and to the counselling process. The TC therefore needs to prepare adequately before the phone rings. If they are troubled by worrying or disturbing thoughts then they need to deal with these in some appropriate way. We are all different and the way in which we prepare ourselves may not work for other people. However,

there are four common ways of preparing for a telephone counselling session. They are:

1. Talk through your own problems with your supervisor.
2. Own your intruding thoughts by telling a colleague that they exist.
3. Use relaxation, meditation or prayer, depending on your spiritual orientation.
4. Engage in physical exercise.

Talking through your own problems with a supervisor

Owning the problems that are troubling you and talking them through with your supervisor is certainly the best approach. By doing this the problems are not just put to one side but are worked through. This is particularly useful, because if you just put your own problems to one side without working them through, then they are sure to re-emerge if the client's problems are in some way similar. Working through them first is clearly the ideal.

Sharing your problems with a colleague

Unfortunately in practice, it is not always possible to talk through one's own problems prior to a telephone counselling session. It may, however, be possible to use a similar method to that described above for face-to-face counsellors, but instead of telling the client that you need to put aside some troubling thoughts you could tell a colleague. It might be sufficient to say to another TC: 'I realise that I have brought with me some troubling thoughts about my family. I don't want to unburden them on to you because you may have needs of your own at this time, but I will talk them through with my supervisor later. Telling you that these thoughts exist helps me to put them to one side for the time being, so that I feel better prepared to answer the phone.'

Use of relaxation, meditation or prayer

The use of relaxation, meditation or prayer can be effective in helping counsellors to feel more prepared for a telephone counselling session. We are all unique individuals and so what suits one person will not be appropriate for another. While some counsellors find the use of structured relaxation exercises helpful, others have learnt techniques for meditating. People who have religious beliefs often find it useful to pray to ask for help in preparing them to receive calls.

Use of exercise

Engaging in physical exercise before a telephone counselling session can be helpful. People who enjoy exercising often find that they are able to feel good and to let go of troubling thoughts in this way. The alternatives are many and include jogging, playing golf, squash, tennis and swimming.

The caller's perspective

Having dealt with the need for appropriate preparation by the counsellor, it is time to consider the caller's position. Callers are often anxious and uncertain about what to expect. The act of picking up a phone and dialling a stranger can be worrying for some people. Some callers, being anxious, may have made a few false starts before finally dialling your number. Consequently the first few words and the way in which you, the telephone counsellor, speak to them are crucial.

The initial contact

Most human beings tend to approach strangers with caution. We are wary and tentative in establishing relationships. Consequently if a TC were to pick up the phone at its first ring and to talk quickly, the caller may feel threatened and be frightened away. We human beings approach each other warily and in our natural caution we draw back when someone tries to meet us at a faster pace than is comfortable for ourselves. We wonder if you have ever felt taken aback when you have called someone and they have answered the phone before you have heard it ring?

We need to be careful to meet the caller at an appropriate pace, so remember to be calm and relaxed so that the process of joining occurs naturally. After two or three rings, pick up the phone and answer caringly in a way that is non-threatening. At Lifeline centres, TCs often start by saying: 'Hello, this is Lifeline. Can I help you?' The words are important and so is the tone and pace. The voice quality needs to be calming and inviting without being gushy.

Responding to 'prank' callers

Some callers, particularly children, may initially behave in a way which suggests that the call is a prank call (see later in this chapter regarding nuisance calls). However, we need to be careful not to respond inappropriately to such callers, because their behaviour may be their way of attempting to access the counselling service and to test the counsellor's acceptance of them. It is important that all callers are treated with respect. By doing this it is sometimes possible to achieve a useful counselling conversation in calls which initially appear to be pranks.

Continuing with the call

After the initial contact, the 'fishing' gets seriously under way. Of course the caller–counsellor relationship is not one of catching someone on a hook, but there is a real similarity with fishing. Inappropriate responses or inappropriate timing will encourage the caller to hang up rather than to continue talking. The counsellor needs to be tentative, and to recognise and make allowance for the caller's hesitancy. They need to explore cautiously what is safe for the caller and what is not. They have to listen intently and to use all their skills and judgment in an effort to build a comfortable non-threatening relationship so that the caller is empowered to talk freely. The counsellor has to maintain such a level of empathic understanding and warmth that the caller will become more at ease rather than be scared away. With some callers this is no problem, but with others, as explained before, the simple act of picking up the phone has in itself been a difficult step. Too much talking by the counsellor is sure to push the caller away, as is too much silence. Yes, telephone counselling is difficult! It involves knowing when to be verbally active, and when to draw back and to listen in silence. Judging the needs of the caller and responding empathically without intruding are what is required. A counsellor who is unable to do this is likely to lose calls.

Hang-ups

One of the advantages to the client of seeking telephone counselling rather than face-to-face counselling is that a caller can easily opt out at any time without embarrassment. Inevitably some callers who are not used to calling telephone counsellors are likely to hang up prematurely in their first attempts to engage in such a counselling process. Don't despair when a caller hangs up, because it is inevitable that this will happen from time to time. Even so, every experienced TC knows how demoralising it can be to lose a call. When it does happen remind yourself that the caller may have achieved a minor goal by learning that they can cope with picking up the phone, dialling the number and starting to talk. Having made what for them may have been a big step, they may then be able to phone back later to talk for longer.

Staying focused

Telephone counselling often requires a high level of concentration with intense listening. Frequently distressed callers will talk quietly and consequently be difficult to hear. For new counsellors, there may seem to be too many things to attend to at the same time. The counsellor needs to listen to the spoken words, identify the emotions underlying them, understand and/or picture the caller's situation, attend to the process of the call, and make suitable responses. Telephone counselling certainly is very demanding for a counsellor but it can also be very satisfying for counsellors who sensibly and properly attend to their own personal needs (see Chapter 38).

Skills needed

The counselling micro-skills described earlier are all needed in telephone counselling just as they are in face-to-face counselling. On the macro scale, the process of a telephone counselling call will be very similar to the process of a face-to-face counselling session as described in Chapter 13. However, there are some differences at both the micro and macro level. Let us look at each of these in turn.

Use of micro-skills

In telephone counselling, all the micro-skills described previously are required. However, in using these skills special attention is required to compensate for the lack of visual and other non-verbal information. The caller can't see your face, your facial expression or your body posture. In our day-to-day communication, the words we say are moderated, amplified or changed in other ways as a consequence of the non-verbal behaviour that accompanies the words. For example, a counsellor may add emphasis to what they are saying by leaning forward as they say it. A caring expression may reassure the client that what the counsellor is saying isn't meant to be hurtful to them although it may be confronting.

Telephone counsellors need to compensate for the lack of non-verbal cues by adding tone and expression to their voices over and above what would ordinarily be required in face-to-face contact. Additionally, whereas a face-to-face counsellor can listen in silence at times, it is important that in telephone counselling the counsellor should regularly give verbal cues that listening is still occurring. Obviously this shouldn't be overdone, but it is reassuring for a caller to hear minimal responses such as 'ah-ha', 'yes', 'mm', coming in response to their own statements. At times during personal telephone calls to friends or family have you ever had to ask, 'Are you still there?' because the other person has been listening silently. Most people find it disconcerting when they get little or no response while talking to someone on the phone. Certainly, in the counselling situation the importance of the caller knowing that the counsellor is still there and listening intently, can't be overemphasised.

Similarly, the TC can't see the caller and will sensibly need to check out with the caller information that would, in a face-to-face session, be obvious from the appearance of the client. Hence in a prolonged silence it may be appropriate to ask, 'What is happening for you right now?' If you suspect that your caller is crying but are unsure, it may be worth waiting for a while and then saying in a quiet, caring tone of voice, 'You sounded very sad as you spoke and I am wondering whether you are starting to cry.'

Finishing a call

Finishing a call is difficult for many telephone counsellors. Generally, terminating telephone calls requires a higher level of skill and determination than terminating face-to-face sessions. See Chapter 10 with regard to the termination of telephone counselling calls.

A macro view: the overall process

The process of a telephone counselling call can often be described by the flow chart shown in Figure 13.1 on page 123. Clearly each call is different, but it is important to recognise, and if necessary influence, the stages through which the call progresses. For example, a counsellor needs to recognise when it is sensible to move from the 'active listening' stage into 'problem identification and clarification', and when to explore options. To do these things a counsellor needs to trust their gut feelings, to be sensitive to the caller, and to be able to recognise whether the overall process of the call is meeting the caller's needs. It is there that experience and supervision are useful.

Influencing the process of a call

While you are attending to the caller, take time to recognise where the call is heading and if appropriate make decisions with regard to the process. For example, it is not going to help a chronically depressed caller if you continue 'active listening' for too long, particularly if you are reflecting feelings and negative thoughts. In fact you may well succeed in helping the caller to move further down into a trough of despair! Recognise the time to move on to 'facilitating attitude change' or 'exploring options' (see Figure 13.1).

It is important, as described in the earlier part of this book, to follow the direction the caller chooses and generally to meet the caller's agenda in preference to your own. However, these guidelines are not inflexible rules and need to be seen in the context of the whole call, the caller's situation, the policies of the counselling agency, and in the context of the counsellor's own goals for the counselling process.

In our view a caller is more likely to feel helped if some progress is made in the call towards an increased awareness such that there is a likelihood of adaptive change occurring for the caller. To achieve this, the TC may at times have to influence the direction and process of the call. Don't forget, however, that change usually occurs through increased awareness rather than through the counsellor pushing for change (see Chapter 22 on facilitating action).

If a caller is repeatedly going through the same material, then it is appropriate to raise the caller's awareness of that process by directly confronting it. It will often be useful to tell the caller what you notice is happening in a call. For example, a counsellor might say to a chronically depressed client, 'I notice that you seem to be sinking deeper into depression.' Once the process has been identified, then the TC has the opportunity to move the call into a new stage. This might mean moving into the 'problem identification and clarification' stage by using an exception-oriented question from solution-focused counselling as described in Chapter 23 and asking, 'Was there ever a time when you weren't so depressed?', followed up by, 'What was different then?' or 'So there was a time when you knew how to beat your depression' and 'Is there anything that you could do now that would be similar to what you did before when you had some control over your depression?' We have used the example of depression because most telephone counselling centres receive a significant number of calls from chronically depressed people. Such people often need to have medical or psychiatric help and it is important to raise this as an option if it is not occurring (for further information on counselling depressed clients see Chapter 26).

You may be surprised that we are implying that telephone counsellors may need to pay more attention to control of the process of the counselling session than face-to-face counsellors. We think that this is true because telephone callers often do not feel constrained by time and when they become comfortable with a counsellor some callers are content to chat rather than focus their thoughts in order to use the interaction constructively. Also, telephone counsellors frequently only have a single interaction with a particular caller so there may be no possibility of ongoing work which more often occurs in face-to-face counselling.

Addressing each caller's personal needs

If we refer back to Figure 13.1 (the process of a counselling session), it is clear that for some callers it may be sufficient to move directly from the active listening stage to termination. For other callers, the other stages listed on the left-hand side of the chart are essential if the caller is to be helped. As each call progresses, a picture of the caller and their situation will emerge and you will need to make decisions about how best to help this caller. You may decide that it is sufficient for the call to stay mostly in the 'active listening' stage with consequent cathartic release for the caller. However, for other calls it may be desirable to gently encourage the caller to move forward into subsequent stages that will enable fuller clarification of the problem, or may facilitate attitude change or the exploration of options.

To be a fully effective and responsible telephone counsellor you need to be able to assess what is most appropriate for each caller. Unlike face-to-face counselling, you may not get another opportunity to work with a particular caller, so you will need to make the most of your opportunity. However, do not think that you have to achieve life-changing results in one call. If the caller finds it useful talking to you then they are likely to use a telephone counselling service again. Each call can be seen as one step in a flight of stairs up which the caller is moving one step at a time.

Solving the caller's problem

A fairy story

Once upon a time in the land of Great Tragedy and Despair there lived a wonderful person who became known as Super-TC. Super-TC was better than most TCs because his calls only lasted a few minutes. He was always able to give good advice and his callers usually politely thanked him for that. His approach was to identify the caller's problem swiftly and then to suggest a solution. Sometimes, when Super-TC couldn't think of a solution himself, although that wasn't very often, he would refer the caller to someone else who might have a solution. Occasionally callers would make it clear that they wanted a longer counselling interaction. In these instances, Super-TC would say to the caller: 'It's clear to me that you have a quite serious psychological condition. You need to make an appointment immediately to see either a face-to-face counsellor or, better still, a psychiatrist.'

At times, particularly when tired, many telephone counsellors will inevitably and inadvertently start behaving in some ways like Super-TC. None of us are perfect. It is always tempting to provide a quick solution rather than to suffer the emotional pain of listening to someone else who is suffering. Of course there are times when it is appropriate and responsible to refer a caller to others. Generally however, before doing that, it is preferable to allow the caller to deal with their emotional issues in the 'here and now'. Often, when this is done a referral will not be necessary.

Some TCs, who have trained specifically for working on the phone, believe that face-to-face counsellors are necessarily more competent than they are, with the consequence that they will refer to face-to-face counselling before helping the caller fully by using the normal counselling skills and processes. Unfortunately, we professional face-to-face counsellors, social workers, psychologists and psychiatrists vary in our competence. Yes, it is appropriate to refer on when you are out of your depth, and it is unethical and irresponsible not to do so. However, give your callers the opportunity to explore their pain fully with you on the phone if that is what they would like to do, in addition to giving them an onward referral if necessary. If you are unsure about what you are doing, then talk to your supervisor.

Unfortunately Super-TCs disempower their callers. By finding solutions for them they have their worst fears confirmed. The implied message they get is: 'You are not capable of running your own life and making your own decisions. You need someone else to tell you what to do.' There are times in our lives when we do need someone to tell us what to do, but usually human beings of normal intelligence prefer to make their own decisions, and can feel good about themselves if they are empowered through the counselling process to do so. If counselling has been really effective, an empowered client might think: 'Counselling wasn't much help, the counsellor didn't tell me what to do, instead I made my own decision. I am an OK person and can run my own life.'

It is clear that finding solutions for clients is not helpful. However it can be very useful indeed to help clients to find solutions for themselves. In this regard readers might wish to use strategies described in Chapter 23 on solution-focused counselling. The solution-focused counselling approach is specifically designed to help clients find their own solutions.

Making notes during the call

It is not easy to give the caller your full attention and at the same time to pay attention to the process of the call so that you can facilitate appropriate changes in that process if necessary. A high degree of concentration is required and it is easy to become distracted and to forget important information.

To avoid losing information, and to help in more fully understanding the caller's situation and seeing the caller's picture more clearly, it can be useful to make notes during a call. Some telephone counsellors add sketches as the call proceeds and find that this helps them to focus on the caller more intently.

If a caller is talking about family problems then it can be useful for a telephone counsellor to draw the family tree in the form of a genogram. Figure 30.1 is a simple example of a genogram. Genograms can be useful in helping the counsellor to more fully understand the caller's background.

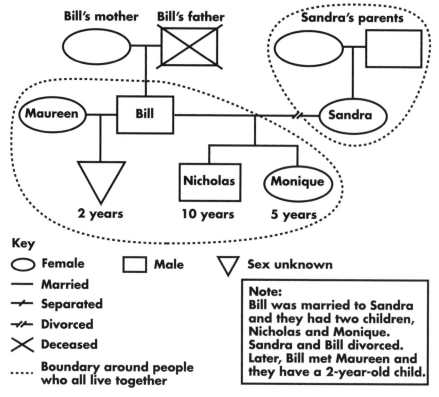

Figure 30.1 *Genogram*

Using your imagination

As a telephone counsellor you can't see your caller but you can, if you choose, imagine them. While they are talking, you can construct a visual picture and imagine yourself in the caller's position in their situation. If you do this you may be able to experience more fully what it is like to be the caller and consequently be able to respond with non-judgmental empathy.

Advantages of telephone counselling

We have made the point previously that in our opinion telephone counselling is harder to do well than face-to-face counselling. It is, however, an extremely valuable form of counselling. Some people who would never come to a face-to-face counselling interview will use the phone. From the caller's perspective, telephone counselling offers the following advantages:

- It is safer for the caller because they can if they wish protect their anonymity. This may help them to feel less concerned about the consequences of sharing private thoughts and emotions with a stranger.
- The caller knows that if they are feeling too threatened, they can hang up. This is far easier than walking out of a counselling room.
- Telephone counselling is easily and immediately accessible (unless the line is engaged) with no waiting list. The caller just has to pick up a phone and dial.
- Generally, telephone counselling is of low cost to the caller.

Setting boundaries

Because telephone counselling provides a safe environment for the client to share their deepest secrets, it also has some hazards. Some people who phone in are alone and have no close friends who can listen to them. Such people can be very vulnerable and may wish they had an understanding friend. Good counsellors are accepting, warm, empathic and non-judgmental with their clients. Lonely callers may build a very skewed picture of the person they are sharing with, perceiving the counsellor very positively. It is essential, therefore, to set clear boundaries so that the caller understands that the relationship is a phone relationship and cannot be extended beyond that. To do otherwise is to set up an expectation in the caller that, maybe, there could be the beginnings of a personal relationship. Remember that lonely, unhappy people are very needy and vulnerable. It is totally unethical to take advantage of them. Further, it is unrealistic to think that you could help them if you were to allow the relationship to change from a counselling relationship into a friendship. To do so would damage their ability to trust the counselling process as a safe one which they could use in the future.

Debriefing

Debriefing is a process used to enable counsellors to let go of the emotions which they inevitably experience as a consequence of listening to a distressed client.

If a counsellor said to you, 'I'm an experienced telephone counsellor, I don't need to debrief because client calls don't trouble me', would you believe them?

All counsellors, however experienced, need to debrief, especially after particularly stressful counselling sessions. Although we are both experienced professional counsellors, we make it a regular practice to debrief after difficult or emotional counselling sessions. If we were not to do so, the service we provide for our clients would inevitably become less effective and we would inevitably suffer burnout symptoms.

Telephone counsellors are particularly vulnerable to the emotional after-effects of their counselling work. When people are in acute crisis, often the first thing they do is to reach for the telephone. Consequently telephone counsellors are frequently dealing with callers who are in extreme distress and/or panic. Additionally, often telephone counselling leads to crisis intervention (see Chapter 28).

Because of the inevitable crisis content of telephone counselling, TCs will sometimes feel drained at the end of a shift on the phone. Their callers' emotional pain will at times inevitably trigger off personal emotional stress for counsellors. Telephone counsellors therefore need to be responsible by CARING FOR THEMSELVES. After a particularly stressful call, we suggest that it is useful to take a break before accepting another call, and if at all possible talk to your supervisor or another counsellor about the feelings you are experiencing. At the end of each counselling shift, debrief once again by talking to your supervisor or another counsellor for a few minutes. Debriefing need not be a long process but it is an important one.

Problem callers

No discussion of telephone counselling is complete unless it gives some consideration to what are best described as 'problem callers'. These are callers who create special problems for telephone counsellors. They may have goals that are incompatible with those of the counselling service and consequently may want to use the service inappropriately. Some of them may want to satisfy particular needs that are not being met elsewhere. However, problem callers are people with genuine needs, so telephone counsellors need to be able to deal with calls from them in a constructive way which fully addresses their counselling needs.

Most problem callers fall into one of the following categories:

- nuisance callers
- regular callers
- chronically depressed callers
- sex callers.

Nuisance callers

Inevitably there will be people who will call in to telephone counselling services with the aim of causing annoyance, or maybe of getting a laugh at the telephone counsellor's expense. Some of these will repeatedly ring up and then hang up, others will be openly abusive, and there will be those callers who make hoax calls. Sometimes angry or abusive callers will repeatedly knock the phone or slam it down. Such calls will naturally tend to make the counsellors receiving them feel frustrated and annoyed. We need to point out that it is *normal* to be frustrated, annoyed and possibly angered by such behaviour. Counsellors are human beings and as such we have our own legitimate emotions. Somehow though, we need to deal with our frustration, annoyance and anger, so that we can feel OK and are ready and able to deal appropriately with these calls and with subsequent calls.

The best way of dealing with emotions resulting from nuisance calls is to talk with someone about them. If this is not possible then we suggest that you might like to try to alter the way you think about the caller so that you are more able to be constructive in dealing with them. Can you think of the nuisance caller not just as an annoyance, but also as someone whose needs are not being fulfilled in an adaptive way which can enable them to have a satisfactory and fulfilling life?

The reality is that any person who finds it necessary to harass a telephone counselling service most probably has a very unsatisfactory and unfulfilled life. Could you be bothered to phone in to a counselling service just to be a nuisance? Neither of us could; we have much more satisfying ways of spending our time.

Here are some suggestions as to why some people make nuisance calls:

- They may be angry and unable to express their anger in a constructive and adaptive way.

- They may be frustrated with life and not know how to deal with their frustration except by annoying others.
- They may be bored and lonely.
- They may be young people who want to bolster low self-esteem by 'playing a joke' on a counsellor to impress friends.
- They may be young people 'taking risks' or acting impulsively but in a reasonably normal developmental way.
- They may be people who are testing the service before deciding whether or not to talk about more serious issues.

All of these people have problems in their lives and are searching for something they cannot find. If you are able to think of nuisance callers as people dissatisfied with their lives who are hurting inside, then you may be able to develop constructive strategies for dealing with them. We don't believe that there can be one correct way of responding to such callers because they are all different. What we try to do is to decide what, if anything, can be achieved when dealing with such callers. We ask ourselves whether any of the following goals are realistic:

- To let the caller know that they are a valued individual.
- To encourage the caller to talk about their real issues.
- To let the caller know why we believe that what they are doing is destructive.
- To let the caller know how we feel.
- To decrease the likelihood that the caller will repeat their nuisance-calling behaviour.
- To deal with the underlying issues that result in this unwanted behaviour.

Can you think of other suitable goals? If you are able to remember your goals then you may be able to deal with such callers constructively and effectively.

At all times, remember that it is not a part of your role as a telephone counsellor to be abused. You have a right to tell any abusive caller that you will not listen to abuse and to hang up if that is what you consider to be most appropriate. Of course, there are times when counsellors deliberately choose to listen to the abuse of an angry caller in order to allow such a caller to vent their anger and then to move on to dealing with constructive issues.

As a counsellor, although the choice about whether to hang up or not will be influenced by the policies of the agency in which you are working, it is ultimately your choice, and you have a right to hang up if that is what you choose to do.

Regular callers

All telephone counselling agencies have problems with those callers who repeatedly call in over a long period of time. Some of these callers have genuine needs that can be appropriately met by counselling. However, many regular callers re-run the same story over and over again.

Others try to engage the counsellor by using a variety of different names and stories, often with an underlying theme to their stories.

Regular callers can cause a considerable problem for telephone counselling agencies because they take up valuable time which could be used in working with other clients. Also, they are likely to cause disillusionment and increased burnout in counsellors. Agencies that employ many counsellors have particular difficulty in dealing with regular callers because their counsellors are sure to find it difficult to recognise the regulars.

Although there are exceptions, we do not think that it is helpful to allow regular callers to talk at length. To do this shuts out other callers. Also, regular callers are more likely to dig themselves deeper into their regular caller's rut if they are permitted to talk for an extended length of time. Unfortunately some regular callers are very adept at manipulating counsellors because they are experienced clients. In this regard, there are a range of statements commonly made by regular callers with the goal of convincing counsellors that they should continue to listen. These include:

'You seem to really understand me.'
'No-one has ever been able to get close to me this way before.'
'You are such a warm person that I feel so comfortable talking to you.'
'I think I'll kill myself now.'
'I just need to ask your opinion about one more thing.'
'Other callers are much more important than me.'

Many telephone counselling agencies have lists of regular callers giving details to assist counsellors in recognising the regulars, and also to give guidelines for handling these calls. If these callers do not receive consistent responses from counsellors then their best interests are not served and additionally they may become a terrible nuisance. It's important to make clear decisions when handling such callers so that their real needs are met and they feel valued as people, but so that they do not disrupt the service so that other callers are disadvantaged.

Most agencies set time limits for calls from regular callers but terminating calls from some of them can be difficult. You may need to be very assertive (see Chapter 23).

Regular callers can be frustrating and annoying at times, but we would like you to consider them from another perspective. Regular callers are often sad, unfulfilled people who would not call in if they were able to lead satisfying lives. Among them are the chronically sick, the mentally ill, people with disabilities, lonely people, people who are grieving heavily as a consequence of broken or lost relationships, the chronically depressed and people with significant past histories of abuse. They are all different from each other and unique as individuals. They each have their personal needs and deserve to be treasured as other clients are treasured. They have a right to receive care and counselling.

David will now describe some examples of regular callers who have been known to him:

CALLER 1:

Some counsellors at a particular telephone counselling agency felt that they were wasting time listening to an old lady who phoned in several times each day. Then one day a woman phoned to say that the old lady was her mother and that she had died. The woman said that she was phoning to tell the counsellors how much her mother had valued the warmth and caring they had offered her during the last few weeks of her life.

CALLER 2:

One day I met face-to-face with a seriously depressed regular caller who was boring TCs with his monotonous conversation. I was confronted by a sad, disfigured and disabled person who had no friends and was avoided by strangers. He had little chance, if any, of improving his lifestyle. He could hardly stand or walk, his speech was impaired, his conversation was uninspiring, he had barely enough income from his pension to survive. He lived alone. Almost his only human contact was by phone with the telephone counsellors who cared enough to listen.

CALLER 3:

Once, to my surprise, a capable telephone counsellor who was well known to me, confided that before becoming a TC she had for a time been a regular caller herself during a very difficult period in her life. Thanks to the counselling process she had been enabled to deal with her problems and to climb out of her trough of despair. She was now helping others.

These examples are, we believe, not unusual. Regular callers are valuable people and require patient caring, although sometimes it is not easy to be either patient or caring when counselling them. It's easy to say, 'Oh, she's a regular caller, and I really don't want to listen to her'. It's harder to say, 'This is a challenge, can I work with this problem caller in a way that will be satisfying for them and for me?'

If you are going to get satisfaction from helping a regular caller then you will need to be clear about your goals for each call. You will also need to be direct in telling the caller clearly what to expect from you. For example, you may say, 'Frank, I'm happy to talk with you for 15 minutes but then I would like to hang up so that other callers also have the opportunity to call in'. By doing this you are being up-front with your caller and can use the call caringly and constructively to achieve a goal. Here are some possible goals:

- To raise the client's awareness of their 'cracked record'.
- To help the client to recognise options.
- To empower the client to do something different, however small.
- To help the client to feel valued.
- To provide a listening ear for someone lonely.

Can you think of other goals?

Counselling goals listed in Chapter 26, entitled 'Counselling the depressed client', may also be appropriate.

Chronically depressed callers

A high percentage of regular callers fall into the chronically depressed category so we have decided to give them special mention. These people have very sad lives and call for a high level of caring from those who counsel them. Strategies for counselling them are in some ways the same as, but in some ways different from, those used in general counselling. Telephone counsellors therefore need to have appropriate strategies for working with such callers. These strategies are described in Chapter 26.

Sex callers

Unfortunately, telephone counselling agencies are frequently troubled by callers who want to use counselling services to satisfy their sexual needs. In our experience almost all of these callers are male and generally they only want to talk with female counsellors. They will either recount a story with a high level of sexual content or may be direct in asking the counsellor if they may masturbate while talking.

It is probable that many of these callers are obsessed by sex and have little or no chance of building a satisfying relationship with a partner. For others, sex may be an escape from the reality of a very unsatisfactory life and they may believe that they have no options to enable them to change their lives. Many of these men lack respect for women and have psychological problems related to their relationships with them.

We can see no justification, regardless of circumstances, for male callers to attempt to use female counsellors for their own sexual gratification. For them to do this is sexual abuse and it can be dealt with as such. However, counsellors need to be careful in assessing whether a caller is a nuisance 'sex caller' or not. There are callers who genuinely seek anonymous counselling help with regard to very personal sexual problems. Some of these would be too embarrassed to attend a face-to-face counselling session and may even be hesitant about talking to a telephone counsellor. Clearly they need counselling help, even if only a sensible referral to a clinic or sex-counselling service. Unfortunately, it's hard to separate these genuine callers from the abusers. If a genuine caller is treated as though they are a sexually abusive caller, then their trust in the counselling process may be seriously damaged. We wish that we could tell you how to distinguish between the genuine and non-genuine caller. We can't. We suggest that all you can do is to use your judgment and if you think that a caller is using you to fantasise sexually or to masturbate, then confront him. If the confrontation is done caringly as explained in Chapter 17, the caller's attitudes may be challenged and there is a possibility that he may seek appropriate help for dealing with his problem.

Obviously, sex callers have genuine psychological or life issues. If they did not, then they wouldn't attempt to use telephone counselling services in such a way. Consequently, a caring counsellor might choose either to deal with the caller firmly but caringly, or to be very abrupt and to hang up. Yes, we do believe that it can be caring to give very direct messages about the consequences of inappropriate behaviour. If you are abrupt and hang up, you do precisely that. Alternatively you may decide to be clear and explicit in telling the person how you feel about what they are doing, explaining that you intend to hang up, and in addition giving the caller an invitation to call back if they want to talk about real-life issues rather than using you as a sex object. However, it pays to be cautious or you may find the same caller pretending to tell you about 'real-life issues' while continuing to masturbate. There are some counsellors who will tolerate this. That is their choice, and if they are able to achieve worthwhile goals then their caring is to be admired. They need to be careful, however, on two counts: firstly, that they are not implicitly encouraging inappropriate behaviour which may be detrimental to other counsellors and secondly, that they are not merely satisfying their own sexual or other needs. Here, supervision can be valuable in identifying the relevant issues.

Certainly, all counsellors need to be aware of their own personal rights and to know that they are fully justified in protecting themselves from abuse by refusing to listen.

TELEPHONE COUNSELLORS ARE SPECIAL PEOPLE!

Learning summary

- Telephone counselling is, in some ways, more difficult than face-to-face counselling because the counsellor has little non-verbal information.
- Telephone counsellors need to prepare themselves personally before taking a call.
- Skill in cautiously building a relationship is paramount or the caller may hang up.
- Hang-ups are inevitable and are not necessarily bad.
- All of the counselling micro-skills are important. However, minimal responses are particularly important in telephone counselling so that the caller knows that the counsellor is attending.
- The telephone counsellor needs to pay attention to the process of each call and if necessary will influence that process with the goal of increasing client awareness.
- Each call can be thought of as one step in a flight of stairs being climbed by the caller.
- The caller needs to be empowered to make their own decisions.

- Making notes and using the imagination helps to bring the client's situation into focus.
- Telephone counsellors need to set clear limits with regard to their relationships with clients.
- Telephone counsellors need to debrief after troubling calls or they will burn out.
- Nuisance callers, regular callers, chronically depressed callers and sex callers cause problems for TCs and appropriate strategies are required for counselling each of these.

Further reading

Hambly, G. 1984, *Telephone Counselling—A Resource for People Who Want to Counsel or Care Using the Telephone*, Joint Board of Christian Education, Melbourne.

Rosenfield, M. 1997, *Counselling by Telephone*, Sage, London.

Waters, J. & Finn, E. 1995, 'Handling client crises effectively on the telephone', in *Crisis Intervention and Time-Limited Cognitive Treatment*, Roberts, A. R. (ed.), Sage, Thousand Oaks.

chapter **31**

Crisis intervention

In this chapter we will look at the following aspects of crisis intervention:
- the nature of crisis
- types of crisis
- the dangers and value of crisis
- the counsellor's personal response to client crisis
- appropriate counselling interventions
- practical responses to crisis
- post-traumatic stress.

The nature of crisis

What comes into your thoughts when you think about the word 'crisis'? We suggest that you might like to stop and think for a moment to explore your own ideas about 'crisis'.

Our guess is that your thoughts might have included remembering a disaster that affected other people or you might have remembered a time when you were confronted by a traumatic experience of your own.

Here are some of the feelings and thoughts that many people associate with the word 'crisis':
- panic
- fear
- horror
- help
- I can't cope with this
- I don't know what to do

- I need to do something in a hurry
- if I don't act quickly there will be a bigger disaster, and
- more panic!

Differing views of crisis

Crisis situations are situations of high risk. In crisis something is happening or has happened to abruptly change the participant's perception of a safe and ordered world. It is as though the bottom brick in a column of bricks is being pulled away so that the whole column will collapse. However, there is another and very different perspective on crisis which we will consider later under the heading: 'The dangers and value of crisis'. Can you think of what it might be? Firstly, however, let's think about the various types of crisis that people typically experience.

Types of crisis

There are several very different types of crisis. Although they are different, they also have similarities. They all raise the stress level of the person or people involved and call for a quick response in order to minimise practical, emotional and psychological damage.

You may wish to stop reading for a moment or two to see whether you can identify for yourself the different types of crisis that people experience before reading on?

We are all familiar with crises which fall into the following categories:

- natural disaster
- accidental
- medical
- emotional
- relationship
- developmental.

These categories are not mutually exclusive or independent of each other, but are useful in helping us to think about the similarities and differences of various types of crisis. We will now consider each of the categories listed.

Natural disaster

TV news has made us all very familiar with the practical type of crisis with physical and emotional consequences which occurs when a volcano erupts, or when there is a bush fire, a flood, an earthquake or when lightning strikes. Sometimes the effects of natural disasters are long-lasting. A drought can cause famine, and the effects may last for years unless there is an effective and timely response. Unfortunately, as with most crises, natural disasters usually occur with little or no warning.

Accidental crises

These crises inevitably occur from time to time. Examples are when a building catches fire, when two cars collide, or when a child falls down some stairs. In the worst accidental crises there is a loss of life.

Obviously, these crises occur without warning with the consequence that those involved are not properly prepared and are often not able to make the most appropriate response.

Medical crises

Some medical crises fall into the 'accidental' category. However, many do not. Medical crises occur when people have strokes, heart attacks, fits, asthma attacks or any of the many medical conditions that afflict the human race. Similarly medical crises occur when people are incapacitated by illness. A migraine headache, for example, may prevent a person from doing those things necessary for their own wellbeing and the wellbeing of others.

Other examples of medical crises are when a woman delivers a baby unexpectedly and there is no-one around to help, or when there are complications with a birth. Similarly, a crisis occurs when a baby becomes sick or when there are problems with feeding a baby.

Medical crises are often very frightening because of high personal involvement at a physical, emotional and psychological level. As with accidental crises, in the most severe cases there can be loss of life.

Emotional crises

An important and valuable human characteristic is our capacity to be emotional. If we were deprived of our emotions we would be automatons–mere machines. Unfortunately, at times the emotions we experience are painfully destructive and prevent us from functioning normally. Rage, sadness, depression and despair can all lead to states of crisis where the individual may be at risk.

Relationship crises

Anyone who has worked for a telephone crisis-counselling service will tell you that relationships are a common factor underlying many crisis calls.

Dysfunctional relationships, broken or lost relationships, and the absence of relationships are probably the most common causes of emotional crisis. However, we are separating 'relationship crises' from other more general 'emotional crises' because this is such an important sub-category.

Time and again people experience crisis when relationships are strained, break up, or are lost through death or unavoidable separation. Often, spouses feel devastated and as though their whole world has collapsed when they discover that their partner is having an extramarital affair. Similarly, those involved in having an affair usually experience a high degree of emotional pain.

Sometimes people experience profound disappointment due to the behaviour of those who are in close relationships with them. Parents are particularly vulnerable to such feelings. Time and again, parents have told us how disappointed and sometimes devastated they were when they learnt that their child was caught stealing or behaving in some other way contrary to their own expectations.

Unfortunately, too often in our present society relationship crises involve physical violence, usually with women and children as the victims. Counsellors are continually hearing about emotional, sexual and physical abuse occurring within families which should provide a safe and secure environment.

Developmental crises

There are some crises that none of us escape. These are the developmental crises that occur naturally and inevitably as we pass through the various developmental stages of our lives.

For most people the first developmental crisis is probably at the time of birth. However, for some there could well be earlier ones when, for example, sudden changes occur within a mother's body. From birth onwards the list of developmental crisis times is endless. Here are a few examples:

- when a child takes a first step
- the first day in child care
- starting school
- the onset of puberty
- starting work
- leaving home
- living with a partner

- getting married
- having a child
- death in the family
- separation
- mid-life crisis
- divorce
- starting again with a new partner
- retiring
- growing old
- dying.

At each of these stages there is risk involved, a raised stress and anxiety level is inevitable, and there will probably be other emotional responses. Often, there is a need for appropriate decisions to be made with consequent action.

There is an inevitability about many developmental crises. They are often a natural and necessary part of growing up and getting older. However, each crisis can be threatening, calls for a response and marks the beginning of a new stage in life.

The dangers and value of crisis

Most crises spell danger. They are fraught with risk. They shake us up and interrupt the comfort of our lives. They call for responsive action and usually this needs to happen without delay. However, crises are not necessarily bad. Although they usually do have emotional consequences, there is another way of looking at crisis. A time of crisis is also a time of opportunity. The impact of a crisis is likely to produce an opportunity for change. A crisis can be the catalyst for the development of something new. It can be a time when we let go of what has been and start afresh.

Surprisingly, even from the most terrible tragedies something of value may possibly emerge. Saying this in no way diminishes the sadness and horror of tragedy, but it is worth remembering that given an appropriate response, something new and worthwhile may grow out of a tragedy. A person may grow stronger psychologically or spiritually, relationships may change for the better, or something in poor condition and of limited use may be replaced by something more useful. Unfortunately though, many people are permanently scarred by the crises which they have experienced.

A good metaphor for crisis, which can sometimes be used with clients, is to describe the crisis experience as rather like going through a doorway from one room into another. If you imagine yourself moving through a doorway between two rooms, you may recognise that you are leaving behind many of the things in the room you are leaving, although you may be taking some things with you. In the new room there will be some unknowns. Consequently you may experience sadness at losing the things you are leaving behind. Also, you may experience apprehension as you wonder about what lies ahead in the new room. If you wish you can focus on feelings of apprehension and this may be threatening. Alternatively, you may be able to give yourself some positive messages about the future so that you feel challenged and consequently energised.

In using this metaphor we need to remember that it is usually not appropriate to tell someone in crisis that something good might emerge! To do such a thing would usually be inappropriate and would not address the person's pain. However, as the person is starting to move out of crisis, it may be appropriate to use the metaphor. At this stage be on the lookout for positive opportunities which may present themselves, so that at the appropriate time these may be fully explored with the client.

It is also useful to remember that in some instances it may be premature and inadvisable for a client to make far-reaching decisions before they have had time to work through the trauma of a crisis. However, the converse can also be true. Sometimes, a crisis provides the opportunity and impetus for sensible and important decisions to be made.

The counsellor's personal response

I, David, remember when I used to work as a crisis-line telephone counsellor. Sometimes, with a suicidal caller, or when a woman with children was trapped in domestic violence, I would feel my hair standing on end. My body would tense, my palms would be sweaty, and I would realise that I was gripping the phone as tightly as I could. It was then that I would recognise my panic.

Panic induces the frightened rabbit syndrome. The rabbit freezes. It can't move and is consequently unable to protect itself or its offspring. Are you a frightened rabbit at times? I am! Rabbits can also run, and use their brains to avoid danger by changing direction. The first step in dealing with panic is to recognise the physical symptoms that indicate the onset of panic. I would usually notice that my whole body was tense.

How do *you* recognise *your* panic? The way to do this is to learn to recognise the messages your body gives you. Then you can easily recognise your frightened rabbit mode and consequently be able to deal with it. Once you have recognised your panic, you are in a position to do something about it.

The first thing I do is to say to myself, 'I'm panicking, and my panic is not helpful'. Next, I consciously relax my body. I loosen the tight grip I have on the phone (if I'm working on the phone). I move my body into a more comfortable position, take a few deep breaths and at the same time let my body relax a little as I breathe out. I follow this by discarding those internal messages and self-destructive beliefs that contribute to panic, and replacing them by internal messages such as:

'I don't have a magic wand.'

'Nobody else has a magic wand.'

'There are limits to what I can do.'

'If I stay calm I will be more likely to think sensibly.'

'The client is more likely to know the solution than I am.'

'Can I help the client to feel calmer and to have some degree of control so that they can use their resources most effectively?'

'What are the client's options?'

'What are my options?'

'What are the limits to what I am able to do?'

Hopefully, I should then be able to attend to the client in an effective and caring way using appropriate counselling interventions.

Appropriate counselling interventions

What's appropriate at a counselling level will clearly depend very much on the nature of the crisis, and whether the counselling is face-to-face or by phone. For example, if a house is on fire and the client doesn't know what to do then it will not be appropriate to spend time reflecting feelings. Practical advice is urgently required! Give it.

Yes, we counsellors generally try to avoid giving advice and instead encourage our clients to make their own decisions. However, as with most rules, common sense is needed about when to apply the rule and when to do the opposite. Sometimes when quick action is needed we have to be very direct in order to prevent a major disaster from occurring. Quick action does not mean acting in panic but means being carefully decisive and giving your client clear instructions.

If as a counsellor you find yourself panicking, then once you become aware of this take action to deal with the panic. Then sensible decisions can be made with regard to the most satisfactory approach.

Similarly, if a client is panicking they will be unlikely to respond effectively and act sensibly. The counsellor's first job in this situation may be to help the client and deal with the panic. A possible counselling response to a panicking client could be:

'I'm catching the panic of this situation. Let's stop and think. Have you any idea what you could do right now?'

What do you think of this response? It joins with the client, may enable them to recognise and deal with the panic, and addresses the need for action. It could be an appropriate response, depending on the situation. Can you suggest some other suitable responses?

Throughout a crisis intervention, try to maintain as much calmness as you can so that your client is reassured. If you are able to do this then the client will feel more secure and will be more likely to believe that a satisfactory outcome will be achieved. They might then be able to match some of your calmness.

As a crisis intervention proceeds, the full range of counselling skills are often required. If you stay with the client, using the normal process of a counselling session as outlined in Chapter 13, then the client will feel supported and empowered to cope. The client will be enabled to experience their feelings in the safety of the counselling relationship and should reach some sense of completeness by the end of the process. Yes, you may leave your client feeling intensely sad, drained and possibly even devastated, but hopefully you will have managed to create a relationship of trust so that the client felt supported through the crisis. If you did, then the client will feel comfortable in coming back to talk with you, or with another counsellor, in the following few days or weeks. It is during this time that the client may well need counselling help as they cope with the emotional, psychological and practical after-effects of the crisis.

Although all the micro-skills are needed, it is worth remembering that the micro-skill called 'normalising' (see Chapter 18) is particularly useful when dealing with developmental crises. Clients often feel relieved to know that what is happening to them is inevitable and normal, even if distressing and painful.

Sensibly, the counselling interventions used must take account of any practical options available to the client and counsellor, so we will now consider practical responses to crisis.

Practical responses to crisis

It is essential that counsellors involved in crisis intervention are clear about the range of practical responses available to them. Because crises usually come without warning, counsellors need to be prepared. As a counsellor you need to know what options you may have when confronted by a client in crisis. You need to have a clear idea of the boundaries within which you work so that you know what you can and can't do. The options available to you and the boundaries that constrain you will clearly depend on the policies and practices of the agency where you are working.

You, the counsellor, will need to know the answer to a number of questions including the following so that you are prepared for client emergencies:

- If a client phones you in crisis, are you able to go out to visit the client or not? If not, is there someone else on your counselling team who is able go? If so, what limitations do they have to their ability to intervene practically?
- Are you permitted, within the guidelines of your employing agency, to ask a client in crisis to come in to see you, or to see another counsellor? Under what circumstances can this be done?
- Can you supply or arrange for transport, accommodation, financial or material assistance, or any other service for your client?
- Does your agency's policy allow you to accompany your client and to give them practical assistance?
- Do you have a comprehensive list of resources available, so that if you can't provide the required help yourself, then you can let your client know who might be able to help?
- Are you permitted to call the police, ambulance, fire brigade or any other service? If so, do you need to have the client's permission in all cases or are there exceptions?
- Can you arrange for women and children in domestic violence to be accommodated in refuges or in other temporary accommodation if refuge accommodation is not available? If so, who will supply the transport? Will someone from your agency or another agency be available to accompany the clients or not?

Clearly, these are just some of the questions you may need to answer and there are countless more. Unfortunately, you probably won't think of some of them until a specific situation arises that is new to you. In training, it's useful to brainstorm and to try to think of every imaginable crisis so that you know exactly what is available, and exactly what you are, and are not, permitted and able to do.

Client expectations

Clients sometimes have unrealistic expectations of counselling services. This is particularly so in the case of crisis telephone counselling services where some callers may expect that counsellors are at all times available to visit clients who would like such a visit. From the outset be clear with your client about the limits of your service so that false and/or unrealistic expectations do not develop. Can you say, 'No'? It's hard, isn't it? You may need to say to your client, 'I'm sorry, but there is no-one available to see you right now, but you are welcome to talk with me on the phone if you would like to do that.'

Practical intervention

At an appropriate stage in the counselling process you, the counsellor, may need to assess whether there is a need for practical intervention. For example, it might be advisable to call an ambulance, the police, the fire brigade, a medical practitioner or some other helper. Alternatively, for example, in a case of threatened suicide, it may be necessary to arrange for a crisis worker to meet urgently with the client.

In many agencies counsellors work under supervision. If you work in such an agency, then you may need to inform or get permission from your supervisor before being able to set in train an appropriate practical intervention. While doing this it is important to stay in touch with your client as much as is possible. A client who phones in is likely to feel anxious if left on 'hold' for even a short time. Be careful to maintain as much continuity of contact with the client as possible and to keep the client fully informed of your actions. In particular, if you are putting a caller on 'hold' tell the caller why you are doing that and let them know how long your absence is likely to be. If you take longer than expected then interrupt what you are doing, go back quickly to the phone and reassure your client.

Be cautious when considering whether it is necessary or not to intervene at a practical level. It is often tempting for a counsellor to take over responsibility from a client when this is not really necessary. Sometimes intervention by a counsellor is very appropriate but at other times it is not.

Consider an example where a client needs an ambulance. In some cases, it may be advantageous for the client, and not the counsellor, to call an ambulance. By doing this the ambulance personnel get a direct message from the client rather than one which might get altered in transmission. Also, it is empowering for a client to take action rather than to be left feeling that they are incapable of doing so. On the other hand, in some cases there may be uncertainty about the ability of the client to perform the task satisfactorily, or the client may be particularly vulnerable and in need of support. In such cases, the counsellor may sensibly decide, with the client's permission, to call the ambulance on the client's behalf. Clearly, sensitive judgment is needed by counsellors in deciding when to intervene and when to encourage clients to take responsibility themselves for any necessary action. There can be no hard and fast rule.

Giving specific instructions

At a time of crisis intervention a counsellor may need to be very directive and very direct in order to avoid an escalation of the crisis. This is particularly so in cases where the counsellor has professional knowledge that will be useful to the client. If we use childbirth as an example, a nursing sister, medical practitioner, paramedic or other trained person may be able to provide crucial information that can be essential for the wellbeing of the mother and/or child. Such a person needs to be clear, concise, concrete and specific in giving directions to the client or helpers. Even so, it is imperative that the counsellor retains the full use of listening and joining skills. It is at times like these that the person undergoing the crisis may have important information to give which could be overlooked unless full attention is given to their verbal and non-verbal communication.

As in counselling generally, it's desirable to stay in tune with your client's feelings, so that any intervention initiated is acceptable to the client. Exceptions to this are situations where the counsellor has a duty of care to the client or others. Clearly, counsellors have a duty of care in cases where clients are out of control of their own behaviour due to psychosis or drugs, or in cases where the safety of another person is at stake.

Post-traumatic stress

Unfortunately a counsellor's work does not necessarily finish when a crisis is over. It is now well documented that people often suffer from emotional and psychological after-effects as a result of severe crisis. These after-effects are generally referred to as post-traumatic stress.

Post-traumatic stress can occur in persons who directly experience a crisis, and in people who act as helpers at a time of crisis, such as emergency service personnel, police, ambulance personnel, medical and nursing staff, counsellors and social workers. Additionally relatives and friends may also suffer post-traumatic effects.

Usually the first evidence of emotional trauma becomes apparent immediately after the crisis, or within a few days. Some people try to shrug off these post-traumatic effects, believing that time will heal all. Unfortunately, time often doesn't heal all, and it is common for those who have been personally involved in crisis, and those who have in some way helped them, to be seriously affected emotionally and psychologically some weeks or months after the event. Post-traumatic stress can best be minimised by those involved undergoing counselling within a few days of the conclusion of the crisis.

Because of the possibility of post-traumatic stress, it is sensible to follow up on clients who have been through a severe crisis. During the days and weeks following a crisis it can be advantageous if the people involved are offered counselling help. Without this, the risk of undesirable psychological effects showing up later may be increased.

As stated previously, counsellors may be affected themselves when they work with clients experiencing crisis. As a counsellor, don't forget your own needs. After counselling someone in crisis, talk to your supervisor or another counsellor about your own experience of the counselling process and the emotional feelings generated within you. Such talking through, or debriefing as it is called, needs to be accepted as necessary and normal after any crisis intervention work. It certainly is not a sign of weakness to engage in such debriefing. On the contrary, it is a sign of maturity, good sense and personal strength.

Learning summary

- Crisis spells danger *and* opportunity.
- Crises occur naturally, accidentally, medically, developmentally, as a result of emotional and relationship problems, and in other ways.
- In crisis intervention counsellors need to deal with panic, be calm, use the full range of counselling skills and sometimes give specific directions to the client.
- Counsellors need to know the limits of their ability to intervene practically. They need to be clear in communicating these limits to clients.
- Counsellors need to be prepared for crisis and to have ready access to information about available resources for practical help.
- There are times when it is appropriate to intervene practically on a client's behalf, and times when it is not.
- Appropriate action is required to deal with the possibility of post-traumatic stress in both the client and the counsellor.

Further reading

Aguilera, D. C. 1998, *Crisis Intervention—Theory and Methodology*, 8th edn, Mosby, St Louis.

Waters, J. & Finn, E. 1995, 'Handling client crises effectively on the telephone', in *Crisis Intervention and Time-Limited Cognitive Treatment*, Roberts, A. R. (ed.), Sage, Thousand Oaks.

part **VIII**

Practical issues

chapter

The counselling environment

In earlier chapters we have discussed the way in which counselling involves the creation of a safe, trusting relationship between the client and counsellor. In order to assist in the promotion of such a relationship it can be helpful, when counselling a client in a face-to-face situation, if the counselling environment is one which will enable the client to feel comfortable and at ease. Similarly, in a telephone counselling situation it is desirable for the telephone counsellor to work from a space which will enable the client to have some reassurance that the privacy of the call is being respected. Firstly, we will discuss the face-to-face counselling situation and then requirements for telephone counselling.

Unfortunately, it is not always possible for counsellors to have the use of a specially designed counselling room. In some situations counsellors are visitors to a home, an agency, school or government department and have to make the best use of spaces that are intended for other purposes. Where this is the case it is desirable for the counsellor to do whatever is possible to protect the privacy of the client. Many adults and children don't like others to know that they are seeing a counsellor. In offices and schools the confidentiality of the counselling process may be compromised at some level by lack of privacy. Clearly, counsellors need to do their best to seek the most private facilities and arrangements as possible.

Special-purpose counselling rooms for face-to-face counselling

Whenever we walk into a room, that room has an effect on us. Is it the same for you? Have you noticed that sometimes when you have entered a room you have felt comfortable and at ease, almost as though the room welcomed you? At other times you may have entered a room that felt clinical, cold and unwelcoming. A well-designed counselling room will have a warm, friendly feel about it. In addition to being warm, pleasant, welcoming and comfortable, it is an advantage if the room can be set up so that it is especially suitable for counselling.

Where a counsellor has their own personal room, that room can reflect something of their individual personality. Our counselling rooms are decorated with plants and pictures. Pictures on the walls are peaceful, showing natural scenes of trees and landscapes. The colours are muted and not harsh, and these combine with comfortable furnishings to provide a welcoming, relaxed atmosphere.

Your room will be different from ours because we are all different and have different tastes. We suggest that you try to make your room an extension of yourself so that you feel at ease in it, and then in all probability your clients will feel comfortable in it too.

Preferably the furnishings in your counselling room should include comfortable chairs for yourself and your client, together with other furnishings appropriate for a professional office. You may need to write reports, draft letters, keep records and carry out some administrative duties. Hence a desk, telephone and filing cabinet will be useful, together with bookshelves for a professional library.

Layout of the room

The sketch in Figure 32.1 shows a suitable layout for a counselling room for the personal counselling of

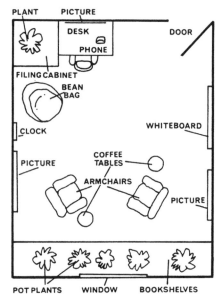

Figure 32.1 *Counselling room arrangement*

individual clients. Notice that the desk and filing cabinet are unobtrusively in a corner facing the wall, where their importance for clients is diminished. When a client is in the room we prefer to sit in a comfortable chair similar to the client's, facing the client and at their level. We avoid sitting at a desk as to do so is suggestive of a power differential. Additionally, we prefer to have open space rather than a table separating us from the client. Using this set-up enables clients to join with us as equal partners as they explore their issues, and we are not perceived as powerful experts separated by a desk. If we do need to sit at the desk to do some written work in a client's presence, we make sure that the desk doesn't separate us from the client.

We don't have a client chair and a counsellor chair, but rather two chairs that are similar. When a client enters the room they are invited to sit in whichever chair they choose. Only if they hesitate will we direct them to a chair. This is a small point, but an important one. Remember that clients are usually anxious when they enter a counselling room, because it is not their space and they may be worrying about the counselling process. They may be more at ease if you make it clear what is expected of them, rather than leaving them to decide what is appropriate.

We try to arrange the chairs so that they do not face directly into light coming from a window. Looking towards a window can be unpleasant, as after a while the glare will cause eyestrain. During a counselling session, the client and counsellor will be looking at each other most of the time, so the background against which each is framed is important for comfort. Preferably the client's and counsellor's chairs will face each other, but at a slight angle with enough space between them so that the client does not feel that their personal space is being invaded.

Equipment needed

We prefer to have a whiteboard in every counselling room. Clients who predominantly operate in a visual mode are likely to focus more clearly and gain in awareness if important statements are written on the board, and if their options are listed there. Sometimes a client's dilemma can be expressed through a sketch that metaphorically describes their situation. A whiteboard is particularly useful for helping clients to challenge irrational beliefs or to construct assertive statements. It may also be used as an aid when carrying out educational and administrative tasks which counsellors inevitably undertake as part of their duties.

We always have a box of tissues in a handy place in our counselling rooms. It is inevitable that some clients will cry and ready availability of tissues minimises embarrassment.

The need for privacy

As discussed in Chapter 36, confidentiality is essential when counselling. A client will not feel comfortable about disclosing intimate personal details unless they are confident that they will not be overheard. If a client can hear voices from outside the counselling room, then they may be justified in fearing that they can be heard by others. It is therefore preferable if counselling rooms are suitably soundproofed, although this ideal is often not achievable.

If at all possible the counselling process should be uninterrupted by the intrusion of people knocking on the door, entering the room or phoning in unnecessarily. For this reason, many counsellors have a rule that when a counselling room door is closed, no attempt should be made by others to enter the room except in unusual circumstances. In many counselling agencies, when a counselling room door is shut, the procedure for contacting the counsellor when unusual circumstances make this necessary is for the receptionist to use the phone. Except in serious emergencies, the receptionist allows the phone to ring a few times only and if it is not answered then the counsellor is left undisturbed. This minimises the possibility that the client might be interrupted at an important stage in the counselling process. It enables the client to feel that confidentiality is assured, and allows them to express their emotions in privacy without the risk and embarrassment of being observed by others.

Setting up your own room

Setting up a counselling room gives a counsellor an opportunity to be creative, and to use their own personal ideas to generate a suitable environment in which clients may feel comfortable and do useful work. We have found that it can be an enjoyable task when we experiment with the layout and decoration of our counselling rooms so that they reflect our personal tastes and are welcoming to others.

Suitable rooms for telephone counselling

The needs of telephone counsellors are obviously different from those of face-to-face counsellors. Sometimes telephone counselling has to be carried out in open areas where there is not much privacy. However, this is not ideal. Preferably, the counsellor should be in a quiet area where others will not intrude. Certainly, if a caller is to believe that the call has some level of confidentiality then it is essential that extraneous noises or voices are not heard by the caller. Additionally, it is unhelpful for a counsellor to be distracted by the activities of other people.

The ideal situation is for a telephone counsellor to work in a separate room so that quietness and privacy are ensured. However, many crisis counselling agencies prefer to use booths for phone counsellors. These provide some level of privacy and have the advantage that they enable the counsellor to make contact with peers and supervisors easily.

Counsellors have personal needs and it is desirable for the telephone counselling space to be an inviting place which is pleasantly decorated. It needs to have adequate lighting and air-conditioning or other suitable cooling, heating or ventilation.

Furnishings and equipment

Telephone counsellors are usually most comfortable if they are seated at a desk so that they are able to make notes and to spread out resource materials. If the desk is facing a wall, information which might be useful for the counsellor can be pinned to a notice board fixed to the wall.

In crisis counselling agencies, it is sensible to provide counsellors with a second phone line, so that in emergencies the counsellor can seek any help which the caller may be unable to obtain, such as an ambulance or police.

Crisis counselling agencies such as Lifeline sometimes provide beds or sofas for counsellors who are working overnight so that if there are quiet times, counsellors can rest and take turns to relieve each other.

Learning summary

- Counselling rooms need to be client-friendly.
- Client and counsellor chairs that are similar and have no barriers between them suit the empathic relationship.
- Looking towards a window is unpleasant.
- If chairs are too close, personal space may be invaded.
- Counselling rooms should ideally be soundproofed, and have whiteboards and a supply of tissues.
- Procedures to ensure that counselling sessions are not interrupted are useful.

Keeping records of counselling sessions

Many counsellors, including ourselves, find the administrative and clerical duties associated with counselling a chore. However, it pays to keep detailed and up-to-date records on each counselling session. Ideally, report writing should be done immediately after the counselling session, while all the relevant information is fresh in the counsellor's mind, and before other inputs have had time to intrude.

In today's society we can either type or dictate records directly into a computer using appropriately formatted software, or keep handwritten records on printed forms or cards. Where records are computerised adequate security measures are required to protect client confidentiality. Similarly, handwritten records need to be kept in secure locations (see Chapter 36).

Identifying the client

Client records need to be clearly identified so that there can be no confusion, because in large agencies it is not unusual to find two clients with the same names. Identifiers might include:

1. client's family name (surname)
2. other names
3. date of birth (if known)
4. address
5. contact phone numbers.

Where handwritten records are kept, it can be an advantage to label each page of the client record with the client's full name so that the possibility of pages being misplaced in the wrong file is reduced.

Additional demographic information about the client

Commonly, when the information is available, records may include any of the following:
1. marital status
2. name of partner or spouse
3. names and ages of children
4. referral source.

Notes about each counselling session

The notes for each counselling session may include:
1. date of the session;
2. factual information given by the client;
3. details of the client's problems, issues or dilemmas;
4. notes on the process that occurred during the session;
5. notes on the outcome of the counselling session;
6. notes on interventions used by the counsellor;
7. notes on any goals identified;
8. notes on any contract between client and counsellor;
9. notes on matters to be considered at subsequent sessions;
10. notes on the counsellor's own feelings relating to the client and the counselling process;
11. the counsellor's initials or signature.

The content of the notes will now be described in more detail under the headings listed above. However, although these headings are discussed individually, in practice, notes often flow together as the headings overlap. Hand-written notes should preferably be legible so that if a client transfers to another counsellor for some reason, notes can be easily read with the client's permission.

1. Date of the session

This heading is self-explanatory. When reviewing a client's progress over time, it's very useful to know the dates of counselling sessions.

2. Factual information given by the client

During a counselling session the client is likely to divulge factual information which may be useful in subsequent sessions. Sometimes small facts which may appear to be insignificant provide the key to unlock a closed door in the client's world, or could, if remembered, provide the counsellor with a clearer picture of the client's background. An example of information that might be included in a counsellor's notes could be:

> 'The client has been married for 13 years and during that time left her husband twice, once two years ago for a period of two weeks, and secondly six months ago for a longer unspecified period. She has considerable financial resources, lacks a social support system, had an affair some years ago and has kept this a secret from her husband.'

3. Details of the client's problems, issues or dilemmas

Keep the record brief, so that it can be read quickly when required. An example of this part of the record would be:

> 'Mary suspects that her husband may be sexually involved with another woman, is afraid to ask her husband whether this is so, and is confused about her attitudes to him. She can't decide whether to pluck up courage and confront him, to leave him now, or to continue in an unsatisfactory relationship with him.'

4. Notes on the process that occurred during the session

The process is independent of the facts presented and of the client's issues, and is concerned with what occurred during the counselling session, particularly in the client/counsellor interaction. For example:

> 'The client initially had difficulty talking freely, but as the counselling relationship developed he was able to explore his confusion and to look at his options. Although he was unable to decide which option to pursue, he seemed pleased by his ability to see his situation more clearly.'

5. Notes on the outcome of the counselling session

The outcome could be that a decision was made, or that the client remained stuck, or that a dilemma was identified. Alternatively the outcome might be described in terms of the client's feelings at the end of the session. Examples of notes under this heading are:

'She decided to confront her husband.'

'She left feeling sad and determined.'

'She said that she could now see things clearly.'

6. Notes on interventions used by the counsellor

Notes under this section are intended to remind the counsellor of particular interventions used. For example, the notes might say:

'Taught relaxation.'

'Coached client in the use of assertive statements.'

'Discussed the anger control chart.'

7. Notes on any goals identified

These may be goals for the client to achieve in the world outside, or in counselling, for example:

'The client wants to learn to be more assertive.'

'She wants to use the counselling process to sort out her confusion and make a decision regarding her marriage.'

'She wants to experiment by taking risks.'

8. Notes on any contract between client and counsellor

It is important to remember any agreements that are made with clients. These may be with regard to future counselling sessions, for example:

'The client contracted to come for counselling at fortnightly intervals for three sessions and then review progress.'

'It was agreed that counselling sessions would be used to explore the client's relationships with people of the opposite sex.'

'I have contracted to teach the client relaxation during the next session.'

9. Notes on matters to be considered at subsequent sessions

Often during the last few minutes of a counselling session a client will bring up an important matter that is causing pain and is difficult to talk about. If this is noted on the card, then the counsellor can remind the client at the start of the next session, thus enabling the client to deal with the issue in question, if they wish. Sometimes, as a counsellor, you will realise at the end of a session that aspects of the client's situation need further exploration. It can be useful to make a note on the record as a reminder.

10. Notes on the counsellor's own feelings relating to the client and the counselling process

These are required to help the counsellor to avoid letting their own feelings inappropriately interfere with the counselling process in future sessions. Such notes can be invaluable in the counsellor's own supervision and may be useful in helping them to improve their understanding of the counselling process. An example is:

> 'I felt angry when the client continually blamed others and failed to accept responsibility for his own actions.'

11. The counsellor's initials or signature

By initialling or signing case notes a counsellor takes responsibility for what is written in them. In many agencies counsellors work together with other counselling team members. In such agencies, over a period of time more than one counsellor may see a particular client. Also, a client may come back to an agency for further counselling after a particular counsellor has left. In such situations it can be helpful to the client if the client's counselling history is available, subject to the normal constraints of confidentiality.

As stated previously, writing records of counselling sessions can be a chore. However, a counsellor who does this diligently will quickly become aware of the advantages. The effectiveness of future counselling sessions is likely to be improved if the counsellor reads the record card before meeting the client each time. By doing this the counsellor is able to 'tune in' to the client right from the start of the interview and will not waste time on unnecessary repetition.

Clearly, records need to be detailed, accurate and legible if they are to be maximally useful. However, when writing records, be aware of the confidentiality issue (see Chapter 36) and of the possibility that the legal system may demand that such records be made available to a court. Also, bear in mind when writing records that clients may later ask to read them. Clearly, clients have the right to read their own records if they wish to do so.

Learning summary

- Ideally report writing should be done immediately after a counselling session.
- Records need to include:
  - the date;
  - factual information and details of the client's problems;
  - notes on the process and outcome of the session;
  - notes regarding interventions used, goals set, contracts made and matters to be considered in the future; and
  - notes regarding the counsellor's own feelings.

part IX

Professional issues

chapter

Cultural issues

Often, counsellors have only limited information about their clients' ethnic, cultural, social, family, community and general environmental backgrounds. This is unlikely to cause problems where the client and counsellor happen to come from the same ethnic and cultural groups but difficulties may arise where the client and counsellor are from different groups. Not surprisingly, it has been found that clients prefer counsellors from their own ethnic group (Tharp 1991). This does not mean that counselling won't be effective unless the client and counsellor are from the same cultural background. However, it does mean that for counsellors to be maximally effective when counselling clients from other cultures, they need to use behaviours and strategies that fit for the client. Additionally, as with any client, they need to try to perceive the world in the way that the client perceives the world. In order to be able to do this with clients from different cultural backgrounds from their own, counsellors need to try to gain an understanding of the client's family, social and cultural environment. This understanding should ideally include information about cultural norms, attitudes, beliefs and values. Additionally, counsellors need to be aware of their own assumptions, attitudes, beliefs, values, prejudices and biases.

For successful outcomes to occur, the most important factor in counselling clients from other cultures is the counsellor's ability to join with the client so that a good, trusting working relationship can be established. Also, strategies and techniques that will fit comfortably with the client's culturally-specific ways of relating need to be used.

Awareness of assumptions, attitudes, beliefs, values, prejudices and biases

As counsellors, each of us need to be aware of our own racial and cultural heritage and to understand how that heritage has affected our attitudes, beliefs, values, prejudices and biases. By being aware of these, it will be easier for us to recognise when the problems we encounter while counselling stem from our own cultural background, or come from some other source. Once we recognise the source of our difficulties, these can be addressed in supervision.

Difficulties facing clients from other cultures

In our modern world many people have to cope with living in a society where the cultural beliefs, values and behaviours prevailing in their country of residence are different from, and in some ways incompatible with, the cultural beliefs of their family and/or close friends. This inconsistency often creates psychological, emotional and behavioural problems for such people with the consequence that they may seek counselling help.

Living within a different culture

A major problem for many clients who live in a cultural environment which is different from that of their families is stress arising from internal conflicts. These conflicts occur when the culturally-determined social and moral values of their families conflict with those of the wider society. While recognising the client as an individual who is experiencing difficulties which might be faced by any other person, counsellors also need to be aware of the possibility that the difficulties being experienced may be related to, or compounded by, issues of race, ethnicity, gender or socio-economic status.

Additionally, counsellors need to be aware of any discriminatory practices at a social and/or community level that may be affecting the client's cultural group so that these can be properly understood if issues relating to them are raised during a counselling session.

Personal search for identity within a different culture

Many people who live in cultures that are different from their own encounter personal identity problems. Waterman (1984) has suggested that there are generally a number of stages during which such people engage in a search for their personal identities. In the first stage, the person from a minority group may accept the values and attitudes of the majority culture in an effort to fit in and be part of that culture. Surprisingly, this often includes internalising negative views of their own group. This stage of identity development may continue until the person concerned has a personal experience of racism or prejudice which forces them to see themselves as a member of a minority group. This awareness may then lead them to a personal ethnic identity search. The search involves efforts to learn more about their own culture and is often likely to be highly emotional. In this stage, emotions such as anger and outrage may be directed towards the majority society.

When a client is experiencing the emotional problems involved in an ethnic identity search, the counsellor needs to try to help the client to achieve a satisfactory outcome with regard to this search, so that the person concerned can develop a deeper sense of belonging to a group.

How culturally different clients view the world

Before considering specific strategies which are useful for counsellors when dealing with clients from cultural groups which are different from their own, we need to consider a number of factors which impact on an individual's perceptions of their world. These factors will influence the person's emotional responses, thoughts, beliefs, attitudes, biases, relationships and behaviours. We will discuss these factors under the following headings:

- individual and relationship issues
- the way decisions are made
- who is perceived to be a natural helper?
- attitudes of the extended family
- gender and gender roles
- perceptions of time
- use of language
- spirituality
- physical or emotional issues
- experience of trauma.

Individual and relationship issues

In Western society we place considerable emphasis on individuality and uniqueness, and a high value on a person's individual rights. In particular, it is generally believed that people have the right to make their own decisions and to follow a lifestyle of their individual choice. Many other cultures place a much greater emphasis on community and see an individual person in terms of the community rather than as a separate entity. In these cultures there is a sense of corporate responsibility and collective destiny. There is often a focus on harmonious blending and cooperation accompanied by a high respect for the role of the elderly. Many families from Southern Italy, China, Japan, Puerto Rico, Mexico and families of African-American and indigenous Australian origin share these views. For example a sense of loyalty to family is so great in Aboriginal people that it is not uncommon for them to confess to crimes committed by their relatives (Eades 1994).

Respect by children for their parents is a very strong value in Chinese families. This respect is shown not only through holding parents in high esteem but also through obeying them. This contrasts markedly with Western culture where elderly people are often not greatly valued but parental obligation to children and respect for children's rights is emphasised as being of great importance. Counsellors need to be aware of cultural differences such as these so that they can recognise conflicts which may arise in clients as a consequence of pressure caused by being exposed to conflicting cultural value systems. Inner conflict may also arise in clients as they are faced with choosing between loyalty to parents and the pursuit of their own individual goals.

The way decisions are made

The way in which people make decisions depends to a great extent on their cultural background. In some cultures making decisions is most appropriately done in the company of other family members. In other cultures, when making decisions, a higher priority is placed on maintaining harmonious relationships than on expressing an individual point of view. This is generally the case for Aboriginal people, where decisions to seek help may be the result of a community concern rather than a response to the personal problem of an individual. Typically when Aboriginal people seek help from non-Aboriginal helpers, they will make the request for help informally and through a casual meeting in an everyday social setting such as a shopping area.

Counsellors who are not Aboriginal themselves and are working with Aboriginal clients also need to be aware of a number of other issues. They may need to use a 'go-between' particularly if the business to be discussed is so sensitive that the client cannot discuss it openly. Additionally, the gender of the counsellor is important because some issues fit into the categories of women's business or men's business and cannot be discussed with members of the opposite sex. Also, it is important that the client be given the choice of the meeting location. In some cases, the client might choose to use a community facility, but in the other cases it may be more appropriate to use a less formal setting. When helping a family it may be more appropriate to use an area outside of the family's home rather than expect to go into the home, particularly as to invite a non-Aboriginal stranger inside the house would be contrary to normal practice (Vicary & Andrews 2000).

Decisions in Chinese families are generally made in quite a different way from the way in which decisions are made in Western families. In many Western families decisions are made through democratic discussion and negotiation. However in Chinese families communication patterns flow down from those of higher status. Consequently, in many families the father makes major decisions with little input from others.

Who is perceived to be a natural helper?

Some Asian cultures put a high value on age and respect for elders, and will consult with the elders when they need advice or counselling help. Because of this, people from these cultures prefer to work with older counsellors, and may find it difficult or impossible to work with young ones. In this regard it is sometimes useful for counsellors to seek the assistance of someone who is aware of cultural norms. This person can then assist by acting as a consultant to provide guidance and information with regard to possible ways of helping a particular client.

When non-Aboriginal counsellors are working with Aboriginal people it can be useful to talk with local elders first. This can be helpful in enabling networks to be developed. Elders can then provide introductions and permission to talk with others. This is useful in building trust which is likely to promote more positive outcomes for the counselling process.

Attitudes of the extended family

Whenever possible, counsellors need to gain an understanding of the social systems in their clients' families. They need to familiarise themselves with family customs and rules, particularly with regard to verbal exchanges between people. For example, Aboriginal families generally include a wide network of people, many of whom are related in ways that could be considered distant in non-Aboriginal society. Relationships within the extended family are characterised by obligation and reciprocity. Strong restrictions are typically imposed on contact or sharing of information between certain categories of relatives. It is also important to note that in Aboriginal societies it is forbidden to say the name of a deceased person, see any photograph of the person, or use anything belonging to the person for approximately six months after the death.

It can be useful for counsellors to learn about the child-rearing practices of their clients if these are relevant to counselling, as these practices vary markedly across cultures. For example, in some cultures there may be emphasis on the nuclear family whereas in others the emphasis is on the extended family.

Generally, in Chinese families, child-rearing practices are focused on emphasising the importance of family ties and obligations. Praise is given for actions that are seen as benefiting the family and guilt-inducing techniques are used to maintain discipline. Children are expected to retain emotional ties with the mother, and a respectful attitude towards the father, even when they have become adults. Consequently, it is not unusual for counsellors to find that some clients will find it difficult to make the choices they would prefer to make because of concern that they may upset their parents. From a Western perspective this concern could be incorrectly perceived as the client being overly dependent. However Western counsellors need to take care when working with such clients, because assisting the client to become more independent may lead to even greater conflict (Lee & Richardson 1991). Clearly, a client's cultural background needs to be respected so that they are empowered to make decisions which fit for them.

Gender and gender roles

The norms regarding relationships between members of the same sex and members of the opposite sex vary markedly across cultures. In order to join effectively with clients when trying to help them with relationship issues it is advantageous if counsellors are able to gain some understanding of cultural norms with regard to relationships. Additionally, gender-based norms regarding behaviour, roles and expectations vary depending on culture. We will now consider a few examples to illustrate cultural differences relating to gender.

In some Aboriginal communities, mothers- and sons-in-law rarely speak directly to each other, and similar taboos also exist between other members such as men and their brothers-in-law (Foley 1984). In these communities certain topics (for example, sexual activity) should not be discussed with a person of the opposite sex. As a result, the fears, expectations and consequences of violating culturally accepted codes will obviously have a large impact on a client's willingness to talk about these issues in counselling.

In Chinese families the mother is usually responsible for socialising the children. If they become rebellious it is seen as reflecting poor parenting on her part. She also has to mediate between the dictates of her husband and the demands of the children. The greatest responsibility is placed on the eldest son as he is expected to help raise his younger siblings and be a role model for them. Daughters are expected to help in the household. Generally fewer demands are placed upon them because they become members of the husband's family when they marry (Lee & Richardson 1991).

Latino culture is hierarchical and patriarchal, placing expectations on boys to be independent and perform outside the home. Girls on the other hand are taught to be selfless and to sacrifice. This passivity and deference to male authority is rewarded in that women are seen as semi-divine, morally superior to, and spiritually stronger than men. Machismo has been popularised as a desirable male characteristic. Having said this, what works in counselling for some Latino clients might not be relevant for others; both group and individual identity need to be respected (Lee & Richardson 1991).

Perceptions of time

For most cultures a linear view of time is appropriate. However for several South American countries, and for Australian indigenous people, time is viewed in terms of 'being'. Previously agreed-upon times for meeting may not necessarily hold. This needs to be remembered and respected by counsellors who come from other cultural backgrounds where time keeping is the expected norm and failure to keep time is considered inconsiderate and impolite. Consequently, when negotiating appointment times with people from cultures where time is not considered to be linear, it is sensible and respectful to recognise the client's perceptions of time and time keeping and to re-adjust expectations. For example, when arranging meeting times with Aboriginal clients, it can be helpful for clients to be invited to select the times that suit them best. It can also be helpful for counsellors to remember that in many traditional Aboriginal languages measurements are defined in qualitative terms, so consequently these languages do not include words to describe many numerals as these are not needed. Thus time and distance are best described by using physical, social and geographical situations as points of reference (Eades 1995).

When working in a cultural environment where time is viewed in terms of 'being', it is generally not advisable to miss or change meeting times, as consistency can be a major factor in promoting trust so that the individual client or family can develop a positive relationship with the counsellor. What is required is consistency with flexibility.

Use of language

The way language is used will have a significant influence on the effectiveness of communication between a client and counsellor. Figures of speech, complex communication, proverbs and quotations may either be familiar or confusing depending on the client's culture. Additionally, it is important to recognise that there may be significant or subtle differences in the vocabulary and meanings of words in different cultural environments. Consequently, the fact that a client is communicating in English with an English-speaking counsellor may be misleading if the counsellor does not realise that there are subtle differences in the use of particular words.

Martine Powell (2000) lists a few differences which can be useful when counselling Aboriginal people. For some Aboriginal people the word *half* may mean a small part but not necessarily 50 per cent. *Afternoon* may refer to the cool part of the day from 4.30 p.m. to dusk. The word *guilty* may be used only in reference to murder. The term *brother* may include cousins and other extended family members. Some Aboriginal groups use *he* and *him* to refer to males, females or objects and to more than one person. Aboriginal groups when referring to past events frequently use the present tense when speaking in English.

When working with Torres Strait Islanders it should be remembered that the word *kill* does not necessarily mean to kill dead.

Spirituality

For many people throughout the world spiritual beliefs hold a very high level of importance. If these beliefs are challenged or questioned the person concerned may well be alienated. As counsellors, when working with people from other cultures, or people who have different beliefs from ours, we need to suspend our own beliefs. In order to join with and help any client we need to try to understand client's spiritual beliefs and to see their world in the context of those beliefs. This may be particularly important with respect to a client's beliefs in the role and function of traditional healers, or in spiritual and religious influences.

Spirituality pervades every aspect of the lives of people from most indigenous cultures. For example, Aboriginal communities have strong spiritual traditions where dreams and beliefs about how mystical forces can influence nature figure prominently.

Physical or emotional issues

When listening to the client's story not all clients appreciate the use of a systematic flow of ideas with careful delineation of issues. To use a metaphor, some prefer to allow their thoughts to wander around rather than to be focused on heading in one direction. However, this process can be useful, as what is likely to occur is that their thoughts will add significant elements to central themes in their story from time to time.

Particular cultural groups who have a common history of past experiences that unite them and help them to define who they are, may also experience emotions which are common to the group. It is useful to understand the common history and the emotions which are associated with that history. For example, counsellors of any ethnic background who see clients with a history of white oppression need to understand, appreciate and respect the anger that this generates, understand their own response to that anger, whatever that may be, and deal with that response appropriately so that the counselling relationship is enhanced.

Issues clients bring to counselling sometimes reflect connections between the individual and the community. For example, the Aboriginal perception of connections between the individual, the community and the land, influences the way in which Aboriginal people view problems. This has implications for counselling. For example, individuals from non-Aboriginal communities might view alcohol abuse as being a personal problem requiring an individual treatment program. However, this solution may make little sense to an Aboriginal person who may perceive the origin of the difficulty as related to external forces such as the stolen generation, poor prospects of employment or racism. It would clearly be counter-productive, and in our view unethical, for counsellors with different beliefs to these to try to change such cultural beliefs. As counsellors, if we are to be helpful to our clients so that we maximise their opportunity to change in ways which are appropriate for them, then we must fully respect and work within the frameworks which make sense to them and which result from their cultural heritage.

Many Maori people view the physical environment as personified with the power to influence physical and emotional healing. Additionally, any insights that a Maori person discovers will be viewed as having a spiritual container (Bowden 2000). Clearly, any counsellor working with a Maori person needs to recognise, respect and understand this.

In traditional Chinese culture emotional expression is restrained and displays of emotional reactions do not typically occur outside the family. Feelings are usually not openly expressed except by young children. Often, if counsellors attempt to encourage Chinese clients to express emotions directly they may be met with resistance and this is likely to be counter-productive. Additionally such clients may lack the experience to identify, acknowledge and communicate emotional states. The emphasis in coun-selling should therefore be on the indirect expression of positive and respectful feelings. For example, interest may be shown in the ways in which members of a family show how they care for each other. This focus on behav-iour is respectful and indirect.

Many Chinese clients express emotional and psychological disturbance indirectly by reference to somatic complaints. They may consider the symptoms of physical illness to cause psychological problems. For example, they may believe that having a headache may result in feelings of depression. This is also true for many South-East Asian families such as the Vietnamese because for them mental disturbance tends to be highly stigmatised so it is much easier for them to talk about physical complaints. Consequently when counselling such clients it would be a bad mistake to discount physical complaints. By encouraging the client to initially talk about these, the client may then be able move on to discuss emotional and psychological problems. Lee and Richardson (1991) suggest that a useful approach is to inquire how the physical complaints impact on the client's family or social functioning. This indirect approach is usually more acceptable for the client than a more direct approach and may lead to the sharing of underlying psychological and emotional issues.

Experience of trauma

The way in which individuals respond to traumatic experiences will differ depending on their cultural beliefs. Clients from some cultures hold the belief that individuals are responsible for their own misfortune. In contrast to this, clients from other cultures may view misfortune as being imposed on an individual by an outside agency such as bad luck, or may view misfortune as the consequence of bad behaviour.

Strategies and techniques when counselling clients from other cultures

As counsellors, we need to develop culturally relevant ways of helping each client. Preferably, counsellors should have knowledge about the client's particular group and culture. However, it is obvious that this will not always be the case. There are many occasions when a counsellor will not have much information about the client's cultural background. In such cases it may be useful to encourage the client to extend their story to include relevant information relating to cultural issues. If a counsellor can do this successfully, they may be able to further their knowledge about the client's family, values, attitudes, beliefs and behaviours. Additionally they may discover information about the characteristics of the client's community, and the resources in that community and in the family concerned, enabling them to understand, join with, and be more helpful to the client.

While exploring cultural issues with clients, it is important for counsellors to recognise their own cultural beliefs so that these do not intrude on the client–counsellor relationship. In any exploration of cultural issues the aim is to produce a better relationship with the client and to understand the client's problems more fully. During a counselling session it is not justifiable for a counsellor to explore cultural issues out of curiosity, or to satisfy the counsellor's own personal needs.

As a counsellor it is essential to avoid stereotyping clients in relation to their racial or ethnic background. We need to remember that all human beings are unique individuals. Even though we each may have particular ethnic backgrounds, the extent of our individual differences makes us all into very different people. However, just as an over-emphasis on cultural issues may obscure the personal and individual issues of the client, an over-emphasis on individuality may obscure cultural issues. As counsellors we need to treat each client as an individual person recognising their individual issues in the wider context of their personal cultural background and the cultural background of the wider society in which they live.

Counsellors need to be aware that not only are there individual differences between the people from a particular ethnic group, but also there may be significant differences between sub-groups within an ethnic group. For example, Aboriginal culture and language differ markedly across different groups, and members within any particular group differ in their adherence to the group's cultural traditions and practices (Powell 2000).

When counselling culturally different clients the counsellor may need to take responsibility for helping clients to understand the counselling process and issues relating to goals, expectations, legal rights and the counsellor's orientation. Negotiation and contracting may be required in order to provide a counselling service that is acceptable and useful for the client.

Counsellors need to be able to engage in a variety of verbal and non-verbal helping responses so that they are able to send and receive both verbal and non-verbal messages accurately and appropriately. In order to do this satisfactorily counsellors need to be aware of the ways in which their own communication styles are different from their clients'. They need to recognise how differences in style may interfere with the counselling process. Counsellors also need to recognise that there is almost always more than one method or approach suitable for helping any particular client, and that some helping styles may be culture-bound. Thus, counsellors need to have an open mind so that they are able to use alternative ways of working. It may be useful for counsellors to consult with, and/or work in conjunction with, traditional healers or spiritual leaders when counselling clients from some cultures.

Establishing rapport

When counselling clients from some cultural groups, joining and engaging may involve a lengthy process. For example, when working with Aboriginal people counsellors need to spend time discussing their own background, where they have lived and worked, and who they might know in other Aboriginal communities. By doing this it may be possible to create an atmosphere of trust by identifying some common connections with other people or places.

Eye contact

Attending behaviours vary from culture to culture and from individual to individual. In fact individual differences among clients may be as important as cultural patterns.

In some cultures, when listening to a person, direct eye contact is appropriate, but when talking, eye contact should be less frequent. This pattern may be directly opposite or may not apply in other cultures. In particular, many Aboriginal people find direct eye contact unfriendly and intimidating.

Body language and physical space

Most counsellors pay a lot of attention to their client's body language. However, as counsellors, we need to be very careful about interpreting body language. The only person who can accurately and consistently interpret a person's body language is the person themselves. Even so, as counsellors, it is important for us to learn what we can from body language cues which clients give us. When a counsellor works with a client from the same cultural background, the meaning of body language is often fairly clear, and this can easily be confirmed by checking with the client. When working with clients from a different culture it is far more difficult to make interpretations regarding body language because there is considerable variation in cultural norms.

In most cultures when two people are holding a conversation they prefer the distance between them to be at least an arms length. However, this norm is not universal. In Arab and Middle Eastern cultures a conversational distance of 150–300 mm is generally the accepted practice. Such close proximity would be uncomfortable for many Western people.

Shaking hands is generally seen as a sign of welcome in Western culture. However it is dangerous to assume that this is the case in other cultures. Indeed, in some cultures if a male gives a female a handshake, this may be seen as giving a sexual invitation.

In Aboriginal culture restlessness does not necessarily indicate inattention. Additionally, eye, head or lip movements may be used to indicate direction of motion, or the location of a person or event being discussed.

Language and translation issues

Clients are able to express themselves more meaningfully in their own language (Ivey, Ivey & Simek-Morgan 1996). It may therefore sometimes be sensible and appropriate for a counsellor to make use of an interpreter in a counselling session. We have done this on a number of occasions with success, but recognise that there are some problems in doing this. Firstly, unless the client feels comfortable with and trusts the interpreter, they may not feel able to disclose important and relevant personal information. Secondly, it is possible that the interpreter's own personal issues might intrude on the counselling process. Additionally, where highly emotional personal issues are raised, it may be necessary for the counsellor to help the interpreter to debrief. If this is not done the interpreter may be left with uncomfortable and disturbing feelings.

When working with an interpreter the counsellor's understanding of the client's and the interpreter's use of language is important. Sometimes, in the transfer of information from the counsellor to the interpreter to the client, and from the client to the interpreter to the counsellor, subtle and important changes in the meaning may occur.

Micro-skills

When working with clients from a different cultural background the most important thing for a counsellor to remember is to focus on creating a trusting relationship. This may mean making progress more slowly rather than attempting to encourage the client to talk through sensitive personal issues too early in the process. It is also important to be congruent and this requires the counsellor to be honest and open about their limitations particularly with regard to their understanding of the client's cultural background.

Once rapport has been developed, it may be sensible and possible for a counsellor to invite the client to give them feedback if the client becomes uncomfortable with any part of the process.

Counsellors need to be familiar with the use of all of the micro-skills described earlier in this book. However, early in the process of relationship-building it may be useful to focus more heavily on active listening than on using other skills. In particular, it needs to be remembered that a question-and-answer style of gathering information is alien to clients from many different cultures, so until you are confident of the client's cultural norms in this regard, it is wise to avoid the use of questions as much as is possible and to use a less intrusive and more indirect style of relating.

Particularly when working with Aboriginal people, direct questions should be avoided, as they are considered intrusive and discourteous. When seeking personal details relating to clients from this group counsellors may gain by sharing information about themselves and then allowing some time for silence. This can give an indirect indication of the type of information that may be useful, without an obligation to respond immediately. This is important, because silence is a positively valued part of Aboriginal conversations. Consequently, Aboriginal people typically take longer to respond. Generally, the most useful information obtained from counselling sessions with them is information which emerges freely in a narrative style of conversation. This is likely to occur when clients are encouraged to provide an account of events or situations in their own words, at their own pace, and without interruption.

Learning summary

- The most important factor in producing successful outcomes when counselling clients from other cultures is the counsellor's ability to join with the client so that a good, trusting working relationship is established.
- Counsellors need to be aware of their own racial and cultural heritage and to understand how that heritage has affected their attitudes, beliefs, values, prejudices and biases.
- The client's emotional responses, thoughts, beliefs, attitudes, biases, relationships and behaviours will be affected by a number of factors including individual and relationship issues, the way decisions are made, who is perceived to be a natural helper, attitudes in the extended family, gender and gender roles, perceptions of time, use of language, spirituality, physical or emotional issues, and experience of trauma.

Further reading

Bowden, R. 2000, 'Psychotherapy as a container for bi-cultural practice in Aotearoa', *Psychotherapy*, vol. 7, no. 1, pp. 10–15.

Eades, D. 1994, 'A case of communicative clash: Aboriginal English and the legal system', in *Language and the Law*, J. Gibbons (ed.), Longman, Essex.

Eades, D. 1995, 'Aboriginal English on trial: The case for Stewart and Condren', in *Language in Evidence: Issues Confronting Aboriginal and Multicultural Australia*, D. Eades (ed.), University of New South Wales Press, Sydney.

Foley, M. 1984, 'Aborigines and the police', in *Aborigines and the Law:*

Essays in Memory of Elizabeth Egglestone, P. Hanks & B. Keon-Cohen (eds), Allen & Unwin, Sydney.

Ivey, A., Ivey, B. & Simek-Morgan, L. 1996, *Psychotherapy: A Multicultural Perspective*, Allyn and Bacon, Boston.

Lee, C. C. & Richardson, B. L. 1991, *Multicultural Issues in Counselling: New Approaches to Diversity*, American Association For Counselling And Development, Alexandria,VA.

McFadden, J. 1993, *Transcultural Counseling: Bilateral and International Perspectives*, American Counselling Association, Alexandria, VA.

Powell, M. B. 2000, 'Pride: the essential elements of a forensic interview with an Aboriginal person', *Australian Psychologist*, vol. 35 , no. 3, pp. 186–192.

Ridley, C. R. 1995, *Overcoming Unintentional Racism in Counseling and Therapy: A Practitioner's Guide to Intentional Intervention*, Sage, Thousand Oaks.

Tharp, R. 1991, 'Cultural diversity and the treatment of children', *Journal Of Consulting And Clinical Psychology*, vol. 59, pp. 799–812.

Vicary, D. & Andrews, H. 2000, 'Developing a culturally appropriate psychotherapeutic approach with indigenous Australians', *Australian Psychologist*, vol. 35, no. 3, pp. 181–185.

Waterman, A. 1984, *The Psychology of Individualism*, Praeger, New York.

chapter **35**

Influence of the counsellor's values and beliefs

In Chapter 2 we discussed the need for counsellors to try to be non-judgmental. Can you imagine what it would be like if you were a client talking to a counsellor and as you were talking you formed the impression that the counsellor was disapproving of you, or of what you were saying? We suspect that in such a situation you would feel inhibited and might decide that it was not wise to talk openly to this counsellor. Alternatively, can you imagine what it would be like for you if the counsellor seemed to be troubled by what you were saying and was questioning whether your values and beliefs were acceptable? Once again, we suspect that you might feel uncertain about continuing to disclose information. Clearly, there is a risk that the counselling process will be compromised if the counsellor appears to be judgmental.

Sometimes it is very hard not to be judgmental. I, David, have found that it is especially hard when I am confused or not clear about my own values or beliefs. When I am not clear, I find that I can easily show disapproval, or get distracted by spending time thinking about my own values and beliefs instead of attending to the client. It is therefore important for counsellors to know where they stand with regard to their own personal values and beliefs.

Sometimes a counsellor's values and beliefs will match those of the client, but often they will not. If I am to be able to help a client with different values from mine, then I need to understand the client's world in the context of their value system and not mine. If I am not able to do this, then I will not be able to join with the client empathically and what I say to them will be likely to jar, confuse or create a barrier between us. At worst, I might get into an argument about values instead of helping my client to sort out their confusion!

I have no right to try to impose my values on a client. However, I believe that there are times when it is appropriate for me to be open with a client about my values in order for me to be congruent.

If I have a clear understanding of my own values, I have an inner strength. I will not need to be defensive in trying to justify my values; they are mine and they will stand in their own right without the need for justification.

If I don't understand and know my own values, I may well be trapped into trying to discover what they are during a counselling session. Instead of being able to concentrate on seeing the world through my client's eyes, I may be distracted by trying to sort out the confusion in my own head. Questions such as, 'Is this morally right or wrong?', may trouble me and prevent me from joining the client in their own struggle to work out what is right for them.

People change as they understand themselves better

The more I work as a counsellor, the more I believe that most people are naturally well-intentioned, caring of others, socially responsible and capable of giving and receiving love. When I meet someone who seems to be nasty, I almost always, as I get to know them better, recognise the damage that has been done to them by past life experiences. As counselling proceeds I usually notice changes occurring as that person comes to terms with past experiences. It is as though a plant that looked like a thistle is changing into something more attractive. With this belief I do not need to try to convince others to accept my values; I just need to understand them better and to help them to understand themselves better.

I remember a friend who trained as a priest telling me that while at university an agnostic lecturer told him that arguments from strongly evangelical Christian students never threatened, or made him question, his agnostic beliefs. However, the lecturer found that my friend made him think about his agnosticism. Rather than confront him with a different point of view, my friend respected him enough to accept him as he was and tried to see the world through his eyes when he talked with him. My friend knew clearly what he himself believed and openly owned his beliefs but did not push them on his lecturer or attack his lecturer's position. As a consequence, he was able to join with this lecturer in a way which allowed the lecturer to explore different ways of thinking in safety and without feeling pressured. The opportunity for change was maximised.

Being non-judgmental isn't easy

As children, our values and beliefs are initially those of our parents and significant others such as teachers. It is appropriate that as young people we accept without question the values and beliefs of those adults who are important in our lives. To use a Gestalt therapy concept, these values and beliefs are swallowed whole. In Gestalt therapy, they are said to have been introjected and are called *introjects*. As we grow up our values and beliefs will change as we accept some of our earlier values and beliefs but modify others in the light of our own experiences. Clearly though, our values and beliefs are likely to be influenced by both the cultural background in which we grew up as children and by the contemporary culture of the societal group within which we live. As counsellors we are therefore likely, at times, to work with clients who may have quite different values from our own.

Being non-judgmental is not so easy at times. Counsellors are sometimes faced with situations where client values strongly conflict with their own. When this happens, it is as though a button is pushed within the counsellor who immediately becomes emotionally aroused by the fear of threat to their own value system.

The first step in dealing with a values conflict between yourself and a client is to recognise it. You will probably be able to do this fairly easily if you remember that the warning sign of a values conflict is likely to be emotional arousal in yourself. If you feel your body tensing, or other bodily symptoms of arousal, then stop and think. Ask yourself, 'What is happening?' Check out whether your values are being challenged. Similarly, if you find that you are starting to disagree with a client and to argue with them, stop and think, to check out whether or not you are involved in a values conflict.

Owning your own value system

It is not going to be helpful to the client, from a counselling perspective, if you deliberately try to change their point of view. As has been emphasised, effective counsellors join with their clients and try to see the world as their clients see it. When you sense that you are encountering a values conflict, then you need to make a choice by asking yourself, 'Can I put my own values to one side in order to join with this client or not?' If the answer is 'Yes', then counselling can proceed. If it is 'No', then to be fair to the client you will need to tell them that while you respect them and their right to have a different point of view, you have different values with regard to the issue in question. If you feel able to do so, it will be useful for you to explain to the client that you are not saying that your values are better or worse than their values; they are just different because you are two different people. You can then offer the client the option of continuing to talk with you if they wish, or of talking with someone else. If the client wants to talk with someone else, then refer them to someone who may be able to meet with them on their own value-ground.

Sometimes you may recognise an important values difference between your client and yourself, but will feel able to put your own values to one side while counselling and suspend judgment. When this happens you may need to continually remind yourself to imagine you are the client, with their world view. When your own values start intruding on the counselling process, recognise this, and once again focus on the client's perspective. If you are able to stay fully tuned in to the client's thoughts and feelings, your counselling will be more likely to be effective. Moreover, you will be more likely to be successful in putting your own values to one side so that they remain intact as part of you.

The need for supervision

Whenever a values conflict interferes with your work with a client, it is important for you to talk with your supervisor about the issues involved. By doing this you will minimise the possibility of future situations where the effectiveness of your counselling might be adversely affected by the particular value in question. Hopefully, if you fully explore the relevant issues, you will be able to work with clients with very different points of view from yourself without your own values influencing the appropriateness of your counselling responses.

As discussed previously, it is very important for counsellors to know, as clearly as possible, what their values are.

Knowing your values

How can you, as a new counsellor, know what your values are? There are so many areas in life where values are important that it is impossible in training to cover all value-laden situations. Inevitably some of these will emerge during counselling sessions. Counsellors have to continually address new issues. Even so, it is possible in training to examine some commonly encountered situations or beliefs where values are of importance.

A values clarification exercise

As an aid to counsellor training we suggest the following exercise in values clarification. This exercise is best done in a group where discussion of differing values can occur. A good way to carry out the exercise is to label one end of the training room 'agree' and the other end 'disagree'. Trainees, as a group, can then be asked to respond to each statement below by individually positioning themselves in the room somewhere on the agree–disagree continuum along the length of the room. Once trainees have positioned themselves in response to a statement, the facilitator can invite comment and promote discussion with regard to their positions in the room.

If you are not in a group, then you may wish to think about each of the statements below to try to work out where you stand with regard to each. Do you agree or disagree with the statement, or stand somewhere between the agree–disagree position?

Please notice that many of the statements below are statements of belief rather than value statements. However, our values are determined by our beliefs, so in determining our values, it's important to also consider beliefs.

Statements for values clarification exercise

Warning!

Some of these statements are intentionally provocative and may offend.

- Unemployment benefits should be terminated after three months.
- People of other nationalities should be treated with suspicion.
- Termination of pregnancy is a woman's right.
- Men are always to blame for domestic violence.
- Women and men are equal.
- Guns don't kill; the people who fire them do.
- Gun laws are for the benefit of the community as a whole.
- With modern contraceptive methods sexual fidelity is no longer necessary.

- Censorship is socially desirable.
- Homosexuality is a normal condition.
- Delinquency is due to parents being too permissive with their children.
- Counsellors wouldn't be needed if people would turn to God.
- Usually one partner is mostly to blame when a marriage breaks up.
- Marijuana should be legalised.
- The Aboriginal people deserve to have land rights.
- Welfare benefits are too high.
- Couples should stay together for the sake of their children.
- Children in two-parent families are happier than children in single-parent families.
- If a person has an affair their spouse should leave them.
- Contraception is wrong.
- People who have had psychiatric treatment are not suitable for leadership positions.
- Lying is sometimes justifiable.
- Charities deserve regular donations.
- Good people should not associate with immoral people.
- Anyone can get a job if they try hard enough.
- Life is to be enjoyed.
- Striving for wealth is wrong.
- Handouts do not help people.
- People can be too honest.
- Sex is overrated.
- Smoking in public places should be banned.
- Love and forgiveness are more important than punishment.
- Alcohol more frequently gives pleasure than it creates problems.
- Alternative medicine is more useful than conventional medicine.
- I don't want to change other people so that they have the same values as I do.
- It's OK for a father to bath his young daughter.
- Chemicals are harmful.
- It's a good idea to build large concrete dams.
- Masturbating is enjoyable and acceptable.
- People should not be allowed to spoil rainforests by tramping through them.

- Sex offenders are nasty people.
- Too much closeness in a family is a bad thing.
- Adult needs should take precedence over children's needs.
- Killing people is wrong.
- The use of four-letter words is offensive.
- The developed countries should feed the developing countries.
- I believe in heaven.
- Oral sex is enjoyable and acceptable.
- Divorce is wrong.
- De facto relationships are moral and acceptable.
- Children who receive sex education are more likely to be promiscuous than those who don't.
- The Bible tells us what is right and what is wrong.
- Single parents shouldn't have sexual relationships with special friends.
- Single parents who have sexual relationships with special friends should be open about what they are doing and should tell their children.
- Hospital births are better for babies than home births.
- Things are either right or wrong; there are no in-betweens.
- Smacking children is unnecessary.
- Only married people should have sexual intercourse.
- It's OK for a 16-year-old to have sexual intercourse.
- You can tell what a person is really like from their appearance.
- It is good to strive for material possessions.
- Money doesn't bring happiness.
- Children should be breastfed until they want to stop.
- Families should have clear rules.
- Children should be allowed to make their own decisions.
- Children are better off in child care than with their mothers.
- We need fewer laws and more freedom.
- Most people are intrinsically good.

When considering your position with regard to the above statements, please remember that we are all unique individuals and different from each other. Consequently, in some ways, your values will probably be similar to ours, and in some ways they will be different. We are comfortable with that. Are you?

Learning summary

- Counsellors need to know their own beliefs and values so that they are not distracted during counselling sessions by trying to sort them out and so that they can respect their clients' value systems.
- Counsellors have no right to try to impose their own beliefs or values on clients.
- Whenever a values conflict interferes with your work, consult your supervisor.

Further reading

Corey, M. S. & Corey, G. 1993, *Becoming a Helper*, Brooks/Cole, Pacific Grove.

Ridley, C. R. 1995, *Overcoming Unintentional Racism in Counseling and Therapy: A Practitioner's Guide to Intentional Intervention*, Sage, Thousand Oaks.

Worthington, E. (ed.) 1993, *Psychotherapy and Religious Values*, Baker, Grand Rapids.

chapter 36

Confidentiality and other ethical issues

The first part of this chapter will be devoted exclusively to confidentiality, because it is one of the most important ethical issues for a counsellor. Other aspects of professional ethics will be considered in the second part of the chapter.

Confidentiality

For counselling to be maximally effective, the client must feel secure in the knowledge that what they tell the counsellor is to be treated with a high degree of confidentiality. In an ideal world a client would be offered total confidentiality so that they would feel free to openly explore with the counsellor the darkest recesses of their mind, and to discuss the most intimate details of their thoughts. As a new counsellor I, David, naively believed that I could at all times give my clients an assurance that what was said in a counselling session was between them and me and would not be discussed with others. I very soon learnt that this was an idealistic belief and found that in practice it is generally not possible, advisable or ethical to offer total confidentiality.

As a counsellor you may at times be troubled by some personal difficulties regarding confidentiality and may need to talk with your supervisor about these. Counsellors are faced with a dilemma with regard to confidentiality. Unless we give our clients an assurance that what they tell us will be in confidence, they are unlikely to be open with us. However, there are limits to the level of confidentiality which we can offer and we need to be clear with clients about these limits. Most importantly, as a counsellor you need to be aware of the limits to the confidentiality which you are offering.

Many experienced counsellors would agree with Woolfe and Dryden who in the *Handbook of Counselling Psychology* (1996) go so far as to say that promising total confidentiality is unethical. It is certainly true that confidentiality is compromised by the following:

- the need to keep records;
- the requirements of the counsellor's own supervision;
- the need to protect others;
- working in conjunction with other professionals;
- participation in educational training programs, conferences, workshops and seminars; and
- cases where the law requires disclosure of information.

The above list will now be discussed in detail.

The need to keep records

As explained in Chapter 33 there are compelling reasons for keeping good records. Counsellors who work in agencies frequently use computerised systems or centralised filing systems for such records. This may make it possible for other counsellors and non-counselling staff such as receptionists and filing clerks to have access to confidential records. Some counsellors omit to note certain categories of sensitive material on their record cards as a way of protecting clients. However, there are obvious consequences if this policy is adopted, as important information may be overlooked or forgotten during subsequent counselling sessions. Clearly, for the protection of clients, computerised records need to be protected by adequate security systems. Similarly, hard-copy records should not be left lying around in places where they can be read by unauthorised people, and should be stored in lockable filing cabinets or in a secure filing room.

Requirements of the counsellor's own supervision

The requirements of professional supervision, as described in Chapter 37, demand that counsellors be free to fully disclose client material to their supervisors. This is essential if clients are to receive the best possible service, and is also necessary for the wellbeing of counsellors themselves. Some counsellors openly talk with their clients about the requirements of professional supervision and sometimes it can be reassuring for a client to know that their counsellor is receiving supervision.

The need to protect others

Experienced counsellors sometimes work with dangerous clients, or with clients who have committed serious offences against other people and may possibly repeat such behaviour. Clearly, counsellors have responsibilities not only to their clients, but also to the community. There may be instances where a counsellor needs to divulge information to protect a third party. For example, if a counsellor knows that their client possesses a gun and intends to kill someone, then it would be unethical and irresponsible if the person at risk, the police and/or the psychiatric authorities were not informed. Where there is doubt about the desirability of informing others, counsellors need to consult their supervisors.

Working in conjunction with other professionals

Professionals such as psychiatrists, medical practitioners, psychologists, social workers, clergy and welfare workers frequently phone counsellors to talk with them about mutual clients. It is sometimes important for the welfare of such clients that other professionals are appropriately informed about their situations. It is also desirable for counsellors to maintain good working relationships with other helping professionals. Sensible judgments need to be made about what information is disclosed and what is withheld. If you believe that it is desirable that sensitive material be disclosed, then you will need to obtain the client's permission first, unless there are unusual and compelling reasons for not doing so. Obtaining the client's permission involves informing the client about what you wish to do and why. Thus the client is able to give *informed consent*. This informed consent should be verified in writing so there can be no misunderstanding. Many agencies have a standard consent form which can be used when information is to be shared. This form is discussed with the client and then signed by both the client and the counsellor.

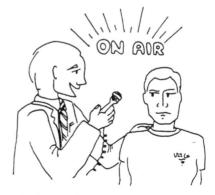

An issue of trust

Sometimes new counsellors think that it is undesirable and unnecessary to ever allow the sharing of such information. However, consider the following example. Imagine that a client comes to see you and that a psychiatrist who is treating another member of the family gives you some helpful and useful information, and asks you to help her by confirming that her perception of the family situation is accurate. It may well be advantageous, in the therapeutic management of both clients, if you work cooperatively with the psychiatrist. In such an instance, it could be appropriate to obtain client permission, and to keep the client informed of ongoing contact with the psychiatrist.

Where two members of a family require counselling help, the need for family therapy is usually indicated. However, if family therapy is not available, or is considered inappropriate, then any helping professionals involved with members of the family are likely to achieve more for their clients if they consult each other, have case conferences and work together as a team.

Sometimes you may discover that a client of yours is also consulting another counselling professional. There is rarely justification for two counsellors working with the same client, and so after discussion with the client it is sensible to contact the other counsellor to decide who will take over the case. There are exceptions to most rules, and sometimes if good contact is maintained between two counsellors it may be possible for them both to remain involved provided that each sets clear boundaries and goals for their work.

Educational training programs, conferences, workshops and seminars

Another problem area regarding confidentiality concerns ongoing training, upgrading of skills and sharing of new techniques. Counsellors need to grow and develop as people and as counsellors. This can partly be done through personal supervision and partly through large group sharing at conferences, seminars, workshops and case conferences. Client material that is presented at such events can sometimes be disguised by changing names and other details, but often this is not possible, particularly when video-recordings of counselling sessions are used. Client material should never be used in this way without the prior written consent of the client. Moreover, there could be legal as well as ethical problems if consent is not obtained.

Where the law requires disclosure of information

Remember that client confidentiality may be limited by legal intervention. Sometimes counsellors are subpoenaed to give evidence in court and in such cases withholding information may be in contempt of court. Additionally, mandatory reporting is required by counsellors from certain professions in some countries and/or states with regard to issues such as child abuse.

Respecting the client's right to privacy

Clearly, from the preceding discussion, there are many reasons why confidentiality in the counselling situation is limited. However, it is the counsellor's task to ensure that client confidentiality is preserved as far as is sensibly, legally and ethically possible. Assure your clients that you will do this to the best of your ability, because they need to feel that whatever they share with you is protected information which will not be carelessly or unnecessarily divulged to others. It is quite unethical to talk about clients or client material to any person whatsoever, except in the circumstances previously described in this chapter. What a client shares with you is personal property and must not be shared around, so if you do have a need to talk about a client or their issues then talk with your supervisor.

You will need to make your own decisions, in consultation with your supervisor, about how best to deal with the confidentiality issue. Our policy is to be up-front with clients and to explain the limits of confidentiality as they apply. For example, if we work for an agency, that agency may have a policy regarding confidentiality. Consequently we need to inform the client of the policy. If we need to divulge information for an ethically acceptable and professional reason, then we obtain the client's informed consent. In a situation where a third party is in danger, we will seek the informed consent of the client but if this is not given we will be direct and open about our intentions to disclose, subject of course to our own safety. This policy seeks to ensure maximum client and community protection.

Professional ethics

The issue of confidentiality has been discussed in some detail. However, there are many other ethical issues for counsellors, and a new counsellor needs to be informed of these. Many counsellors belong to professional associations with codes of ethical conduct. These codes are readily available on request, and it is sensible for a new counsellor to read through the relevant code for the relevant profession. Some of the more important ethical issues are included in the list below, and these will be discussed in subsequent paragraphs:

- respect for the client
- limits of the client–counsellor relationship
- responsibility of the counsellor
- counsellor competence
- referral
- termination of counselling
- legal obligations
- self-promotion.

Respect for the client

Regardless of who the client is, and regardless of their behaviour, the client has come to you for help and deserves to be treated as a human being of worth. If you treasure your client then, through feeling valued, they will be given the optimum conditions in which to maximise their potential as an individual. Most helping professionals agree that within each of us is the potential for good, and for that potential to be realised we need to feel OK about ourselves. Counsellors therefore have a responsibility to help their clients to feel OK about themselves, and to increase their feelings of self-worth.

If we try to impose our own moral values on clients, then we are likely to make them feel judged and to damage their self-worth. Moreover, they are likely to reject us as counsellors and to reject our values too. Paradoxically, if we are able to accept our clients, with whatever values they have, we are likely to find that as time passes they will move closer to us in their beliefs. This is inevitable because, as counsellors, we are, whether we like it or not, models for our clients. We have a responsibility to be good models. In this regard, it can be useful to create opportunities for clients to give feedback about their experience of the counselling process. This will demonstrate respect for their views and their right to have some influence in the counselling relationship.

We need to remember that the client's interests must take precedence over the counsellor's during the counselling process. It is not ethical to use counselling sessions with clients to work through our own issues. The correct time for working through our issues is in supervision sessions.

Respect involves protecting the client's rights. Clients have a right to know when information about them is being recorded and if the records are on a computer system. Further, the client has the right to see records concerning themselves if they wish. This right is covered by legislation in specific situations in various countries and states.

Limits of the client–counsellor relationship

In all our relationships we set limits. Each of us has a boundary around us to preserve our identity as an individual. The strength of that boundary, and its nature, depends on who the relationship is with, and on the context of the relationship. The client–counsellor relationship is a special type of relationship, established by the client for a particular purpose. The client enters into the relationship entrusting the counsellor with their wellbeing and expecting that the counsellor will, throughout the relationship, provide them with a safe environment in which they can work on their problems.

As discussed previously, the client–counsellor relationship is not an equal relationship and inevitably, whether the counsellor wishes it or not, they are in a position of power and influence. They are often working with clients who are in highly emotional states and are consequently very vulnerable. The way in which a counsellor relates to a client is uncharacteristic human behaviour. A counsellor devotes most of their energy to listening to and understanding the client, and so the client sees only a part of the counsellor's character. In these circumstances, a client may perceive a counsellor as unrealistically caring and giving. The counsellor's power and the client's biased perception combine to make the client very vulnerable to offers of friendship or closeness.

The counsellor is also vulnerable. In the counselling relationship, the client often shares innermost secrets, and so inevitably there may develop a real closeness between the client and counsellor. Counsellors learn to be empathic, and so they develop special relationships with their clients. If they are not careful they too become vulnerable to offers of closer relationships than are appropriate. Counsellors therefore need to be careful not to discount sign-posts that the counselling relationship is being compromised.

Unfortunately, it is almost always unhelpful and damaging to the client when the client–counsellor relationship is allowed to extend beyond the limits of the counselling situation. If such an extension occurs, the counsellor's ability to attend to the client's needs is seriously diminished, and there may well be serious psychological consequences for the client.

As a counsellor, it may at times be hard to refuse invitations to get closer to your clients than the counselling situation allows. Remember that if you do not set appropriate boundaries you will merely be satisfying your own needs at the expense of the client. You will have abused your special position of trust as a professional, and you will have to live with that knowledge, and with any more serious consequences. When counsellors breach appropriate boundaries they may damage or diminish the usefulness of the counselling process and reduce the possibility that the client will seek further counselling help. Be aware of the danger signals when your relationship with a client is becoming too close, and bring the issue into the open by discussing it with your supervisor and with the client, if that is appropriate.

Counsellors need to exercise care if they touch a client in any way. Unwelcome touching is not only unethical but also can result in sexual harassment charges.

Responsibility of the counsellor

Counsellors frequently experience a sense of conflict between their responsibilities to the client, to the agency which employs them and to the community. You will at times need to make your own decisions about which of these responsibilities needs to take precedence, and in our view the decision is unlikely always to be the same. If you are in doubt about any particular decision, consult your supervisor.

Clearly, the counsellor has a responsibility to the client and needs to directly address the client's request for counselling help. When a client comes to you for confidential help, you have an implied contract with them to give them that, unless you tell them something to the contrary. Clearly though, you cannot ethically fulfil the client's needs if doing so would:

- involve working in opposition to the policies of the organisation that employs you
- involve a breach of the law
- put other members of the community at risk
- be impossible for you personally.

However, in these situations you need to be clear with your client about your own position, so that they understand the conditions under which they are talking to you.

Counsellors who are employed by an organisation or institution have a responsibility to that employing body. All the work they do within that organisation or institution needs to fulfil the requirements of the employing body, and to fit in with the philosophical expectations of the employing body. For example, when I, Kathryn, worked in a part-time capacity for the Child and Youth Mental Health Service in Queensland, it was my responsibility to comply with the policies of the Queensland Department of Health. If I had not been able to do that, then I would have had an ethical responsibility to discuss the issue with my employers, or to resign.

Counsellors at all times have to be aware of their responsibilities to the community at large. As discussed earlier, this raises problems with regard to confidentiality. Whenever a member of the community is at risk, or property is likely to be damaged, or other illegal actions are likely to occur or have occurred, then a counsellor has an obligation to take appropriate action. Often decisions do not involve choosing between black and white, but rather between shades of grey, and sometimes counsellors find it difficult to decide what is most appropriate in order to serve the needs of the client and community in the long term. At these times the sensible approach is for a counsellor to talk through the ethical issues with their supervisor.

Counsellor competence

A counsellor has a responsibility to ensure that they give the highest possible standard of service. This cannot be done without adequate training and supervision. All counsellors need to attend to their own professional development and to have supervision from another counsellor on a regular basis. Failure to do this is certain to result in the counsellor's own issues intruding into the counselling process, and this will be to the detriment of the client (see Chapter 37).

A counsellor also needs to be aware of the limits of their competence. We all have limits professionally and personally, and it is essential that as counsellors we are able to recognise our limits and to be open with our clients about those limits. The client has a right to know whether they are seeing someone who has, or does not have, the abilities necessary to give them the help they require.

Referral

When a client's needs cannot be adequately met by a counsellor, then that counsellor has a responsibility to make an appropriate referral, in consultation with the client, to another suitable professional. However, it is not appropriate for a counsellor to avoid all difficult and unenjoyable work by excessively referring clients to others. There is a responsibility on all counsellors to carry a fair load, and to be sensible about referral decisions. Such decisions are best made in consultation with a supervisor.

It may sometimes be appropriate for a counsellor to continue seeing a client while under intensive supervision, instead of referring. If this happens, then the counsellor has a responsibility to inform the client.

Often, referral is useful where people have special needs. For example, people with particular disabilities, people from other cultures and people who speak another language may benefit from referral to an agency (or professional) which can provide for their specific needs.

When referring clients to others, it may be useful to contact the professional to whom the referral is being made, with the client's permission, to ensure that the referral is acceptable and appropriate.

Termination of counselling

Termination of counselling needs to be carried out sensitively and with appropriate timing (see Chapter 10). It is not ethical to terminate counselling at a point where the client still needs further help. If for some unavoidable reason (such as leaving the district) you need to do this, then it is incumbent upon you to make a suitable referral to another counsellor who can continue to give the necessary support.

Legal obligations

Counsellors, like all other professionals and every other member of the community, need to operate within the law. Therefore, as a counsellor, you need to familiarise yourself with the relevant legal requirements for your profession. It is particularly important to know whether mandatory reporting of specific behaviours such as suspected child abuse is required.

Self-promotion

Most professional associations for counsellors have specific rules about advertising. There is clearly an ethical issue with regard to the way in which counsellors describe themselves and their services. It is unethical for a counsellor to make claims about themselves or their services which are inaccurate or cannot be substantiated. Counsellors who do this not only put their clients at risk, but may also face the possibility of prosecution.

Learning summary

- For counselling to be most effective a high degree of confidentiality is required.
- Confidentiality is limited by the need to keep records, professional supervision, the law, the protection of others, participation in training conferences and cooperation with other professionals.
- Professional ethics relate to issues such as respect for the client; limits to the relationship with the client; responsibility to the client, the employing agency and the community; competence; referral to others; termination of counselling; legal obligations; and self-promotion.

Further reading

Corey, G., Corey, M. S. & Callanan, P. 1998, *Issues and Ethics in the Helping Professions*, Brooks/Cole, California.

Shillito-Clarke, C. 1996, 'Ethical Issues in Counselling Psychology', in *Handbook of Counselling Psychology*, Woolfe, R. & Dryden, W. (eds), Sage, London.

Woolfe, R. & Dryden, W. (eds) 1996, *Handbook of Counselling Psychology*, Sage, London.

chapter **37**

The need for supervision

Clients are people with real needs. They need to be valued and given the best available help. It is therefore not ethical for a client to be seen by a new counsellor unless that counsellor is being adequately supervised. Additionally, our belief is that all counsellors, new and experienced, should have ongoing supervision. There are several important and quite different reasons for this including the following:

- to enable the counsellor to work through their own personal issues;
- to enable counsellors to upgrade their skills;
- to provide an external review of the counselling process for particular clients; and
- to address issues concerning dependency and professional boundaries.

We will now consider each of the above.

To enable the counsellor to work through personal issues

You may be surprised at the suggestion that supervision is required to enable the counsellor to work through their own personal issues. You may be asking, 'If counselling is for the benefit of the client and not the counsellor, why should the counsellor use counselling supervision in order to deal with their own issues?' The answer is simple: unless a counsellor owns and deals with their own issues, these issues are quite likely to interfere with the counselling process to the detriment of the client. Frequently, a counsellor will feel emotional pain when their client discusses issues similar to the counsellor's own unresolved emotional issues. Consequently, when issues issues are discussed which are painful for the counsellor as a result of unresolved issues, the counsellor may consciously or unconsciously avoid their own pain in a number of ways:

- The counsellor might deflect away from the painful issue by encouraging the client to talk about something else.
- The counsellor might try to comfort the client rather than to help the client to deal with the issue.
- The counsellor might attempt to encourage the client to pursue a course of action that in some way satisfies the counsellor's own needs. The counsellor may wish, for example, that they had taken a particular course of action in their own life and may encourage the client to take a similar course.
- The counsellor may avoid facing both their own issue and the client's by failing to recognise the issues and subconsciously suppressing them.

A perceptive supervisor will spot counsellor behaviour that demonstrates avoidance of painful issues and will ask the supervisee to explore whatever was happening emotionally within them when the avoidance occurred. This means that counsellors need to be prepared to own and explore their own issues on an ongoing basis. Otherwise these issues are likely to diminish the effectiveness of counselling.

Most people don't look closely at their own emotional problems unless they are causing them considerable distress. It is a natural human defence to suppress uncomfortable feelings and not to delve into them without good reason. However, a counsellor must delve into uncomfortable feelings, because if they have a problem that they can't face, then it will be quite impossible for them to help a client with a similar problem. As counsellors, therefore, we need to explore and deal with all of our own painful issues as they come into our awareness. The spin-off for us is that our personal growth is enhanced when we do this.

To enable counsellors to upgrade their skills

Even experienced counsellors find it useful and valuable to learn from other counsellors. We all have a different range of skills and use differing styles when counselling. During my, David's, counselling career I have discovered that my own style has continued to change. This has enabled me to integrate new skills into my work and to continue to take a fresh approach to my counselling work rather than sink into a rut and become stale.

I find that it is sometimes useful for me to receive input from counsellors who use quite a different framework from mine. By doing this I usually find that I discover some new ideas for enhancing my own work.

Although didactic learning can be useful for counsellors, it seems to me that the experience of personal supervision is more powerful in promoting professional development. Learning through supervision can integrate skill training with personal growth. Additionally, the counsellor is reminded in supervision of how it is to be a client. This can be helpful in enabling a counsellor to continually meet with the client as a person of equal value.

To provide an external review of the counselling process for particular clients

Often clients can't see what is obvious to the counsellor because they are personally and deeply involved in their situation. In comparison a counsellor, after joining with the client and trying to see the world in the way the client does, can stand back to take a more objective view and thus see more clearly. A parallel process happens when a counsellor is being supervised. The supervisor is able to view the counselling process and the case details in a different way from the counsellor. The supervisor may recognise processes which are occurring for the client or the counsellor which have been unrecognised. Thus a supervisor is able to provide useful input on ways of working with particular clients. Additionally, supervisors hopefully have considerable experience which can be a source of useful information for a new counsellor.

To address issues concerning dependency and professional boundaries

As discussed in the previous paragraph a supervisor may recognise processes that have not been recognised by the counsellor. Of specific importance are issues of dependency and respect for professional boundaries.

It can sometimes be hard for new counsellors to recognise when the time for terminating a series of counselling sessions has been reached. This may be partly due to issues of dependence that inevitably will develop in some counselling relationships (see Chapter 10). Sometimes it is hard for a counsellor to recognise whether the client really does have a need for further counselling or whether dependency is occurring either on the part of the client or the counsellor themselves.

Dependent clients sometimes produce new material for discussion when the counselling process is moving towards closure. This may be as a consequence of a subconscious or conscious desire to prolong the counselling relationship. By discussing cases in supervision, a supervisor may be able to recognise when dependency is interfering with appropriate termination processes. Additionally a supervisor may be able to help a counsellor devise suitable strategies for managing dependency issues.

Some counsellors have difficulty in recognising when their own personal feelings towards a client could result in behaviours which would inappropriately transgress professional boundaries and consequently interfere with the counselling process. Additionally, new counsellors sometimes have difficulty in knowing how to respond to direct and/or indirect client invitations for friendship and closeness. Once again, supervision can help a counsellor to recognise inappropriate processes that are occurring and to develop appropriate strategies to deal with these processes.

What does supervision involve?

There are a number of ways in which supervision can occur:
1. by direct observation with the supervisor in the counselling room
2. by direct observation through a one-way mirror
3. by observation using a closed-circuit TV
4. by use of audio- or video-recording and analysis
5. by direct observation together with audio- or video-recording and analysis
6. by use of a verbatim report

These methods will be discussed in turn.

1. Direct observation with the supervisor in the counselling room

Trainee counsellors are usually apprehensive about seeing their first few clients. A good way to help them adjust to the counselling environment is for trainees to sit in on counselling sessions conducted by their supervisors. Naturally, the permission of the client is required. Student counsellors who are allowed to do this need to understand what their supervisor expects of them. Initially I, David, prefer my students to take a low profile and to sit quietly out of the line of vision of the client. This reduces the necessity for the client to feel the need to interact with two counsellors simultaneously, leaves me free to conduct the session in the way that I choose, and enables the trainee to observe without feeling pressured to participate. As the trainee's level of comfort increases, some participation by them can occur. Adopting this approach allows them to observe me as a model, and to feel at ease with a client and me in the room. The method allows the trainee gradually to make the transition from being a passive observer to being an active counsellor under supervision.

The process just described is excellent for raw beginners who have had no previous counselling experience but there are problems connected with having both the trainee and supervisor in the room together. Obviously, some of the intimacy of the counselling relationship is lost, and as a consequence the client may find it difficult to deal openly with sensitive issues.

2. Direct observation through a one-way mirror

The one-way mirror system as shown in Figure 37.1 provides a better alternative. Many counselling centres have a pair of adjacent rooms set up like this for training purposes and for family therapy. The one-way mirror allows a person in the observation room to watch what is happening in the counselling room without being seen. A microphone, amplifier and speaker system provide sound for the observer, so that they are able to see and hear what is happening. Ethically, it is imperative that a client who is being observed from behind a one-way mirror is informed in advance about the presence of the observer or observers, and that consent is obtained for the session to proceed in this way.

The one-way mirror system can initially be used to enable a trainee or trainees to watch an experienced counsellor at work. Later the trainee can work as a counsellor while being observed by their supervisor, and possibly by other trainees also. The system has the advantage that the supervisor is not present in the counselling room and therefore does not intrude on the counselling process. However, they are available

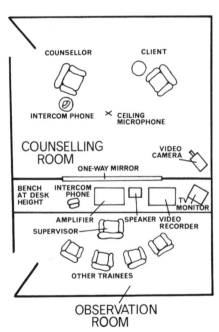

Figure 37.1 *Counselling and observations rooms*

to take over from the trainee if that becomes necessary, and they can give objective feedback after the session is completed.

3. Observation using a closed-circuit TV

A similar method to the one-way mirror system is to have a video camera in the counselling room connected to a TV monitor in another room. However, this method doesn't provide as much visual detail as is obtained with the one-way mirror system. It is often difficult to see facial expressions if the camera has a wide-angled lens to enable most of the room to be in the picture.

One of the best methods of supervision is by use of video-recordings. Audio-recordings can also be used although their usefulness is more limited because non-verbal behaviour cannot be observed. Video-recordings of counselling sessions are a rich source of information. Not only may selected segments of a session be viewed repeatedly, but it is also possible to freeze the picture so that non-verbals may be studied.

Whenever an audio- or video-recording is made it is essential to obtain the prior written consent of the client, and to tell them who will have access to the recording and when it is to be erased. Many agencies have standard consent forms for clients to sign. It is sensible to have such forms checked for their legal validity.

4. Use of audio- or video-recording and analysis

Sometimes counsellors audio- or video-tape sessions without their supervisor observing at the time. Such tapes provide an excellent opportunity for supervision. The supervisor and counsellor can then review and analyse parts of the tape. Often it can be useful for the counsellor to review additional tapes on their own in order to recognise unsatisfactory processes and to improve their counselling techniques.

5. Direct observation together with audio- or video-recording and analysis

A combination of a one-way mirror system together with audio- or video-recording is a very powerful arrangement for counsellor training. Trainees can be directly observed during practice sessions, and may later process their work in detail with their supervisors by analysing and reviewing the audio- or video-recordings.

6. Use of a verbatim report

Another method of supervision is by use of the verbatim report. A verbatim report is a written report which records, word for word, the client's statements and the counsellor's responses. It may be produced from memory, or as a transcript of an audio recording. Here is an example of a verbatim report. Note that this example is invented and does not relate to a real client or counsellor.

Verbatim report
Name of counsellor: Fiona Smith
Name of client: Simon Anonymous
Date of counselling session: 19.2.01
Background information about the client: Simon is 36 years old, has been married twice and has two children. These are a girl, 12, and a boy, 10. Both children are in the custody of Simon's second wife. He lives alone.

This was Simon's second visit to see me. He came a week ago feeling tense and depressed. He told me that he was worried about his inability to build relationships with women, and he couldn't understand why.

My feelings and attitudes prior to the session: I was feeling good and was looking forward to working with this client again. I believed that I had built a good relationship with him during the previous session and that this would enable him to talk freely with me.

What occurred prior to the responses given below: When Simon arrived for this session he looked pale and was very subdued. During the first 15 minutes of our time together his body looked tense and he seemed reluctant to talk. After a few minutes of silence, I felt as though he had put a barrier between us and I spoke.

F1   Seems like there's a barrier between us. (Said quietly.)
S1   *Ah what . . . what da ya mean? (He sounded defensive to me.)*
F2   Like we're separated by a barrier. (I used my hands to suggest a barrier.)
S2   *Separated? (Said with non-verbals that suggested disbelief and questioning. I felt very shut out from Simon now.)*
F3   Yes, I feel shut out by an invisible barrier. Sometimes you open it up a . . . (Simon interrupted heatedly.)
S3   *No, no, it's a double brick wall with a door in it. The door is usually closed and that's because it keeps me safe.*

F4   That brick wall's important to you!

S4   *It sure is!*

F5   It protects you. (Simon started to talk freely and easily after this.)

S5   *Yes, it does . . . (He went on to explain how vulnerable he would feel without the wall, and then started to cry. I waited.) . . . You see, I've been hurt too much in the past, and I'm scared that if I'm me, if I'm really me, and open up, then I'll be rejected again.*

F6   The barrier protects you from the pain of rejection. (Long pause.)

S6   *It also prevents me from getting into a relationship and I'm not sure that I like that. (Said carefully, slowly and firmly.)*

F7   You don't sound sure about whether you want the barrier or not.

S7   *Well, it would be hard to tear it down. I'm so used to it now. You know I realise that the barrier's been there for a long time now. Goodness knows what might happen if I didn't have it there.*

F8   It would be risky to tear it down.

S8   *It would. (He paused to think for what seemed a long time. I had difficulty staying silent because I wanted to tell him what he was discovering for himself.) . . . You know, I would get hurt for sure, and what's worse, I'd have to take responsibility for the ways I hurt the women I get close to. (He laughed.) That's worse. That's worse! I can't bear it when I hurt someone I love.*

F9   Getting close involves lots of hurt. (He interrupted, fortunately, before I was able to take him off track by suggesting getting close could also involve pleasure. I was bursting to tell him!)

S9   *Yes, it seems like that to me . . . (He then told me in detail about his pain at losing his second wife. He couldn't understand how he hurt so much when he had left her.) . . . It's not over yet. How can I still be hurting after so long?*

F10   I get the impression that you're still grieving.

S10   *I should be over her by now! (Said despairingly.)*

F11   It takes time to grieve. Can you give yourself time?

From here on the process flowed naturally as he dealt with his grief. I got the strong feeling that his barrier would gradually disintegrate as he worked through his grief.

My feelings after the session: I felt good because Simon had moved forwards to a fuller awareness of himself and his behaviour. I felt I had been infected by some of his sadness though.

What I have learnt from the session (or things I would do differently another time): I learnt that it was helpful for the client when I shared with him my own feelings (of separation, see F1, F2 and F3). Because he interrupted (F9 and S9), I discovered that it was better to follow his path. If I had brought the focus on to the pleasure associated with closeness then I would have made it more difficult for him to address the underlying issue of his grief. I learnt that my desire 'to make the client feel good' could have been counter-productive. I'm pleased he interrupted and prevented me from doing this.

Structure of the verbatim report

As you will see from the example of a verbatim report, the report begins with background information about the client, his problems and his emotional state. The first part of the report may also summarise the process and outcome of previous counselling sessions.

The next section of the report concerns the counsellor's own feelings and attitudes prior to the counselling session. This information is required because a counsellor's behaviour and performance is often influenced by their mood, feelings generally and feelings towards the client, and their preconceived ideas and attitudes concerning the client and the client's behaviour.

A central component of the verbatim report is the section containing client statements and counsellor responses. This section usually contains only about 10 to 20 responses from each person. It would be very laborious to write out a transcript of a substantial part of a counselling interaction and this is unnecessary. Preferably the trainee counsellor will select a portion of the session that demonstrates some important learning or highlights some difficulties. Often a new counsellor will find that a part of the interaction seems to 'go wrong' inexplicably. Such a segment provides ideal material for a verbatim report and subsequent discussion in supervision. Notice that responses are numbered and identified by the initial letter of the person's name. For example, statement F7 is Fiona's seventh in the report. After each statement other significant information is recorded, in parentheses, including non-verbal behaviour, silences and the feelings and thoughts of the counsellor.

Immediately before the verbatim client and counsellor statements is a description of what occurred in the session prior to them, and immediately after them is a brief description of what occurred in the remaining part of the session. These descriptions are required so that the statements that are recorded verbatim are seen in the context of the whole session.

The verbatim report concludes with sections that describe the counsellor's feelings after the session and what they have learnt for the future. It is then signed.

The value of verbatim reports

Verbatim reports enable a supervisor to tap into trainee issues that might have blocked them from satisfactorily helping the client to work through their issues. Such reports also enable the supervisor to identify unsatisfactory processes and inappropriate counsellor responses and to help the trainee discover better ones.

Confidentiality

Audio-recordings, video-recordings and verbatim reports require the same level of protection as client records in order to ensure that confidentiality is preserved (see Chapters 33 and 36). It is essential that tapes and reports are not left in places where they might fall into the hands of unauthorised persons.

In conclusion

By using any of the methods described in this chapter, a supervisor can help a new counsellor to improve their skills and to understand the process that occurred during a particular counselling session. This chapter has discussed ways in which you may be supervised as a new counsellor. Your initial training is just the beginning, and there is no end to the ongoing need for further training. A good counsellor never stops learning from their own experiences and from what others can teach them. In order to improve, it is advantageous to continue in supervision even as an experienced counsellor.

The counselling strategies described in this book are the basic ones. Once you have mastered them, you may wish to continue to learn from experienced counsellors who have advanced skills or who are skilled in specialised counselling techniques. We believe that ongoing training can best be carried out through experiential training in workshops and seminars, together with hands-on experience under the supervision of a qualified and experienced practitioner.

Learning summary

- It is not ethical for a new counsellor to see clients without adequate supervision.
- A counsellor's own unresolved issues will adversely affect the counselling process.
- Common supervision methods involve direct observation, observation using a closed-circuit TV, audio- or video-recording and analysis, and use of verbatim reports.

Further reading

Carroll, M. 1996, *Counselling Supervision: Theory, Skills and Practice*, Cassell, London.

Feltham, C. & Dryden, W. 1994, *Developing Counsellor Supervision*, Sage, London.

Holloway, E.L. 1999, *Clinical Supervision: A Systems Approach*, Sage, Thousand Oaks.

chapter  38

Looking after yourself

A counsellor's own wellbeing is of paramount importance. Firstly, counsellors are human beings with their own needs so it is appropriate for them to be sensible in caring for themselves. Additionally, from a professional point of view, it is important for counsellors to look after themselves because counsellors who are not feeling good are unlikely to be fully effective in helping their clients. Counselling can be draining, so counsellors need support; otherwise they are likely to find themselves emotionally depleted. If they are to feel good they must resolve their own personal issues satisfactorily while receiving the support they need. This can be done as described previously, through regular supervision from an experienced counsellor (see Chapter 37).

In recent years, it has become clear that all counsellors at times experience what is known as 'burnout'. Burnout is disabling, but if it is recognised in its early stages, then it is comparatively easy to take remedial action. Even experienced counsellors fail at times to recognise the onset of burnout and try to convince themselves that the symptoms they are experiencing are due to some other cause. It is difficult for many counsellors to admit to themselves, let alone to others, that they are burning out, even though there is now general acceptance that burnout is a common problem. The first step in dealing with burnout is to be aware of the symptoms.

Burnout symptoms

There is a wide range of symptoms that come under the general heading of burnout. These symptoms give an indication that the counsellor is becoming drained emotionally by the counselling work and is wanting to draw back.

Counsellors may experience a feeling of being totally overworked and of having no control over their workload. They may perceive themselves as swimming against the tide and unable to keep their heads above water. This leads to feelings of hopelessness and helplessness.

Physical and emotional symptoms

Counsellors experiencing burnout are usually tired physically, emotionally and mentally. They start to feel that they can't face meeting another client. Typically, a counsellor may say to themselves during a counselling session: 'I really can't bear to be here. I wish the client would just go away.' They may experience being physically debilitated and find it hard to drag themselves to work. Their enthusiasm has evaporated and they may have physical symptoms such as headaches, stomach-aches, skin disorders, high blood pressure or back and neck pains. Their susceptibility to viruses and other infections is increased.

Negative attitudes

Burnt out counsellors may develop strong negative attitudes towards clients. They may develop a cynical attitude to their clients and blame them for creating their own problems. They may even start to treat their clients in an impersonal way, as though they were objects and not human beings. Consequently, the counselling relationship will suffer and counselling will become a chore, rather than an interesting, challenging and creative activity. Such counsellors no longer find satisfaction in their work. Negative attitudes may also be experienced towards fellow workers, supervisors, other staff and the employing organisation.

Disillusionment

Disillusionment with the counselling process is a major burnout symptom. Counsellors start to question the value of their work and begin to wonder if what they are doing is worthwhile. Burnt out counsellors will often be unable to see any evidence of success in their work. They feel frustrated by their inability to bring about change in their clients and are dissatisfied with their job, believing that it involves giving and getting nothing in return. This leads to feelings of failure and low self-esteem. The demands of clients become too great and the counsellor may just want to withdraw from the helping situation. In the advanced stages of burnout, the counsellors start taking days off sick, and may start frantically looking for a new job so that they can resign.

Personal consequences

One of the sad consequences of burnout is that it is likely to affect the counsellor's personal life. As a counsellor's self-esteem diminishes, their personal relationships may be put in jeopardy and other people may become targets for feelings of anger, frustration, helplessness and hopelessness.

A major cause of burnout

What is the primary cause of burnout? Well, we can't be certain, and in any case all counsellors are different, but it seems likely that a major cause of burnout is the stress of the interpersonal counselling relationship. This is an unbalanced relationship, with the counsellor doing most of the giving and the client doing most of the receiving.

In the early chapters of this book, heavy emphasis was put on establishing an empathic relationship, and on the need to join with the client. It is essential that, as a counsellor, you learn to do this effectively, because *empathy* is one of the essential ingredients of successful counselling. However, *being empathic can be hazardous to a counsellor's health!* That is, unless proper precautions are taken.

Clients are often in a highly emotional state, and if a counsellor listens with empathy and effectively joins with an emotional client, then the counsellor is likely to be infected by the client's emotional state. Emotions, like viruses, are catching, which is probably why people who aren't counsellors try to calm their friends down when they are emotional. After all, who wants to be emotionally distressed? In contrast to most friends, many counsellors encourage people to experience and express their emotions fully. Empathic counsellors are certain to experience, at some level, emotions similar to those of their clients. Clearly, no counsellor can afford to be emotionally distressed for a significant part of the working day, because to allow this to happen would be certain to result in burnout. Counsellors who are working mainly with emotionally disturbed clients are therefore very much at risk and need to take special precautions to avoid burnout.

Protecting yourself

With experience, you will learn how to walk beside a client with empathy and also how to protect yourself from the excesses of emotional pain by at times moving back for a while, grounding yourself, and then joining more fully with the client again. Certainly, if you are to protect yourself from burnout, you will need to learn how to do this. I, David, will describe the technique I use for myself, and then you will need to experiment for yourself, to find out what works best for you.

In a counselling session, when I notice that I am starting to experience a client's emotional pain excessively, I immediately set about grounding myself. This grounding process takes only a second or two to happen, but will take longer to describe.

Using an imaginary space-bubble

I imagine myself to be encapsulated by a plastic space-bubble which separates me from outside emotions, but enables me to observe them, and allows me to respond to them appropriately. I then slow down my breathing and relax my body, so that my troubled emotional state is replaced by tranquillity. In my imagination, I float, in the space-bubble, upwards and backwards to a position several metres behind and above my body. It is as though the part of me in the bubble is able to observe both the client and the physical me, which is still sitting in my counselling chair. I am still able to concentrate fully, but am more detached and less involved. In this position, I can make sensible decisions with regard to the counselling process. However, I can in a split second travel back in my imagination to my counselling chair, to give empathic attention and empathic responses to the client.

Clearly I have a powerful imagination, and have trained myself to relax quickly, when necessary. You will need to experiment for yourself, to devise an effective way in which you can protect yourself from emotional damage due to excessive exposure to client pain.

Despite the above discussion, there will inevitably be times when, as a counsellor, you *are* affected by the emotional traumas of your clients. Personally, I don't think that it is helpful to let a client know that I have been emotionally affected by what they have told me. Most clients are caring people who do not like to upset others. Consequently, if a client thinks that I have been emotionally disturbed by what I have heard, then they may be less likely to tell me about other disturbing information. Counsellors therefore need to control the expression of their own emotions appropriately, so that clients feel able to talk freely.

Recharging

If you are left in an emotionally disturbed state after a counselling session, talk to your supervisor about your feelings as soon as possible. Remember:

the counselling relationship is substantially a one-way relationship, in which the counsellor is the giver and the client is the taker. Such a relationship will inevitably drain the counsellor of emotional energy. Clearly, unless a counsellor recharges, they will experience the symptoms of burnout as they become drained.

Other factors which lead to burnout

The dangers of over-involvement

It is important to be aware of the dangers of over-involvement with clients and their issues. We all have different personalities and differing capabilities for coping with emotionally stressful situations. Some counsellors get over-involved with their clients and take their client's problems home with them, whereas other people are more philosophical and are less affected by their counselling work. I, David, have trained myself so that when I leave my place of work, I will allow myself to think about client material only until I reach a particular set of traffic lights. Once I have passed these lights, I give myself the option of going back to my place of work to think about clients, or of forgetting them and continuing my journey. I invariably continue my journey.

Suicidal clients

Experienced counsellors who deal with suicidal or violent clients have an extremely stressful time and are particularly prone to burnout. A counsellor who has a high case load of suicidal clients has little option but to accept that, even with the use of properly accountable practices, eventually a client may succeed in killing themselves. This knowledge creates anxiety in the counsellor and increases the likelihood of burnout. Remember that it is not appropriate to blame yourself for what you are unable to prevent. Protect yourself, as a new counsellor, by ensuring that such clients are referred for appropriate professional help.

Isolation

Being isolated and working alone puts a counsellor at increased risk of burnout, because of a lack of peer support during the working day. After all, if I'm being drained of my energy, I need to be able to get some back by interacting with others who can meet with me in more equal two-way relationships.

Personal stress

A stressful personal life may make a counsellor more susceptible to burnout because of diminished emotional resources.

Combating burnout

As stated before, many counsellors are afraid to admit to themselves, let alone to other people, that they are starting to experience burnout symptoms, because they feel that it would be an admission of failure. This is understandable for many reasons. Firstly, most of us have learnt from childhood to appear to be strong enough to cope with our load, whatever that may be. That learning is based on a myth that human beings are inexhaustible, which is obviously not true. Secondly, new counsellors invariably start counselling with very high ideals and unrealistically high expectations of what they will be able to achieve.

Having realistic expectations

Our own experiences as counsellors lead us to believe that usually the outcomes of counselling interventions are helpful for the client. However, there are times when a client does not seem to be helped by the counselling process and when this does happen, it would be easy for us to become disillusioned. At times like this we remind ourselves of the need to look at the overall picture.

Outcomes with clients are often different from what the counsellor would prefer, and it is therefore necessary to have realistic expectations in order to avoid disillusionment. The idealism of the new counsellor can easily be eroded and lead to later dissatisfaction if unrealistic expectations are not fulfilled.

Giving with no expectation of return, caring for people unconditionally, and being dedicated to counselling work are all attitudes that are implicitly absorbed as part of many counsellor training programs. These attitudes conflict strongly with feelings that may be experienced during burnout. It is therefore not surprising that counsellors find it difficult to own burnout feelings.

Accepting that burnout is normal

It is strongly recommended that counsellor training programs always include education for trainee counsellors about the inevitability of burnout occurring at times, even in the most dedicated counsellor. If counsellors realise that burnout feelings do occur in normal, competent, capable and caring counsellors, then they will be able to start accepting their own burnout feelings and to share those feelings with their peers and other professionals.

Burnout comes in cycles and it is helpful to expect these cycles to occur. It is healthy to say, 'Ah-ha, I'm starting to recognise some of the symptoms of burnout.' By making that simple statement, a counsellor is able to admit truthfully what is happening and is then empowered to take the necessary action to deal with the problem.

Most counsellors start their job with some feelings of nervousness, but very soon this is followed by enthusiasm and excitement. However, it doesn't take long for other feelings to set in. These may be feelings of stagnation and apathy, or even of frustration and annoyance. In other words, the counsellor's initial enthusiasm and excitement will, from time to time, be replaced by feelings associated with burnout. In the same way, by using sensible burnout management techniques, the initial enthusiasm about counselling can be re-experienced.

Actively dealing with burnout

Quite often people look for a new job or resign as a result of burnout. That is one way of dealing with it, but it is not necessary to do that if you recognise the symptoms early enough and do something positive to deal with them. Experiencing burnout is not a disaster if it is recognised and dealt with effectively. For a counsellor, dealing with burnout can be compared to a car owner servicing a car. The car needs to be serviced regularly or the car will not function well. Similarly, as a counsellor take steps to continually look after your own needs. If you become aware of burnout feelings, take the appropriate action to recharge yourself, to regain your enthusiasm and the excitement you experienced at the beginning of your counselling career. This can be done time and again, so you can work as a counsellor for a lifetime if you choose by recharging yourself and starting afresh from time to time.

Here are some suggestions for dealing with burnout:
1. Recognise and own the symptoms.
2. Talk with someone about your feelings.
3. Re-schedule your work.
4. Cut down on your workload.
5. Take a holiday.

6. Use relaxation or meditation.
7. Use positive self-talk.
8. Lower your expectations of yourself, your clients, your colleagues and your employer.
9. Allow yourself to enjoy life and have a sense of humour.
10. Use thought-stopping to stop worrying about clients when not at work.
11. Use your religious or other belief system for support.
12. Care for yourself as a person by doing some nice things for yourself.

Consider some of these ideas. Firstly, it is interesting to note that simply admitting that you are experiencing burnout will affect your behaviour and enable you to cope better. Talking with your supervisor or someone else may also be helpful, as by doing this you may be able to clarify your options more easily with regard to suitable methods of intervention.

It can be helpful to re-schedule your work so that you have a feeling of being in control. You may need to be assertive if your boss doesn't understand your need for a reduced workload. Reducing your workload may not be sufficient initially, and you may need to take a few days off, to have a holiday or to take some days off sick. Help yourself to feel more relaxed, more in control and fitter. Build into your lifestyle proper times for rest, recreation, exercise, light-hearted relief and relaxation. Doing relaxation exercises or meditating can be helpful. Use positive self-talk to replace negative self-statements and challenge the negative self-statements you make about others. This involves changing your expectations of yourself, your clients and your peers.

A useful way to deal with burnout is to take a less serious view of life, to allow yourself to have a sense of humour and to be less intense in your work. Be carefree and have fun. Most importantly, do not take client problems home. If you do catch yourself doing this, practise thought-stopping. The first step in thought-stopping is to recognise that you are thinking about client problems when you should be relaxing. Then recognise your choice, to continue thinking about these problems or to focus your attention on something in your present environment. This may involve doing something physical or it may involve concentrating on some-

thing specific such as listening to music. Focus all your energy and attention on the 'here and now' to block out the intruding thoughts. Sometimes you may find that the intruding thoughts recur and catch yourself saying, 'If I don't think about this client problem now, then I will never deal with it and that will be bad for the client.' If such a thought comes into your mind, then write a note in your diary to deal with that issue at a particular time when you are at your place of work, and say to yourself, 'OK, at 10 o'clock tomorrow morning, at work, I will devote half an hour to thinking about that problem, but right now I will get on with doing and thinking about things that are pleasant for me.'

Many counsellors find strength in their religious beliefs and gain through prayer and meditation. They find that by doing this they receive an inner strength that enables them to be more effective in their work. Similarly, people with other philosophical belief systems can use their philosophy of life as an aid in combating burnout.

If you care for yourself, and take appropriate action to attend to your own needs by leading a less pressured and more balanced life, then your burnout symptoms are likely fade and you will be able to regain your energy and enthusiasm. However, if you are like most counsellors, you will have an ongoing struggle with burnout which will come and go. There will always be times when you will give too much of yourself, and then need to redress the balance so that your own needs for recharging are adequately met.

Gaining satisfaction from counselling

If you are pro-active in caring for yourself then you will be more able to care for others. You will be likely to get satisfaction from counselling and to enjoy being a counsellor. I hope that you, the reader, will gain as much personal fulfilment from counselling as we have. We wish you all the best for your work.

Learning summary

- All counsellors need regular supervision because:
  - counselling can be emotionally draining for the counsellor; and
  - counsellors need a way to resolve their own issues and without supervision they are more likely to burn out.

- Burnout includes the following symptoms: feelings of disillusionment, being emotionally and physically drained, somatic symptoms, and negative attitudes to clients.
- Burnout comes in cycles and with self-awareness and adequate supervision recharging can occur.
- Methods for dealing with burnout include:
  - recognising the symptoms and talking with someone about them;
  - changing your workload or schedule;
  - taking a break;
  - using relaxation, meditation or positive self-talk;
  - lowering your expectations;
  - taking life less seriously and having a sense of humour;
  - using thought-stopping; and
  - using your religious or other belief system for support.

Further reading

Carter, R. 1994, *Helping Yourself Help Others: The Caregivers Handbook*, Times Books, New York.

Grosh, W. N. & Olsen, D. C. 1995, 'Prevention: avoiding burnout', in *A Perilous Calling: The Hazards of Psychotherapy Practice*, M. B. Sussman (ed.), Wiley, New York.

Schaufeli, W. B., Maslach, C. and Marek, T. (eds) 1993, *Professional Burnout: Recent Developments in Theory and Research*, Taylor & Francis, Washington.

Index